FAITH IN A CHANGING CULTURE

Creating churches for the next century

JOHN DRANE

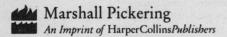

Marshall Pickering
An Imprint of HarperCollins*Publishers*

FOR ROB AND JULIE BANKS

Marshall Pickering is an Imprint of
HarperCollins*Religious*
Part of HarperCollins*Publishers*
77–85 Fulham Palace Road
London W6 8JB

First published in Great Britain
in 1994 by Marshall Pickering
under the title *Evangelism for a New Age*
This revised and expanded edition
first published in Great Britain
in 1997 by Marshall Pickering

3 5 7 9 10 8 6 4 2

A catalogue record for this book is
available from the British Library

0 551 030747

Printed and bound in Great Britain by
Caledonian International Manufacturing Ltd, Glasgow

CONTENTS

PREFACE

This book is a revised and extended edition of *Evangelism for a New Age*, which first appeared in 1994. The fact that it is being reprinted such a short time after its first publication and includes two entirely new chapters and significant changes throughout, is symptomatic not only of the great interest shown in the original edition, but also of the many developments in my own thinking on the subject of faith in relation to our ever-changing culture.

This is a very personal book (probably more so than anything else I have written), in the sense that its arguments and conclusions have emerged out of my own faith journey rather than out of intellectual reflection on theology *per se*. Not that the two are unconnected, of course; in the New Testament itself discipleship comes first, and theological reflection is primarily focused on the nature of the experience of following Jesus. Theology must be done first, and analysed later.

The ultimate origins of this book go back to 1984 when I was invited to become Mission Convener of the Scottish Churches Council. Few people find spiritual renewal by joining church committees but, as I review the last 12 years, I have no doubt that is what happened to me. In 1984, I was a traditional academic – trained to do theology the way others had done it for centuries before. I was reasonably good at it, and had written a number of books on the Bible to prove it. But as I got down to the business of working out what we would need to be and do to share the Christian faith effectively at the end of the twentieth century, I soon discovered that I had a lot to learn about myself, about contemporary culture, about the world Church and about God.

It is a truism to say that we are all in the process of becoming someone, but there can be no question that as I have worked through these and other related issues, I have become a very different person from what I was before. I still have a lot to learn but just now, towards the end of the 'Decade of Evangelism' and on the threshold of the new millennium, it seems the right time to share with the wider Church some of what I think I have discovered.

The opportunity to put my ideas into some kind of coherent form first came in 1989 when my friend Raymond Fung, who was then Evangelism Secretary to the World Council of Churches, invited me and my wife Olive to participate in a series of international Schools of Evangelism that he was planning. The first took place in Adelaide, Australia, in July 1990. At the time, what I had to say seemed to me so commonplace and obvious that I wondered how it could be worth travelling halfway round the world to say it. But I forgot that by then I had been living with these thoughts for a few years, and what was commonplace to me was new to others. What I had to share was given such a warm reception that I soon realized it had the potential to become a significant new model for evangelism in the postmodern situation.

I was particularly encouraged by the response not just from Western church leaders (some of whose churches are in such serious decline that they would grasp at anything), but also from the leaders of huge and fast-growing churches in places like Korea, Africa, Malaysia and South America. In the years since then, I have had the opportunity to present this material in a wide variety of different contexts, evangelical as well as ecumenical, and always with the same, positive response. If it is genuinely a new way forward, then I can only say it is also a return to our historical origins, for it is rooted in the teaching and practice of Jesus.

It is also a reflection of the experience of the world Church, and for many of its insights I am indebted to non-western Christians, not least Raymond Fung himself. If I were to single out others who have had a significant input into the writing of this book, I would mention especially the Revd Maitland Evans, General Secretary of the United Church of Jamaica and Cayman, who invited Olive and me to lead seminars on liturgical renewal in early 1995; we found it to be one of those occasions when we learned at least as much as we handed on. The School of Theology at Fuller Seminary in California has also played a significant role in the development of my thinking, not least by providing a space for my practical exploration of various themes through the course: 'Spirituality and Creativity for Evangelism and Worship', which Olive and I developed and which we continue to teach there.

This is not a 'how-to' book that will provide blueprints of evangelizing strategies, although I have no shortage of specific ideas as to how its principles can be put into practice, and I have a pretty good idea of how this model might work out in different contexts. But what works for one church cannot necessarily be transplanted somewhere else with the same effect. Congregations can waste much time and energy trying to copy others. This is why the focus here is on an overall approach to and understanding of evangelism that can easily be transferred from one culture to another, whereas specific ideas generally cannot. Moreover, I believe that a particular set of attitudes can be identified from within the New Testament itself, especially in the teaching and example of Jesus, and that these attitudes are sufficiently distinctive to justify a book to themselves.

Few academic theologians ever get around to writing a book on evangelism. Given the extensive international interest that has been expressed in what I am writing here, I am sorry to admit that the world of British theological education still struggles to find useful ways of incorporating much on mission within its regular curriculum. But for better or worse, I straddle these two worlds of academic theology and the international Church, always hoping that somehow the two might yet be brought together. I explain all this so that readers will understand my particular perspective. I can only be who I am, though I recognize that some people will find my insistence on critical scholarship irksome, while others will find my use of popular materials uncritical.

Finally, it is worth pointing out that this book is unlikely to be the last word on the subject. I am not claiming that I know all the best answers, merely that I think I have found some of the right questions, and that struggling with these questions will be essential if Christians are to have something relevant to say to the world of the new millennium. I will have got some things wrong, just as I know I have got some things right. Michelangelo always believed that even in the roughest piece of rock there is an angel waiting to be released. As I have shared these ideas around the world, I have found the Spirit of God releasing angels of unexpected beauty from some of the clumsiest concepts, and if that is the experience of my readers then it will have been a worthwhile enterprise.

John Drane
October 1996

CHAPTER 1

FAITH, CULTURE
AND THE 21ST CENTURY

From time immemorial, the start of a new century has always been a thought-provoking occasion, and the celebration of the dawn of the twenty-first century is no different. Many people are finding it is a time for reflection on what is past, and a time for a sense of pride in all the good things that have happened in our generation and that of our parents and grandparents. It is also an occasion for regret, as people reflect on the hopes and aspirations that went unfulfilled, and on the mistakes that were made.

The twentieth century has witnessed more violent conflicts than any other century in history. The sheer scale of destruction and human misery has been mind-blowing; human life and well-being has so often been threatened by the very inventions that were supposed to improve them. In the process, the nature of human confrontation has changed significantly. The terrifying mechanization of warfare in the 1914–1918 conflict looked decidedly primitive by the time Hitler hatched his demonic scheme to use industrial processes to annihilate an entire nation. More recently, the digitalization of mass destruction now makes it possible for combatants to engage in warfare without ever physically coming face to face with another human being. All these things are leading people to face the future with increased pessimism and a feeling that, since so much is so uncertain, probably the only way to get through life is to live for today and leave the future to take care of itself – if there is a future; we have not even mentioned the destruction of the planet, the alarming rise in child exploitation throughout the world, and increasing urbanization, with its rising tide of poverty and marginalization for many people. Yet at the same time, the human spirit is ever hopeful that somehow things might get better. Ironically – though predictably – the new century is also engendering a new spirit of expectancy, as people throughout the world close an old chapter and begin a new one.

Wherever we look, people's horizons are being widened and their vision inspired by the realization that a new age (whatever that might mean) is about to dawn, and that maybe this time we will get it right. Indeed, the possibilities this time around seem much greater than they have ever been. Of all the generations that have gone before us, we are uniquely privileged: we stand not only on the threshold of a new century, but of a new millennium. Since people started counting time, only one generation before us has initiated a new millennium, and that was a long, long time ago – when the year 999 gave way to the year 1000. Though the purists have debated exactly when a new millennium truly begins, and the consensus of informed opinion places the end of the twentieth century as 31 December 2000, for most people the party begins on New Year's Eve, 1999. Hotels and public buildings around the world have been booked up years in advance. Multitudes of people are looking forward to the big day; as it comes ever closer we must expect an intensification, not just of the celebration but also of the serious questions that human beings will have to face in the twenty-first century.

As we begin to limber up for the starter's pistol, more and more of us are trying to gaze into the future to discern the trends that will shape the way we run our lives in the new century. Big business is already planning millennial marketing strategies, and the hype is about to begin. Of course, it is not all exciting news. The scenario described so far is very Western, and prosperous Western at that. For other people, their deepest aspiration is that the dawn of a new century might bring an end to the suffering and injustice imposed on them by corrupt warlords and politicians. Their cry for fairness finds a ready echo among many thinking Westerners, who are questioning the very fabric of civilization as we have known it for the past three or four centuries. At the same time, those for whom the next century means the most – today's children – can often be heard wondering if there will be a future for them, or whether it is yet another cruel illusion; and whether, instead of ushering in a golden age, the twenty-first century might see the whole world system fall helplessly into the abyss of ultimate environmental disaster.

People have always had an insatiable appetite for knowledge of the future. Every significant civilization of the ancient world had its soothsayers and astrologers: kings were unable to rule without their constant support; armies never went into battle without first consulting them; and ordinary people were both inspired and terrified by their apparently supernatural power to look beyond the mundane and the everyday and to see the bigger picture that had its effect on everyone's lives. A thousand years ago, as the first Christian millennium was about to give way to the second, there was much feverish speculation about when the world would end; the last 150 years has seen any number of groups all asking the same question. Most have flourished for a time, and then disappeared. Some – such as the Plymouth Brethren – sprang up within the framework of the Christian Church, and have since lost their apocalyptic distinctiveness by merging with the Establishment to become just another church. Others, such as the Theosophical Society established in the mid-nineteenth century by Helena Blavatsky, sprang from different spiritual roots, but they too have been domesticated and accepted as part of the religious (albeit non-christian) scene. A few have fallen into the control of dangerous autocrats and have brought untold misery and exploitation – even death – to their followers.

NEW QUESTIONS – SURPRISING ANSWERS

Historically, those people who were attracted to join such groups have been ordinary people who were just apprehensive about what the future might hold. Many were loners who, for a variety of reasons, found themselves on the fringes of Western culture. But that is no longer the case.

As we approach the end of the twentieth century, such activity has intensified rather than diminished. The London *Financial Times* regularly carries adverts from clairvoyants who offer advice about how money can be invested in stocks and shares, and presumably enough people seek it to make it financially worthwhile offering the service. Every day, phone-in programmes on radio and TV feature astrologers whose opinion on deeply personal and potentially life-changing decisions is highly prized. Callers look to the stars and planets for the solution to their problems of employment, relationships, infertility, health and well-being. Nor is this concern for knowing the future restricted to the inadequate and the gullible. Royalty and politicians also pay more than lip service to the belief that the future can both be known and influenced by tuning in to the right sources of cosmic information. Back in 1988, former White House chief of staff Donald T. Regan claimed that the US president and his wife used an astrologer to plan their lives. According to a report from Associated Press dated 3 May 1988, it had been on such astrological advice that President Ronald Reagan insisted on signing a nuclear disarmament treaty with the Soviet leader Mikhail Gorbachev some six months previously, at exactly 1.33 p.m. on 8 December 1987. Though the President himself denied making policy decisions on such a basis, his wife's press secretary subsequently confirmed that she regularly consulted 'a friend that does astrology'. No one was surprised. After all, Reagan (like many US politicians) had been strongly influenced by fundamentalist groups who specialized in understanding the future. In a world where millions of us call astrological helplines to get detailed advice about the most intimate of relationships, and certain types of churches give credence to their own version of it, why should the president of the USA be any different? Or the British Royal Family?

Christians hold a variety of opinions on all this. Many smile and think of it as a harmless pastime, one that is unlikely to do much harm, even if it does no good. Others perceive the influence of dark, demonic forces behind it all. For either reason, it is easy to dismiss people who seem more interested in the future than the present and regard them as, at best, escapists or, at worst, seriously maladjusted. Increasingly, however, those who are now talking of 'the end of the world as we know it' in our generation are not members of fringe religious groups, nor are they unbalanced, insecure individuals who seek assurance about the future because they are incapable of coping with the present. Wherever we look – in government, in education, as well as among ordinary citizens – there is a fresh awareness of the fact that as we approach the beginning of a new millennium this is the time to ask some serious questions about the future of the human race. Indeed, maybe this will be our last chance before chaos descends. For as the ruthless exploitation of the earth's resources continues unabated, and the gaps in the ozone layer expand annually, even scientists are getting concerned that we might be fried alive in our own lifetime as a result. At a more immediate level, many of the world's large conurbations are literally in danger of being buried beneath their own trash, while a rising tide of crime and violence threatens the safety and security of people all over the world, even in their own homes.

In their understandable eagerness to avoid being identified with some of the more bizarre doomsday sects, Christians should beware of not taking seriously enough these very real concerns. If the Christian gospel is to be 'good news' (as its name means), then this is the time for a more profound engagement with this generation's hopes and fears than we have hitherto known. That will not necessarily entail setting up our own millennial task forces to broadcast a 'Christian vision'. For Christians, sharing faith should always begin with recognizing their solidarity with other people. Time taken to reflect on where we might be heading in the new millennium will not be time wasted. On the contrary, it might enable us to hear what others are saying, and to empathize with the crisis that is moving relentlessly through our culture at this time.

When I was a child 30 years ago, in the middle of the social revolution of the 1960s, it seemed as if we had finally cracked it. If we didn't know the answers to all the world's questions, then at least we thought we knew where to look for them. The philosophical and practical foundations laid by the scientific and technological revolution in previous centuries had proved substantial enough to support a whole new concept of the world, of human nature and destiny; we all took it for granted that the Western values and lifestyles being affirmed then would be the ultimate and only answer to humanity's search for the good life. Today, all that is gone. As we move to the beginning of the twenty-first century, the frenzied search for a new world order grows in intensity almost daily. Not many people support the old order any more, and this frustration and disillusionment is widespread not just among the popular media, but also in most disciplines of academic scholarship. Let me suggest three factors that are contributing to this surprising about-turn.

THE YEAR 2000 IS A DEFINING MOMENT

This, of course, should be so obvious as hardly to be worth saying. But considering the fact that this is the 2000th anniversary of the birth of Jesus Christ, most Christians seem unbelievably casual about it. To call it a 'once-in-a-lifetime' opportunity is to belittle its enormous significance for the whole of the human race.

There are any number of organizations already moving into top gear as they plan their celebrations and marketing promotions for this unique point in time. As long ago as 1992, I attended a meeting to discuss the most effective ways for the mass media to mark the arrival of the new millennium. The occasion was chaired by an executive from a TV company, and included people from all walks of life in Scotland: education, industry, finance, commerce, as well as government. The person in the chair posed a simple question: 'Why is the year 2000 so special anyway? What is it that makes it worth celebrating?' The answers were interesting, if slightly predictable. A clear majority saw it as a chance to make a new start, to forget all the mess of the past century, turn over a new page in human history and begin to construct the kind of world society we all profess to admire and long to enjoy. There was much idealistic talk of getting rid of injustice, poverty, famine, violence, abuse and all the other things that have scarred so many people of our generation. But one thing surprised me. Not a single person mentioned – not even vaguely or in passing – the fact that these 2000 years are counted from the time when Jesus Christ was born. After about 40 minutes of brainstorming, I eventually threw this observation into the discussion. Predictably, perhaps, it was a conversation-stopper – at least for 20 or 30 seconds. Two things were obvious: first, that those present already knew that it would be the 2000th anniversary of the birth of Jesus. But even with the best will in the world these people (who were not anti-christian, and some of them were church members) could not really see how that fact would have much relevance for the task of inspiring and equipping people for life in the new century.

So where are the Christians? There are, of course, several Christian groups using the year 2000 as part of their marketing strategy. But with few exceptions, they do not seem to be drawing attention to the distinctly Christian dimensions of that year. If my experience is typical, none has penetrated the corridors of power in the mass media. Yet if so many people are looking at the year 2000 as the opportunity for a new beginning, when the mess of the past can somehow be cleaned up, is that not an open invitation for people of faith to share their vision for what the twenty-first century might become?

'THINGS CAN'T GO ON LIKE THIS
FOR MUCH LONGER – CAN THEY?'

No one should be surprised that the dawn of a new millennium might be a chance for humanity to make a new start. After all, most of us vow to do that on the first day of every new year! But the desire for fundamentally new directions for our culture runs much deeper than just the sentimentality and impermanence of a new year's resolution. Even serious academic thinkers are acknowledging that things cannot go on the way they are for much longer. There is a growing feeling that things are slipping away, the Western world is in a crisis and the condition is probably terminal. The philosophies that have guided and controlled our thinking for the last 500 years have run their course.

The year 1992 was the 500th anniversary of Columbus's voyages of exploration, which took him and others out of their European homelands and to every corner of the planet. But it was scarcely celebrated, either in the old European homelands or in the 'new worlds' which were 'discovered' – and certainly not in the grand style that one might have anticipated. Sensitive and thinking people found themselves embarrassed and distressed by the long-term results of the great age of discovery and so-called enlightenment; at best, the heritage of this 500-year period has become a liability from the past that no longer holds the power to inspire and give direction for the future.

In *Das Athanäum*, the eighteenth-century German diplomat Friedrich von Schlegel remarked that 'a historian is a prophet in reverse'. There is a lot of truth in that. Yesterday, today was tomorrow, and being aware of our past can help us to be better equipped to deal with the present and the future. As we reflect on the crisis apparently gripping our civilization today, it is worth taking time to consider the roots of our culture. In a more profound way than we often realize, modern Western thinking does indeed go back to the days of Columbus and his contemporaries. Excited by their discoveries of 'new' lands, sixteenth-century European visionaries soon began to wonder what other unknown horizons were waiting to be explored. A new age of scientific investigation was about to dawn. Within a very short time, there was a veritable explosion of new knowledge that soon encompassed the whole range of human experience and changed our understanding of ourselves and the world for good. Copernicus (1473–1543) challenged the old idea that the earth was the centre of the universe, and convincingly demonstrated that the sun was the centre. When the Italian astronomer Galileo (1564–1642) popularized the idea, he soon found himself on a collision course with the Establishment. In due course, however, the new idea was accepted and an alternative view that had prevailed since ancient times was discarded. There was a paradigm shift of massive dimensions, that merely served to give permission to others to ask further questions, not only about science but about human nature.

In the middle of the seventeenth century, Sir Isaac Newton wondered why apples always fall downwards and not up, and came up with the law of gravity to explain it. His notion that everything worked according to carefully defined and unchanging laws of nature heralded another paradigm shift, as people came to think of the universe as a gigantic machine. Science and technology were born and, with the Industrial Revolution, such discoveries were put to creative use for the benefit of ordinary people. No wonder that this period of history soon came to be referred to as 'the Enlightenment'. For that is just what it seemed to be. Compared with what was now being discovered, the old world of the Middle Ages and the ancients was nothing but darkness – full of superstition and ignorance. Before, people had believed their lives to be hemmed in by cosmic forces beyond both their control and their understanding. Now, new possibilities seemed to stretch out endlessly, and the only limit to progress would be human ingenuity. There were still many uncertainties, but for the first time in the whole of human history it looked as if people would be able to control their environment, rather than the environment controlling them. Great voyages of discovery became commonplace, together with the imperialistic expansion of Britain and other Western powers into virtually every part of the globe. These were heady days, when it seemed that human endeavour could achieve just about anything.

Today, of course, all that has been swept away. The old certainties of the Enlightenment are no longer secure, and science and technology have failed to deliver the goods. In the twentieth century, the very things that were supposed to bring progress have often led us to the brink of destruction, and in the process have inhibited and devalued significant areas of human experience and understanding. No one would wish to turn the clock back, nor to deny the usefulness of the advances in human knowledge there have been in the last two or three centuries; there has been tremendous progress, and much of it has been enormously beneficial to the entire human race. But it is also undeniable that when we look more closely at this golden coin of modern progress, more often than not the flip side is heavily tarnished.

A 100 years ago, the invention of the internal combustion engine was beginning to revolutionize daily life. It was unquestionably a great discovery which made life easier for all succeeding generations. But it has not all been good news, and the very machines that make modern transportation so efficient are in danger of destroying both our social environment and ultimately, perhaps, the planet itself. Consider modern agriculture, for example, where artificial pesticides and fertilizers enable us to grow food crops with predictable regularity, so that every vegetable in every supermarket throughout the Western world can be guaranteed to be of a particular shape, size, colour and quality. If that seems a dubious advantage, then remember that although too many are still starving, such technology has enabled us to feed far more people than our ancestors could ever have believed possible. Yet in many places, the same fertilizers and pesticides that have had such generally beneficial effects have also poisoned the most basic human food resource of all, namely the water supply.

Think of medical science. No one would wish to go back to the days before the discovery of anaesthetics and antibiotics. But conventional Western medicine often treats patients as if they are no more than dead bodies that happen to be still breathing. People are seen as machines, and illness is defined as malfunction of the parts. Doctors restore 'health' by tinkering with the defective organs to make them work properly.

There is nothing at all wrong with that, except that it is only half the picture. Most people do not think of themselves as machines, and they instinctively know that having a perfectly functioning body does not automatically produce wholeness and well-being. People are not just bundles of spare parts, but have emotions and relationships that have their own crucial part to play in ensuring human satisfaction. It is taking traditional Western medics a long time to accept this, and in the meantime increasing numbers of suffering people look to complementary therapists of various kinds who seem better equipped to take account of the more personal and spiritual aspects of wholeness.

On his return from the Soviet Union in 1919, the US journalist Lincoln Steffens reported, 'I have seen the future and it works.'[1] That sentiment would not be shared by many people today. As we approach the dawn of a new millennium, there is a sense in which we have already seen the future, we know it doesn't work and we want to make radical changes before it's too late. Moreover, these changes need to be more than cosmetic. It is not just that the Enlightenment vision has become dimmed, but that the foundational concepts on which the Enlightenment was based are themselves part of the problem. Think for a moment of three of the key philosophical notions on which Western culture has been founded. There is 'rationalism', the idea that the only things worth knowing are things you can think about. There is nothing wrong with thinking, of course, but the way we have tended to focus on this to the exclusion of all else has left millions of Western people emotionally powerless. Then there is 'materialism', the belief that the only things worth thinking about are what you can see and touch – an attitude that has cut us adrift from any sense of spiritual moorings. Finally, there is 'reductionism', the idea that you understand things by taking them to pieces – a procedure that has led, amongst other things, to personal alienation, and is at the root of much of the destruction of our natural environment. No wonder that many see our culture in terminal crisis. The vision that inspired the past can never provide answers for the future, because it is itself part of the problem. Somewhere along the line, something significant has been lost – a sense of our own humanity, values, and spirituality.

'MORE SPIRITUALITY AND LESS MATERIALISM'

You might be forgiven for thinking this would be the phrase of a religious leader. But you would be wrong. It was not a bishop or Christian leader who used it. It comes from the autobiography of British actress Joanna Lumley, who went on to say, 'In the 1990s we're going to start finding our souls again. We've gone through a very non-spiritual time this century.'[2] A mid-decade issue of the youth magazine of the British TSB Bank put it this way: 'After the '60s and Hippies, after the '70s and Rock 'n' Roll drugs, after the '80s and post-mod radical chic 'OK Yah' materialism, after everything…there's a more spiritual way to guide us through to the '90s and beyond.'[3] Smile at the journalistic hype if you please, but remember that these are not the words of some cranky religious cult leader. Financial institutions are a central part of the Western Establishment, and when the Establishment speaks in this way you can be sure there is a growing conviction that we need spiritual answers to some of the apparently intractable problems which we now face. In more reflective – but no less committed – vein, American psychology professor Marilyn Ferguson wrote as long ago as 1980 that 'the entire culture is undergoing trauma and tensions that beg for new order.'[4]

You might suppose this renewed awareness of the spiritual is good news for Christians. But the exact opposite is the case. The Western Church is actually in a weak position, for the very simple reason that to most people it is a part of the same, institutionalized authority structure that helped create the mess in the first place. Among the leaders of today's generation, there is an insistent and growing belief that Christianity is irrelevant. Modern Western thinking, it is said, has largely been dominated by Christian values, and these must therefore have contributed to our present predicament. That being the case, it stands to reason that we will not solve things by doing more of the same. It can be debated whether Christian values shaped the Enlightenment, or whether it was the other way round, and the Church has allowed itself to be taken over by essentially secular values.[5] Either way, the practical outcome is no different: Christianity is very firmly perceived as part of the old order, and therefore something to be discarded rather than trusted for the future.[6] As a result, people searching for a spiritual dimension to life today are unlikely to have much expectation of finding it in the Church. In medical circles, for instance, there is a concerted effort to identify ways of including 'spirituality' within the healing process, but it is generally taken for granted that, whatever 'spirituality' is (and there is a good deal of uncertainty over that), it has nothing at all to do with the work of hospital chaplains and organized religion. They are all seen as part of a system that has failed us, and the way forward will be in our exploration of and openness to alternative ways of ordering things and understanding the world.

This explains why there is so much interest today in other cultures. If, as is claimed, we need to rediscover spirituality in order to put things right, and if (as is also believed) the traditional sources of spiritual wisdom in the West (the churches) have dried up, then there is nowhere else to look but to other cultures and worldviews, or within ourselves. For some, this takes the form of studying major non-western thought systems such as the great religions of the Orient. For others, it means a concern to rediscover and preserve the native cultures that were displaced when white people first invaded the Americas, Australasia, or Africa. Yet others see the solution in a kind of reversal of history, by jumping backwards over the last 1000 years or more into the dim and distant pre-Christian past of Europe itself, to embrace and affirm the long-lost values and worldviews of our own pagan ancestors. As a result, a dazzling and bewildering array of different spiritualities compete for attention, each of them claiming to be able to offer something that will help us find our souls again, and chart a safe course for the future. The goods on offer in this religious marketplace range from messages from spirit guides and extra-terrestrials, to neo-paganism, celtic mythology and aboriginal spirituality – not to mention renewed interest in astrology and a vast range of psychological therapies offering the prospect of a renewed, holistic humanity.

Back in the middle of the first century, the Roman satirist Petronius observed that 'the gods walk abroad so commonly in our streets that it is easier to meet a god than a man.'[7] The same thing could be said of many cities in the West today. History is coming full circle. The complacency of Christians in this situation both amazes and horrifies me. For people who should be operating at the cutting edge of our culture, far too many Christian leaders seem almost totally unaware of this enormous spiritual movement of our day. Yet most of my junk mail relates to it, in one way or another! Even those who are aware of it rarely engage with this spiritual search in any constructive or serious way. It is easy to dismiss all this by sticking labels onto it. To call it the 'New Age Movement' makes it sound like the work of a minority pressure group that sooner or later will disappear. There is undoubtedly a great deal of movement and change around today, and the present spiritual search is by any definition an eclectic phenomenon that is in a state of constant flux. But it is not a movement in the sense of being a passing fad. Without question, this is the shape of things to come, and when the people of 2020 look back to the 1980s and 1990s, I believe they will see that we have been in the middle of a paradigm shift as significant as those inaugurated in the past by Copernicus, Newton or Einstein.

Wherever we look, from industry to the home our institutions are collapsing – including, above all, the traditional Western spiritual institutions (the churches). At a time when traditional answers no longer seem to make sense, it is inevitable that sensitive and thinking people will turn to other things. Even so, the spiritual about-turn has been dramatic. Just 20 years ago, a rationalist–materialist worldview still dominated the lives of most people, and precluded the possibility of belief in any sort of mystical or spiritual dimension to life (whether Christian or otherwise). Today, it is no problem to find practising shamans in the main streets of Western cities, while statistics show that in the former West Germany alone there are something like 90,000 registered witches and wizards.[8] Europe is poised on a knife-edge, and may be entering a new socially-regressive dark age, not only with the rise of ethnic strife but also the re-emergence of neo-Nazi movements. Given the close connections of Hitler himself with spiritistic practices, it is difficult to resist the conclusion that these two forces go hand in hand.[9]

This whole phenomenon is both the greatest single threat to Christianity in the West and also its greatest single opportunity for many decades. There is a tremendous – and growing – interest in the supernatural, the mystical and the spiritual among younger people in particular. Western governments struggle to encourage more school-leavers to take up careers in science and technology. But there is a strong tide running in the opposite direction, and universities in many countries are faced with the unexpected phenomenon of massive growth in the numbers of students wanting to study religion. After 300 years of dominance, the Enlightenment values are crumbling fast, for very few of today's students are rationalists or materialists of the kind that were commonplace even a decade ago. Not long ago, I gave an address in one of Britain's most ancient universities. It was about the so-called 'New Age' phenomenon, and after I spoke the person chairing the meeting (which was part of a Christian mission) asked for questions and comments. A man in his forties jumped up right away: 'I am a professor of chemical engineering,' he said, 'but I've been a wizard for the last 15 years, and I'm thinking of becoming a Christian.' The chairperson was lost for words! The combination of being a university professor, a wizard *and* a potential convert to Christianity was simply mind-blowing. But in the course of further conversation, I discovered it was all true. In his professional life, this man was a successful science professor, but at home he lived like a medieval alchemist. His apartment was full of magical potions, books of spells, sacred bones and feathers – even a witch's broomstick. Yet he wanted to be a Christian! What then transpired was like a scene from the New Testament as he took all this paraphernalia outside and burned it. That episode encapsulates the evangelistic opportunity that is presented to the Church today. Here was an intelligent, educated person, a leader in society, who spent his spare time in magic and spiritistic practices, and yet was more than open to Christian faith once he knew what it was about. But when he stood up and made that statement in public, the Christians who were there all disappeared into the woodwork as fast as they could! It is difficult to know whether to be more alarmed by the nature of the spirituality rising in our culture, or by the apparent inability of most Christians either to understand or relate to it.

CHALLENGES FOR THE CHURCH

The picture so far has been sketched out using broad brush strokes. Now we need to be a little more specific. Where exactly are we heading, as we move ever closer to the new millennium? It is impossible – and unwise – to make detailed predictions, and maybe only one thing is certain anyway: wherever our destination, we are definitely going there in the fast lane. Change in a very big way is the name of the game, and whereas in the past changes took decades to filter through, today's new idea is often superseded even before it has a chance to establish itself.

This presents new challenges, especially for institutions like the Church. At one time, society could move slowly, accommodating change gradually by making small adjustments as one generation succeeded another. In that climate, it was possible for the Church to catch up gradually with the culture in which it had to minister. Today, that is no longer possible. Any institution that is not at the cutting edge of change is soon going to find itself cast on one side as irrelevant and unhelpful, no matter how grandiose its claims to truth may be.

> The more the rate of change increases, the more the problems that face us change and the shorter is the life of the solutions we find to them. Therefore, by the time we find solutions to many of the problems that face us, usually the most important ones, the problems have so changed that our solutions to them are no longer relevant or effective ... In other words, many of our solutions are to problems that no longer exist in the form in which they were solved. As a result we are falling further and further behind our times.[10]

That was written back in 1981 about secular business organizations, though its appropriateness to the Church is obvious. Since then, cultural change has accelerated fast, and the challenge will only intensify as the new millennium approaches.

What are the needs of the world to which the Church should respond in order to minister effectively to people of the twenty-first century? The search for a new worldview that can provide a credible ideological foundation for Western culture is obviously fundamental, and we will return to that theme throughout this book. But in terms of everyday life, changing assumptions and values generally take a different, more personal form. Simone Weil once wrote that 'the future is made of the same stuff as the present',[11] and some of today's significant issues will undoubtedly dominate the agenda for the foreseeable future – though we must always expect the unexpected, even if we cannot plan for it.

POLITICAL AND ECONOMIC CHANGES

The world is not the same today as it was 40 years ago. Europeans need look no further than their own continent for proof of that. In both East and West, Europe has little clear sense of either identity or purpose. Who would have believed in 1980 that communism would be in a state of terminal decline only 10 years later? The steady forward march of this totalitarian system seemed set to continue without visible end, dominating not only its traditional strongholds in Eastern Europe, but extending its influence into many countries of the developing world. Even with the insights of someone as skilful as Mikhail Gorbachev, the communist system proved to be incapable of effective reform. In its European version, it is now a thing of the past; Westerners should be reminded, however, that (so far) it has managed to survive elsewhere, including China – the world's most populous nation. The fall of the Berlin Wall and the disappearance of other obvious physical signs of communist oppression was greeted with euphoria in Western European capitals, but the demise of the communist system has not given birth to the democratic, capitalist Utopia confidently predicted for so long by its enemies. In many previously communist states, one form of exploitation and state-inspired terrorism has merely given way to another, as ethnic tension and violence have again risen to the surface of European politics. Ancient animosities that seemed long-since dead have been resurrected, and the brutality with which rival armies have opposed one another in places like Bosnia has rivalled even Hitler's Germany for savagery and inhumanity.

The countries of Western Europe have, in general, escaped the worst horrors of this social turmoil, but the European Union wrestles with its own problems. Back in the 1970s, its creators believed it could be the solution to all of Europe's problems. Today, that hope seems, at best, impossibly optimistic. Economic, social and political co-operation – let alone union – are little more than elusive shadows, and the inability of the EU even to form an effective policy in relation to the tragic events played out on its own eastern borders only serves to highlight a major failure of nerve, and identifies bigger and more disturbing questions. What exactly is 'Europe'? In what sense is Europe an identifiable place? Is it a geographical unit at all, or are these countries bound together only by the fact that for centuries their histories have impinged on one another? Could it be that the idea of 'Europe' as a unified concept had its origins not in geography or ethnicity, but in religion and ideology? Was 'Europe' a notion that only made sense as long as Christianity was the binding force holding these otherwise disparate nations together, giving them a common worldview and set of values? Is it going too far to wonder if a Europe bereft of its Christian foundations can ever be a cultural unity at all? Will Europe, in the twenty-first century, revert to being what it physically is – an appendage to Asia?

Things are no more clear-cut in that other superpower of the twentieth century, the USA. Following the Second World War, American values and national identity were largely shaped by the perceived threat to world peace coming from the old Soviet Union and its satellite states around the world. Despite all the rhetoric about upholding traditional American standards, what President Ronald Reagan once dubbed the 'evil empire' was in effect calling many of the shots in US policy, domestic as well as foreign. The demise of the Soviet Union has forced the USA onto the defensive in trying to redefine its role and identity in the new world order. Early in his presidency, Bill Clinton gave a newspaper interview in which he admitted, 'I even made a crack the other day. I said, "Gosh, I miss the cold war"...'[12] Moreover, the USA faces the same kind of internal ambiguities as the Europeans. Who exactly are the Americans? That might sound like a silly question, but it was at the heart of the nation's ambivalence about celebrating the 500th anniversary of Columbus's voyages of exploration to the so-called 'new world'. To those who already lived there, it never was the 'new world', and so the USA is still struggling with profound questions about its own national identity. Though the reins of power and influence are largely held by people from a Caucasian background, there are other significant groups with at least as much right (if not, in some cases, more) to be regarded as 'real' Americans. This great country is an amalgam of native Americans, African Americans, Asian Americans, Hispanic Americans, as well as Caucasians, all living together in what, in cultural terms, is a somewhat uneasy truce that needs little provocation before the cracks begin to show.

While Europeans and Americans are looking within to patch up their failing vision, the whole world centre of gravity is moving elsewhere. The economic power of the West has been in decline for the last 40 years or more, but because of the inherited wealth and traditions of the preceding 500 years, it was possible for Westerners still to behave as if they were truly in control of things. That is no longer the case. The majority of the world's people have always lived in the two-thirds world. Today, they are getting influence commensurate with their numbers, and many of the most significant decision-making and trend-setting processes have moved east. The Pacific Rim is now the world's economic powerhouse, and we can expect other parts of the two-thirds world increasingly to take responsibility for setting the agenda in the next century and beyond.

The influence of the two-thirds world will not just be economic, for alongside the economic growth there are some significant religious and social factors. Everyone knows about the rise of so-called Fundamentalist Islam. At least, everyone knows what the Western media – who are generally militantly anti-Muslim – report of it.[13] Yet clearly, Islamic values are not as alien to Western people as the media would have us believe. How, otherwise, can the growth of Islam in the West be explained, especially when many of the converts are white, Western people with no ethnic or other ties to traditionally Islamic nations? Such converts are clearly affirming the positive usefulness of Islamic values as they attempt to make sense out of the jumble that is modern Western culture.[14] Christians who become paranoid about the growth of Islam in the West are often uncritically accepting the distorted (and, arguably, racist) media view of this ancient faith.

The fact is that there are still far more Christians in the world than there are adherents of any other faith – just over 2 billion of them. At a time when an average of 7,500 people leave the Church every day in Europe alone,[15] there is no denying that Christianity is disintegrating in the West, though there is no evidence that this is in any way linked with or leading to a significant expansion of Islam. On the contrary, there is every reason to believe that the failure of the Church is more closely paralleled by the rise in popularity of new forms of home-grown spirituality. In world terms, talk of Christianity in decline is absurd. One of the ironies of our time is that as Westerners question and reject Christianity, the ever-increasing populations of the two-thirds world are embracing Christian faith in vast numbers. Some 60% of all the world's Christians now live in the developing world, and are not white Westerners. Though there is still a significant Christian missionary enterprise, it is rapidly moving into reverse gear as Christian missionaries are now travelling from places like Africa and South America to share their faith in the traditional Christian heartlands of Europe, North America and Australasia.[16]

In parallel with the shift in the world's economic centre of gravity from the West to the Pacific there is another great shift in the centre of gravity of Christian faith. For its first 1000 years, Christianity was the faith of the Mediterranean lands where it originated. During its second 1000 years, it was the faith of people in Europe and the lands to which they emigrated, predominantly North America and Australasia. At the beginning of its third millennium, Christianity is without question the faith of the people of the two-thirds world. Western Christians who wish to take their evangelistic calling seriously will need to take account of the fact that the majority of the world's Christians are no longer like them. While the Western churches decline, Christianity elsewhere is expanding very fast. There must be lessons to be learned from this which can benefit the Western Church, but it will be a painful process for Westerners to learn how to accept new insights from those who have all too often been regarded as spiritually inferior and unsophisticated.

LIFESTYLE CHANGES

If anything, the pace of change in Western lifestyles is even faster than in other areas we have mentioned. As a result of new opportunities for worldwide travel, people are becoming more aware of different cultures than their own. This is having a profound effect on what we eat, the kind of medicine we practise, and the ways in which we expect to make sense out of life. We now know that Christianity is not the only possible religious faith, and there is growing admiration for the achievements of other cultures as people discover that for the past few centuries it is the West that has been the aberration, not the rest of the world. For while Westerners confidently supposed that religion was dead, most of the world's people continued to find meaning and significance through religious faith. Coupled with a genuine search for personal identity, meaning and purpose in life, appreciating that has encouraged people in the West to adopt a much more open-ended approach in their search for personal fulfilment.

The information and communication revolution has also changed the outlook of most people. Every day, increasing numbers of us access data files all across the world using nothing more than a personal computer and a phone line. Of course, the accessibility of so much information raises new questions, not least how to find enough time to process and use it all. But the problems raised for the Church by what is essentially a non-book culture are enormous. The growth in the entertainment and leisure industries have the same impact. Even in my lifetime we have gone from cracked gramophone record to compact disc and interactive video. There are so many options now open to us for our leisure, that people can even become stressed by making decisions about how to enjoy themselves. In fact, the nature of leisure itself is changing, as people seek to define their identity through what they do in their own personal time rather than what they do in paid employment. We will not be far into the twenty-first century before it will be the norm for people to design their own lifestyle portfolio of part-time work, voluntary service, and self-expressive leisure activities – partly because of increasing concern about the quality of life, but also because changing patterns of business organization are providing fewer and fewer full-time job opportunities.[17] In this climate, churchgoing and religious involvement will inevitably be sidelined unless they appear to offer the promise of something that is worth giving one's time and talents for. The major challenge for evangelism will be how to reach the person who says they can live quite well without God.

Family structures are also changing rapidly, and while many agree that a major cause of social suffering today is the disintegration of the traditional family, there is no consensus about what can be put in its place. Single parent families, blended families, multi-generational households, even street gangs, are the norm for many of today's children. Some children literally have no idea who their real parents are, as partners remarry, divorce and cohabit with increasing speed. The dysfunctional family is widespread, with abuse and violence found at all levels of society. Then there is the fact that cohabitation is increasingly favoured in preference to marriage, at least on a short-term basis, while recent figures suggest that one in four of all mothers over 40 in the UK are now unmarried, by choice.[18] Is this a genuine change in our culture? It is certainly symptomatic of a real search for new ways of community, but have Christians taken it all seriously enough to be able to have something useful to say?[19]

This, then, is the confusing, yet dynamic jungle that we live in as we approach the end of the millennium. This is where today's Christians are called to be salt and light, sharing the good news of which Jesus spoke. What does it all mean? How can the Church respond in ways that will be culturally appropriate, while still reflecting the ultimate values of the gospel? These are big questions, and we will be doing well if we can even set up a few signposts by the end of this book. As we seek new vision and empowerment for the task, I am reminded of a story told by Australian sociologists Peter and Sue Kaldor:[20]

Once upon a time there was a mighty river. It flowed gracefully and elegantly across the landscape. Along its banks it gave life and sustenance to the tribes of aboriginal Australians who camped by it. For many generations this river was a central focus for life. Then, gradually, the river ceased to flow, becoming a stagnant pool. With the heat of summer it started to dry up. Around the banks of the disappearing symbol of their security, the people watched aghast. What could be happening to them? By the dried-up riverbed many sat, waiting for the river to flow once more.

Yet others thought to look around and discovered that the river was not gone. Still flowing, it had simply changed course upstream, creating a billabong on the curve at which they sat.

Most Christians in the West can see that things have changed, and that the world has moved on. But too many are still sitting by the dried-up riverbed, hoping the water will flow back the way it once did. It takes neither faith nor courage to do that. It is more demanding to step out and take risks, to experiment in order to discover where God's life-giving Spirit is moving in today's world. To move away might mean the dismantling of our institutions or the sacrifice of some sacred cows, and that is always painful. But if the experience of the world Church is anything to go by, it might also mean a rediscovery of the gospel and some exciting surprises. Whatever the cost, this could be where God is calling the Church to go. For the size of the opportunity more than matches the dimensions of the challenge:

> The future of humanity could easily be more dependent on our moving with this moment of grace than on anything else being done in the world today. If we truly believe that Jesus is the God-sent answer to our human needs but fail to share that answer with others, the next millennium could become the last.[21]

CHAPTER 2

WHERE DO WE GO FROM HERE?

There are some times and places that, no matter how hard we try, are impossible to erase from the memory. Many people of an older generation remember exactly where they were when they heard the news that US president John F. Kennedy had been assassinated in 1963. For me, one of the days I shall never forget is Wednesday 13 March 1996.

On that spring morning, life in the normally quiet Scottish rural city of Dunblane was changed forever by a crazed gunman's brutal murder of 16 young children and their teacher, as they began what would otherwise have been just another day at school. The repercussions of that event spread far and wide. The world's media descended on this small community, only a five-minute drive from my home, and in a matter of hours a place most people had never heard of was making the headlines in news bulletins on every continent. For some, it was a time of great tragedy and crisis, as those families who had lost the most came to terms with the fact that their lives would never be the same again. For the whole community, and for many more beyond Dunblane and Scotland, it was one of those defining moments when ultimate questions about the meaning of life and death took on a new significance; it was a time to reflect, and above all to do whatever seemed possible and practical in order to support those who were suffering. Within 24 hours, the streets of this tiny community were lined with floral tributes, children's toys and cards of condolence sent from people in distant lands, as well as those closer to home. Two days later, Dunblane's ancient cathedral was packed to capacity not once, but several times, as thousands of people sought a place of quietness and spiritual consolation in the midst of their grief.

One of the things that struck me most in that situation was that alongside the natural question, 'Why do bad things like this happen to innocent people?' there was also a spontaneous outpouring of popular spirituality, motivated not so much by a desire to blame God, as an almost primal need to rediscover where God might be found within the terror and uncertainty of that awful moment. During that particular day, I must personally have prayed with literally hundreds of people whose lives were touched, and who sought solace in God. They were not, for the most part, regular Church attenders, and it was a new experience for me to walk down the street and be accosted by complete strangers who just wanted to be held in silence and assured of God's presence with them in their shock and sorrow.

By the end of the day, I knew I needed some space to reflect for myself, and just before midnight I made my way to the school gates which had become a centre of devotion, transformed by the floral offerings and other tributes placed there by residents and strangers alike. As I approached, the street outside the school was deserted apart from a handful of police officers and a gang of youths aged, I suppose, about 17–20. As I watched, they took from their pockets 16 small candles and one larger one – one for each dead child, and one for their teacher. Kneeling on the damp pavement, they arranged them in a circle, then carefully lit them, using for the purpose glowing cigarettes removed from their mouths with almost sacramental precision. They stood around the candles for a moment, until one of them said, 'I suppose somebody should say something.'

As they wondered how to do it, they caught sight of me, identified me as a minister, and called me over with the words, 'You'll know what to say.' Of course, the reality was quite different. As I stood there, tears streaming down my face, I had no idea what to say, or how to say it. Words had not been especially useful to me, or anyone else, in this crisis. So we stood, holding onto one another for a moment, and then eventually I spoke. I have no recollection of what I said. It certainly was not a formal 'Churchy' kind of prayer, but it provided the catalyst that enabled them to start praying. A question came first: 'What kind of world is this?' Another asked, 'Is there any hope?' Someone said, 'I wish I could trust God.' 'I'll need to change,' said a fourth one. As he did so, he looked first at me, and then glanced over his shoulder to the police who were on duty. He reached into his pocket and I could see he had a knife. He knelt again by the ring of candles, and quietly said 'I'll not be needing this now,' as he tucked it away under some of the flowers laying nearby. One of the others produced what looked like a piece of cycle chain, and did the same. We stood silently for a moment, and then went our separate ways.

You might be forgiven for wondering what relevance all this has to a book on faith and culture. Just this. The street outside that school had become holy ground for those youths that night. They were meeting God in a profound way. Though they would not have used this language, they were repenting. They were reaching out. They were searching for a better way of living – for God's kingdom. And they had identified a culturally relevant way of expressing their spirituality. You might imagine that incident should be good news for the Church. But in reality, it presents Christians with a profound challenge. For what kind of Churches would we need to develop in order to create a space to accept and encourage the growth of the kind of spirituality I met that night on a deserted street in a mourning community? Put simply, I want to suggest that the Church is in love with words, doctrines, rational arguments and statements about faith, whereas those youths instinctively expressed their spirituality not through words, but through symbols. Could it be that we Christians are somehow imprisoned in a kind of cognitive captivity, which is inhibiting our mission, and maybe even keeping Christ on the fringes of the Church?

The significance of all this came home to me during a visit to the USA some three or four months after that experience in Dunblane. I was visiting a thriving mainline Church, with a large congregation of several hundred people. Following the custom of the particular denomination, a talented and gifted woman rose to her feet to tell a story to the many children who were present. She began her talk by pulling a large sheet of paper from her bag, commenting as she did so that 'This story is so important that I decided to write it down.'

For me, that was a defining moment of a different sort, because for the first time I heard a Church leader give verbal expression to something I had long suspected to be true, and which highlighted a major feature of much Western Church culture, which in turn reminded me of a major reason why it is so difficult to communicate the gospel to those millions of people who are engaged in a spiritual search, but have not been conditioned to accepting the way Churches do things. For Christians, all the truly important things are written down: in books, in confessions of faith, in liturgies, even in sermons which, for the most part, are spoken forms of essentially literary communications. More than 30 years ago, Marshall McLuhan taught us that 'the medium is the message'.[1] Among other things, that means the medium we choose has a subtle effect on the substance of what we are passing on. When the medium is written, literary, bookish and wordy, then by definition the most important things are going to be things we can think about, reflect on and analyse, and the unimportant things are going to be intuition, experience and the concerns of the spirit – none of which can adequately be communicated through words.

LOOKING BACKWARDS

A traditional Chinese proverb advises, 'Whoever does not know the village they have come from will never find the village they are looking for.' If the Church is to find its true calling in the new world order of the twenty-first century, there will need to be some honest heart-searching about the past. What is the village we have come from? The European Enlightenment has had a profound and far-reaching impact on Christian thinking. To a much greater extent than many Christians care to admit, for the last several centuries the Church has been dominated by the ideological values of an essentially secular culture. As a result, Christians have taken it for granted that faith is a matter of private opinion, with no direct relevance to the real world of politics, science or economics. They have accepted the basic rationalist understanding of how things might be known, and what is worth knowing. They have promoted a materialist attitude to the mystical and the numinous, and theological scholarship and education has applied a reductionist methodology in a more thoroughgoing way than almost any other intellectual discipline.[2]

When some contemporary critics of Christianity claim that the Church has become so hopelessly identified with the problems in our culture that it has no useful contribution to the search for new solutions, they frequently exaggerate and over-state their case.[3] But their analysis is not completely inaccurate, and as Christians face up to the challenge of the re-evangelization of the West, they will need to own and deal with the intellectual and social baggage inherited from past generations. A revisionist version of Christian history will be seen for what it is: a whitewashing of previous mistakes, and an attempt to avoid any sense of shared responsibility for them.

Where might we begin that process of critical and creative reflection on our past? Descartes (1595–1650) is as good a starting point as any, with his Latin dictum *cogito ergo sum*: I am thinking, therefore I am. This understanding of human nature has had a profound and dominating effect on the whole of recent Western history. Personhood has been defined in relation to what people think, and the processes of rationality and argument, rather than how people feel. Doing has been more highly prized than being. Of course, this notion is not of specially recent origin. Centuries before Descartes and the Enlightenment, the same idea was espoused by Greek philosophical thinking in an even more radical way, which denigrated the whole of physical existence in favour of the 'reason' that was believed to be at the centre of all things. The Renaissance rediscovery of the classical heritage played a key role in the articulation of this doctrine for modern times. Within that cultural stream, thinking was often set in opposition to feeling. The Jewish philosopher Philo of Alexandria, a near-contemporary of Jesus, wrote that 'we must put down our feelings as we put down the working classes.'[4] It may be politically incorrect to agree with the second part of that statement today, but the first assumption is still widely taken for granted. The marginalization of feelings has been a key characteristic not just of Western Christianity, but through it of the whole of Western society – to such an extent that many Western people, men in particular, simply have no life skills with which to handle emotions and feelings, or to relate to the numinous and the spiritual.

CHALLENGING THE CONSENSUS

Of course, our culture as a whole is waking up to the impoverishment of spirit induced by this kind of reliance on just one way of seeing the world. Part of the paradigm shift that is undoubtedly taking place today is a movement away from the traditional Western consensus, and towards a different worldview, the precise shape of which is unclear as it is still emerging, but which – for that very reason – Christians need to take seriously and with which they must urgently engage in constructive dialogue. One of the most obvious challenges to the traditional Cartesian view has come from modern brain science. To put it simply, we now know that to be Western in this traditional sense is literally to be half-witted, because it values and uses only one half of the human brain.[5] Western culture has been dominated and directed by those skills that are located in the left hemisphere of the brain – skills of analysis, of logic, of abstract thinking, of speech and of grammar. But we cannot be whole persons unless we learn to use all our brains, and that means valuing the different kinds of skills that are controlled by the right side of the brain: imagination, feeling, metaphor, colour, texture and so on.

All this is, of course, a well attested physiological fact. But many people are now using the imagery of left- and right-brain not so much to speak literally of the brain itself, but of two different – though complementary – ways of being and of understanding the world and society. This has been encouraged and facilitated by the rapid shrinkage of the world in real terms, as we are becoming more aware of different cultures and the possibilities of other worldviews presented by them. At the beginning of the twentieth century it was still possible to imagine that being Western, and accepting Western values and lifestyles, was the only way to live the good life. But it is now obvious to all but the most blinkered that the Western worldview is not the only possible one, and that in historical terms the majority of the world's people in all times and places have lived their lives according to quite different principles. Indeed, one can arrive at the same understanding of worldview options by an entirely different route through Western linguistic philosophy.[6] The following diagram highlights some of the major contrasts:

SCIENTIFIC WORLDVIEW	POETIC WORLDVIEW
Precise	Imprecise
Reason/intellect	Emotions/intuition
Permanent	Provisional
Physical	Spiritual
Absolute	Ambiguous
Science/technology	Values
Propositional	Approximate
Western Culture	Ethnic worldviews
Rational	Intuitive
Men	Women
Literal	Symbolic
Church	Spiritual quest
Worship	Personal needs

To a large extent, the two columns can be identified with the qualities of left-brain thinking (the 'scientific worldview') and right-brain thinking (the 'poetic worldview'). Though there is a good deal of debate about the precise difference between Hebrew (biblical) thinking and Greek (secular) thinking, it would not be misleading to identify, in addition, the scientific column with the Greeks and the poetic column with the Hebrews, at least if we use these terms in a typological sense.

The various headings then identify not only the philosophical notions underlying these distinctions, but also some of their practical repercussions. The diagram itself will repay further reflection, but anyone can see that the development of Western Christianity has been wholly dominated by the values and concerns of what is here labelled 'scientific'. Moreover, contrasts of this kind can also be expressed in other, more overtly spiritual ways. With greater knowledge of Eastern philosophy and religion, the notion of forces of *yin* and *yang* and the need for balance between them for true wholeness in life has entered the vocabulary and thought world of more and more people. Forget for a moment the metaphysical origins of these concepts, and reflect on them as a typological understanding of two opposed ways of being, and you can construct a diagram like this:

YANG	YIN
Masculine	Feminine
Demanding	Contractive
Aggressive	Responsive
Competitive	Co-operative
Rational	Intuitive
Analytic	Synthesizing

It hardly needs any further comment for the similarities between the two diagrams to become immediately apparent, nor for the repercussions of this for Christian faith to be obvious. In each case, the column on the left represents those characteristics that arguably have created most of the tensions in the world today, not only those tensions between people but also that most crucial tension of all, between people and the environment. The column on the right, by contrast, highlights a different way of living and relating, which looks to be gentler and more relevant to life in the new millennium, and ultimately more redemptive in terms of healing the wounds of the world and its people. The question is: has the Church become trapped in the wrong place?

Before we address that question more directly, it is worth mentioning, however briefly, the revolution in pure science that has also led to the questioning, if not the complete abandonment, of the Enlightenment understanding of what is worth knowing and how it can be known. When I was a student in the late 1960s, it was a common opinion that science dealt with facts, whereas religion was only about opinions. That perception led many of my contemporaries to atheism; although, even then, cutting-edge science had dealt the death-blow to such an understanding. Today, however, it is taken for granted that science does not have the answers; indeed, that as traditionally practised in its Newtonian and Baconian forms, it scarcely knew the right questions. By 1994, in a throwaway aside that he felt no need to justify because he knew no one would fundamentally challenge it, management professor Charles Handy could write of 'the myth of science, the idea that everything, in theory, could be understood, predicted and, therefore managed'.[7]

Science no longer claims to tell us how things really are in some objective sense, certainly not within the context of a closed-system view of the universe. The whole agenda now seems to be wide open. Following the groundbreaking work of Einstein, Heisenberg, Gödel, Mandelbrot and, more recently, Stephen Hawking, literally anything seems to be possible, at least in theory. Some of the leading spiritual commentators of our day are also scientists. I am thinking here of people like biologist Rupert Sheldrake and physicist Fritjof Capra, or astronomer Barry McWaters, who explains his own search for new light on the human condition in the following terms:

We are listening for messages of guidance from every possible source; tuning in our astro-radios, talking to dolphins, and listening more and more attentively to the words of those among us with psychic abilities. Is there help out there? Is there guidance in here? Will anyone respond?"

Christians who are also scientists are often inclined to dismiss such statements as unscientific and unrepresentative, but the fact remains that all these people hold university chairs in their respective disciplines, and so the average person trusts them to know what they are talking about. Even Stephen Hawking, arguably the greatest scientist of our day, writing in the foreword to Lawrence Krauss's book *The Physics of Star Trek*, comments that 'To confine our attention to terrestrial matters would be to limit the human spirit', and in the process tacitly endorses the possibility of time travel.⁹

DIAGNOSING THE PROBLEM

In the midst of all this upheaval in Western culture, and the growing conviction that we need a new paradigm to take us forward into the next millennium, a widely-held understanding of what is going on would run along the following lines:

Our present predicament is due to mistakes made by our forebears during the last 500 years or so. In particular, they so marginalized spiritual and personal values in favour of a mechanistic, rationalist, reductionist outlook that what once seemed to be the major strength of Western culture has now turned out to be its greatest liability. At the root of our problem is a loss of spiritual perception and sensitivity. Any effective resolution of the ideological crisis facing the West must therefore start by reversing that trend, and hence with the recovery of spirituality. Furthermore, if there is a way out of the mess, traditional Western sources of spiritual guidance will be of little help in finding it. As part of the old cultural establishment, the Church as we know it is incapable of playing any constructive role in redefining the future, because the defective Enlightenment worldview was little more than the logical outcome of classical Christian beliefs and values.[10]

There is no question that the relationship between Church, Enlightenment and Western culture is a good deal more complex than that analysis implies. But there is enough truth in this understanding to give it plausibility in the eyes of growing numbers of people, and at this purely pragmatic level the Church cannot afford to split hairs over the inaccuracies it may contain while ignoring what is correct about this diagnosis. A particular concern ought to be the implication that the Church is part of the problem, and therefore cannot be part of the solution to it. This focuses especially on the area of spirituality. For whereas 10 years ago, people were inclined to dismiss the Church as dull, boring, old-fashioned or irrelevant, today an increasing chorus is insisting the Church is 'unspiritual'. It is not always easy to define what 'spirituality' might mean in this context, and I am not going to try, though later chapters will hopefully provide some materials out of which some kind of frame of reference might be constructed. But it is obvious that, if the Church is the last place today's spiritual searchers will go for spirituality, then Christians face a major problem of credibility and integrity.

So where are the places people are visiting to find spirituality today? To provide a comprehensive route map through all the intricacies of the Western spiritual search would be complex and – probably – impossible, if only because the exact shape of the territory is changing all the time. Nevertheless, it is possible to establish some compass points that may help to give a sense of direction while not being prescriptive about the actual path that any given person might choose to follow. As indicated in the previous chapter, I believe we can trace four dominant polarities through which transformational philosophies and experiences are being actively pursued at the present time.

1 NON-WESTERN WORLDVIEWS

By this I mean the traditional worldviews of Eastern religions. A simplistic view of things says that if the problem is created by what is modern and Western, then the way to deal with it is to find solutions in things that are ancient and Eastern. Consequently, many Western people are committing themselves to Eastern paths, particularly Taoism and Buddhism, but also others.

2 FIRST NATION BELIEFS

Others question whether we need to look so far away. In places like North and South America, Australia and Aotearoa New Zealand, other ancient nations flourished long before white Westerners arrived in those lands. Insofar as anyone can tell, their worldviews and lifestyles were spiritually-oriented and environmentally friendly – but they were brutally suppressed and devalued by the imposition of Western culture.

With the benefit of hindsight, it can now be seen that native Americans and other aboriginal peoples had much spiritual wisdom. Could it be that by reaffirming them, Western people might not only expiate some of the guilt of their own past, but also find new ways forward into the future? Certainly, one does not have to look far today to find young people reconstructing native American medicine wheels that their own great-grandparents destroyed just a couple of generations ago, and adopting their religious mythologies as a way of addressing issues of modern living.

3   GOING BACKWARDS

Perhaps we do not even have to look as far as that. In the European heartlands of the West, there were spiritual cultures long before the arrival of classical 'Western' values, reinforced through Greek philosophy and, later, the development of Christendom. Could we maybe get things right by leaping backwards, as it were, into our own history and seeking to rediscover afresh the kind of worldview that motivated our own long-forgotten ancestors? This possibility accounts for the renewed interest in ancient Celtic spirituality, goddess worship and the increasing popularity of neo-paganism in its many forms – all of which are perhaps the fastest-growing types of popular spirituality in northern Europe today.[11]

4   GOING WITHIN

Many of those searching for new ways of being are not at all attracted to anything that might be labelled 'religion'. For them, religion in general – not just Christianity – is the problem. If we are to make sense of life, we will need to go within, recognizing that ultimately we ourselves are the only resource we have. The development of psychotherapies of various kinds   foremost among them the rise of transpersonal psychology – is providing this kind of 'secular' person with access to the same kind of transformational experiences as mystical religious traditions offer, but without the initially unwelcome baggage of religious dogma.[12] Hence the popularity of transformational video and audio tapes, bodywork, and other related therapies.

❊   ❊   ❊

Even within these so-called 'new age' spiritual circles, there are different attitudes to what is going on. Starhawk, for example, is a self-styled witch who is very much a part of the revival of goddess worship and neo-paganism. But she expresses real doubts about the validity of what happens when people try and construct their own eclectic spiritualities out of such diverse materials, dismissing them as misguided and insensitive people who, because of the spiritual starvation they experience in Western culture 'unwittingly become spiritual strip miners damaging other cultures in superficial attempts to uncover their mystical treasures'.[13] Others, though, are much more optimistic about the possibility of combining disparate materials into a new worldview, and on the whole they are the ones who are attracting most followers. David Spangler and William Irwin Thompson are typical representatives of such optimism:

> ...this new planetary sensibility or culture will be less a thing and more a process that nourishes our creativity and wholeness and provides sustenance for building the bodies of tomorrow...we are reimagining our world. We are taking hunks of ecology and slices of science, pieces of politics and a sprinkle of economics, a pinch of religion and a dash of philosophy, and we are reimagining these and a host of other ingredients into something new...a reimagination of the world.[14]

In the midst of such euphoria, though, we need to note that not everyone even believes the effort to create such a 'postmodern' worldview is worth making, as this quotation from social psychologist Ernest Gellner makes plain:

> Postmodernism is a contemporary movement. It is strong and fashionable. Over and above this, it is not altogether

clear what the devil it is. In fact, clarity is not conspicuous amongst its marked attributes ... all this seems to be part of the atmosphere, or mist, in which postmodernism flourishes, or which postmodernism helps to spread.[15]

The introduction of the word 'postmodernism' provides an opportunity to summarize where we find ourselves today. Three ages, or stages of development, may be discerned in Western culture. First was the period of the pre-modern (which in fact was most of history): a time dominated by superstition and mythology, and other pre-critical ways of understanding things. Then, with the Renaissance, the development of modern science and the Enlightenment, came the period of modernity, with its commitment to the critical application of reason as the way to get things right, and a consequent devaluing and demythologizing of what were perceived to be 'primitive' magical and religious worldviews. We now seem to be somewhere in the transition from modernity in that classical sense to whatever may follow it, conventionally labelled 'postmodernism', though there is a good deal of uncertainty as to what exactly that means.[16]

Some things, though, are clear: the cultural climate in which we now find ourselves is increasingly post-critical, in the sense that it is questioning – even rejecting – categories of reason and rationality. It is giving a much greater place to intuition, and is rapidly remythologizing our understandings of the world, not only through the spiritual search in the narrow sense, but also in modern science. In one sense, this is just a different way of expressing the same thing as the two diagrams used previously in this chapter.

CHURCH AND CULTURE

Where does the Church find itself in all this? Dean W. R. Inge (1860–1954) is credited with the observation that 'A church which is married to the spirit of its age will be a widow in the next.' On all the indicators that I can identify, there seems to be no doubt whatever that the Church, an essentially conservative institution, has so firmly and fully committed itself to the worldview of the Enlightenment – in itself collapsing with accelerating speed – that it is being left behind by the pace of change, and is finding it increasingly difficult to be taken seriously by the new emerging mainstream Western culture.

The Church's indebtedness to Enlightenment thinking is beyond question. Writing of the development of the modern evangelical movement, David Bebbington observes that

> It is extremely hard to resist the conclusion that the early evangelicals were immersed in the Enlightenment. They were participating fully in the progressive thought of their age ...[17]

For him, that is a strength of evangelicalism, and a commendation of its achievements. But from the standpoint of effective mission in the new millennium, it is arguably the taproot from which stem most of the Church's problems – both in empowering its own members to live in ways that will bear witness to gospel values, as well as in sharing Christian faith with unchurched people.

At the very least, the Church's alignment with classical Western culture (and it is a Church alignment, not just – or even predominantly – an evangelical phenomenon) is a double-edged sword. For we need to put the currently fashionable rejection of the Enlightenment in a proper perspective. Some scholars today write as if the Enlightenment was the greatest disaster ever to befall the human race. But no one can seriously believe that. Despite the current emphasis on holistic healthcare, for example, who would really want to turn the clock back to the medical practices of 300 years ago, or return to the way things were before the invention of mass transportation systems? The Enlightenment and its values are not all bad news, and in our eagerness to distance ourselves from some of the mistaken excesses of the past, it does no harm to be reminded of the positive side.

Take, for example, the emphasis on reason, and the consequent insistence that faith needs to have a rational foundation. A couple of generations ago that led to the conclusion that, in religious terms, nothing could possibly be worth believing. With the questioning of that outlook, much contemporary speculation on spirituality seems to have swung to the opposite extreme, and we now live in a culture where everything and anything seems to be worth believing; for some people, the more bizarre and unlikely it is on a rational level, then the more value there is in believing it. To bear witness to faith in a generation that is increasingly attracted to the irrational as an alternative to materialist rationalism might need to be started by underlining the importance of thinking. Being rational about things is not necessarily the same as being a rationalist – nor for that matter is irrationality the only alternative to an over-confident rationalism. There is more to the human personality than a left-brained analytical understanding of things; the non-rational or right-brained side, as experienced and expressed through the emotions and intuitions, is undoubtedly more important than Western people have typically allowed. Even traditional Western science has sometimes relied on intuitions for significant advances! In 1865, for example, the German chemist August Kekule had a dream in which the benzene molecule was like a snake whirling around biting its own tail. He remembered his dream and as a result of taking its images seriously, not only described the chemical structure of benzene for the first time, but also came up with a hypothesis that explained otherwise incomprehensible aspects of organic chemistry.

However, if we depend only on our non-rational intuitions for everything it is all too easy to misrepresent and misunderstand things in a way that will effectively undermine any serious spiritual search for truth. Many people today seem unable to tell the difference between fact and fantasy, and bearing witness to the gospel in our generation might need to begin with an insistence that there are at least some objective realities out there! The critical attitude engendered by the Enlightenment emphasis on reason is far from being all bad news!

Having said that, however, it is undeniable that on the whole Christians have related to the forces of modernity and Enlightenment in a very uncritical way. They have accepted without question its weaknesses as well as its strengths, and the impact of this is devastating, especially now we are faced with a fast-changing cultural context. In its ways of knowing and definitions of what is worth knowing, not to mention prevailing attitudes to anything remotely mystical, numinous or supernatural, Western Christianity looks increasingly like one of the final resting places of a rationalist–materialist worldview. As a consequence, the Church often has a fragmented vision of itself, and its theology and spirituality suffer from a cognitive captivity that inhibits the development of a truly holistic gospel that will speak authentically to the needs of people in a postmodern world.

If this analysis seems unduly negative and critical, then I need to remind readers that I am writing from within the mainstream of the Christian Church, and many of my conclusions arise from what I know to be the painful cultural discontinuity that is experienced not by those on the fringes of the Church, but increasingly by those who are the most committed as they struggle to be true to themselves on the one hand, and faithful to the gospel of Jesus Christ on the other. Not that we need to rely solely on that kind of anecdotal evidence to support this point of view. It is a truism that most people in Churches get their theology out of hymns, rather than from Bibles or books of doctrine. And if anyone doubts the influence of Western culture on the Church, they need look no further than this hymn by Addington Symonds, still found in the standard hymn books of most denominations (even those whose official pronouncements express completely contrary sentiments!):

> These things shall be: a loftier race
> Than e'er the world hath known shall rise
> With flame of freedom in their souls
> And light of knowledge in their eyes.
>
> They shall be gentle, brave, and strong
> To spill no drop of blood, but dare
> All that may plant man's lordship firm
> On earth, and fire, and sea, and air.

What is this, if not a manifesto for the Western imperialist vision? The sentiments of these verses, in particular, quite overtly disseminate the seeds of racism and of environmental exploitation, not to mention innuendoes along similar lines contained in subsequent stanzas. Rudyard Kipling, writing in the year of Symonds's death (1893), discerned the close connection between the power of empire and the beliefs of the Church in his poem 'McAndrew's Hymn':

> Lord, Thou hast made this world below the shadow of a
>   dream,
> An', taught by time, I tak' it so – exceptin' always Steam.
> From coupler-flange to spindle-guide I see Thy Hand, O God –

Predestination in the stride o' yon connectin'-rod.
John Calvin might ha' forged the same – enorrmous,
   certain, slow –
Ay, wrought it in the furnace-flame – *my* 'Institutio'.

Clearly, Western Christians have a lot of baggage to sort
through in order to have an effective gospel for the twenty-first
century. And dealing with it in a positive way will require a
much more extensive tool-kit than the Church is accustomed to
using. Abraham Maslow once commented that 'If the only tool
you have is a hammer, you tend to see every problem as a nail',
and that fairly sums up where the Church finds itself. We have
only one tool – or, more accurately, several different models of
what is the same basic tool. They are all oriented towards rational, cognitive, left-brained ways of doing things. Using a hammer to remove a screw is a very difficult enterprise. Not
impossible, maybe, but if you try it there is a high risk that you
will damage the wood, destroy the screw, and probably harm
yourself into the bargain. The analogy holds good in the
Church. Older people, who were educated in a system which
saw everything as decided by human reason, often simply cannot understand the concerns and questions of younger people
who are truly a part of postmodern culture – and 'older' in this
context means roughly people over forty. Trained in a different
generation, they find it hard to comprehend the extent to which
reason is no longer dominant in today's world. Writing about
her own spiritual worldview, Shirley Maclaine says that 'It
seems to be all about feeling, not thinking.'[18] Bhagwan Shree
Rajneesh went further, and insisted that: 'It is not that the intellect sometimes misunderstands. It is not that the intellect sometimes errs; it is that the intellect is the error.'[19] I have selected
these quotes from popular writers, because this is where most
people look for guidance. But the same general sentiments
could as easily be quoted from regular scholars of literature or

history, many of whom would share the same distrust of reason, even though they owe their positions to their own exercise of it.

NEW OPPORTUNITIES

This is not just an arcane philosophical issue: it is something of vital importance to the Church's mission at this time. Philosophy professor Jacob Needleman is perhaps a classic example of today's spiritual searcher, who is not against the Church or Christianity, but cannot see its relevance because it is

> only a matter of words, exhortations and philosophy rather than a matter of practical guidance for experiencing directly the truth of the teachings ... We are looking for the Christianity that works, that actually produces real change in human nature, real transformation.[20]

Needleman wrote that back in 1980, but George Barna discovered exactly the same concern among young adults in his 1994 study of what in the USA are called 'baby busters' (people born between 1965 and 1983). He reports an interview with a 20-year-old called Lisa Baker, who commented:

> I honestly tried the Churches, but they just couldn't speak to me. I'm not against Churches or religion. I just don't want to waste my time in places that have no real wisdom, only to discover that when I'm 50 or something. All I want is reality. Show me God. Help me to understand why life is the way it is, and how I can experience it more fully and with greater joy. I don't want the empty promises. I want the real thing. And I'll go wherever I find that truth system.[21]

✳   ✳   ✳

Later on, he concludes that 'Busters believe what they can feel, taste, see, hear and touch – and very little else.'[22] All my own experience points in exactly the same direction. But in the average church, how much is there to feel, taste, see, hear and touch?[23] Of course, some will ask: how much should there be? We will return to Jesus as the model evangelist in a later chapter, but for the moment reflect on the fact that, when asked to summarize his message, he quoted the book of Deuteronomy to the effect that 'you shall love the Lord your God with all your heart, and with all your soul, and with all your mind, and with all your strength ... you shall love your neighbour as yourself' (Mark 12:30–31).

Both parts of that statement are important, but let us single out the first part here. Whatever else may be said, this presents a holistic vision of discipleship that has largely been sidelined in traditional Western Christianity. We have done a wonderful job of loving God with our minds, while to varying degrees we have either dismissed altogether or been embarrassed by the possibilities of a spirituality that expresses itself through the heart (emotions), or the spirit (harder to define, but definitely something mystical/numinous) or the strength (physical bodies). Of course, thinking and rational processes are not unimportant, but even with a simplistic view of what Jesus is saying, that only constitutes 25% of the total demand of the gospel. Whereas we typically offer people something to think about, the kind of all-embracing discipleship of which Jesus speaks is an invitation to explore a balanced spirituality that engages every part of the human personality. If the Church is to be effective in communicating the gospel today, it will be through the rediscovery of that holistic balance. In particular, we will need to affirm that spirituality comes before theology, and allow experience of God to take precedence over metaphysical speculation. After all, the New Testament shows that following Jesus is the first act, and reflecting on the meaning and significance of that following comes subsequently.

Moreover, we will need to insist that this is no new-fangled notion dreamed up by a few trendy end-of-century theologians. Not only can such teaching be traced back to Jesus himself, but it can also be found in the Western theological tradition. Anselm of Canterbury (1033–1109), for example, put it this way: 'I do not seek to understand that I may believe, but I believe that I may understand...unless I believe I will not understand.' Unless I am much mistaken, today's Christians will be judged more by the quality of their spirituality than by the truth of their message. I am not saying that truth is not important. But our entire apologetic seems to be directed towards 'proving' the truth of the gospel using the tools of an essentially secular worldview going back to Enlightenment rationalism. For me, that would raise questions even if people were making enquiries that could be addressed in that way. But on the whole, they are not. Most spiritual searchers are not first asking whether Christianity is true in some absolute sense, but what difference it might make to them if they choose to follow Jesus. If they come and follow Jesus, how will that impact lives and help people be more fulfilled people?

Discerning how to address questions like that, while being faithful to Jesus, is the major agenda for much of the rest of this book. Without pre-empting later discussions, it seems obvious that a fundamental need will be the rediscovery of community as a central part of Christian faith and practice, and a realignment of the relationship between theology and spirituality. This will be a huge challenge to the status quo, for it will require us to put into reverse gear the way most of our Churches operate. We typically invite people to believe first (accept the creeds, sign statements of faith or, more simply, but nevertheless cognitively, 'believe in Jesus'), and then we say that they can belong to the community of God's people. The need of our culture (not to mention the gospel imperative itself), however, is for us to create a community where people can feel comfortable to belong, and then to be continuously challenging and encouraging one another to follow Jesus, whatever that might mean. This is not merely accommodating the gospel to the spirit of the age (it will be no more advantageous to marry postmodernism than it was for a previous generation to fall in love with modernity), but it seems to me it is a scriptural way of being Church, deeply rooted not only in the teaching of Jesus himself, but in the fundamental Christian doctrines of creation and incarnation, as I will argue later.

One of the interesting features of this present moment is that many lines of research seem to be converging to point to appropriate ways forward through which the Church might engage with today's rising culture and the spiritual search which is an integral part of it. My own starting point has been the history of ideas, and the relevant cultural trends as we move into a new paradigm that may, for want of a better term, be called postmodernism. But several pieces of research aimed at identifying the felt needs of ordinary people are pointing in the same direction. In the survey of young adults already mentioned, George Barna observed that

the spiritual journey of [today's generation] is based upon a desire to grow personally through the discovery of personally beneficial truths and practices. What most Churches and religious organizations fail to offer is a tangible means of becoming a more completely whole individual. The religious faiths that will win … support … are those which enhance relationships and lifestyles … Allowing a faith to be positioned as a series of rules, traditions, or punishments is antithetical to the search … A faith that becomes positioned as a means of growing

personally through deeper relationships and understanding would be more attractive.[24]

A British survey carried out by the Christian Research Association on behalf of Churches Together in England reached
almost identical conclusions, namely that unchurched people
'are more interested in relationships than in receiving information about God or Church...need churches that are caring
– not just friendly...are more likely to respond to churches
that are interested, than to those that are interesting...are
looking for relevance, not history...want practical answers to
life's hard questions.'[25]

Matthew Fox generally comes up with better questions
than answers, but he puts his finger on the fundamental
dilemma when he writes:

So much of religion in overdeveloped countries is in
books, academic institutions, degrees, sermons, and
words. *While learning is certainly essential to healthy religion,*
it is no substitute for praxis. Thinking about God is no
substitute for tasting God, and talking about God is no
substitute for giving people ways of experiencing God...
Fewer and fewer persons are attracted to Christianity in
the 'First World' countries because there is so little practice, so little spirituality in religion...When the mystics
start gathering again in worship, the young and the
alienated will return, for there is nothing so natural to
the human heart than the desire to give thanks. Once the
wounds are healed so that people can feel awe and wonder again, the yearning for occasions to praise and give
thanks will flow with the opportunities for effective
compassion.[26]

✳　　　✳　　　✳

And those who would be inclined to question his optimism could do worse than turn to Douglas Coupland's outstanding book, *Life after God*. Having taken more than 300 pages to highlight in his inimitable story-telling style the plight of those in what he calls 'the first generation raised without religion', he finds himself in the quietness of a temperate rain forest in his native British Columbia, about to plunge into a cool stream of water where he hopes to find a fresh angle on life and its meaning:

Now – here is my secret: I tell it to you with an openness of heart that I doubt I shall ever achieve again, so I pray that you are in a quiet room as you hear these words. My secret is that I need God – that I am sick and can no longer make it alone. I need God to help me give, because I no longer seem to be capable of giving; to help me be kind, as I no longer seem capable of kindness; to help me love, as I seem beyond being able to love.[27]

He speaks for millions of young people all around the Western world today – and it is for the sake of Christ's mission to them, that those who are already Christian need to take a long, hard look at their own lifestyles, beliefs, and practices, to prize what is good and jettison what is unworthy, and be willing themselves to follow Jesus, wherever that may eventually lead them.

CHAPTER 3

BACK TO THE BEGINNING

Effective Christian worship and witness requires an understanding of our cultural context, sensitivity to the needs of people, awareness of the radical demands of the gospel and a willingness to commit ourselves to it. So what more obvious thing for today's Christians to do than to go back to their roots in the New Testament and the life of the early Church for inspiration? Surely, if any Christians ever knew the secrets of successful mission, it must have been the apostles and their associates.

It is easy to be excited by the heroic exploits of those first disciples of Jesus Christ, and modern Christians often wistfully imagine that if only they could get back to what was happening then, the Church's present problems would disappear. The massive expansion of the earliest Christian communities is certainly a remarkable story. Beginning with an untrained rabbi from Nazareth, assisted by a collection of hill-billies from rural Galilee, it is the kind of rags-to-riches story that appeals to romantics and visionaries the world over.

Though Galilee was probably not as unsophisticated as some modern commentators assume, the reality is that these people had very little going for them.[1] Their homeland was on the extremities of the Roman Empire, and had it not been for its strategic position on the eastern frontier its inhabitants would undoubtedly have been dismissed as 'barbarians' by the sophisticated Romans and Greeks. As it was, they were always regarded as a cultural enigma: their long history, fierce nationalism and unfamiliar religious attitudes were all but totally incomprehensible to Roman soldiers and politicians.

Even within this maligned and misunderstood nation, Jesus and his disciples were out on the fringes. Galilee had an unenviable reputation, and in spite of being home to several leading rabbis it was frequently dismissed by the Jewish religious authorities as a place of no consequence. Moreover, most of the followers of Jesus were very ordinary people, with little educational background or personal career prospects. Without exception, they were the kind of people whom one would expect to make a minimal influence on their own culture, let alone the whole world. Yet that is what they did, and within a generation of Jesus' death these same people had facilitated the establishment of Christian communities in every major population centre of the Roman Empire. Ultimately, of course, their mission was to result in a change of direction for the whole of world civilization.

USING THE BIBLE

Faced with such extraordinary achievements, it is natural for modern Christians to look to the New Testament as the obvious starting point for all talk about evangelism. There are several good reasons for doing so. In terms of their practical performance, the earliest Christians – following Jesus' example and teaching – were singularly successful. Their strategy worked, and there must be something that later generations of Christians can learn from them. In addition, in terms of the message itself, today's Church needs to have a sense of continuity with Jesus and the first disciples. How otherwise can modern Christians be sure that what they are doing is *Christian* evangelism?

But things are rarely quite so simple and straightforward; we also have to face some obvious, challenging facts about the Bible. We are not the only people to be inspired by the stories of the New Testament. Nor are we the first. If Christian witness was just a matter of reading and understanding what is in its pages, and then acting on it, the world would presumably have been evangelized long before now. There is the further fact that the Bible by itself seems to be of limited value in the evangelistic task. People do become Christians through reading it, of course. I was one of them. But that is exceptional. Bibles have been readily available throughout the Western world for the last 100 years or more. The UK has one of the highest rates of Bible availability anywhere in the world, yet its churches are in serious decline. It is not without reason that the Bible has been dubbed 'the least-read best seller', and despite the multiplicity of modern translations now available people still pronounce it difficult to understand. Even when people get around to reading it, they understand the Bible in different ways.

We will return later to some issues related to the role of the Bible and its authority for today's Church. But, restricting our consideration for the moment to the practical issues that surround its use in evangelization, it is a fact that the Bible does seem to mean different things to different people, and within the cultural context all these various ways of reading its stories are perfectly valid. To make progress in communicating the Christian faith, the Church needs to take seriously the possibility that there may be no such thing as *the* message of the Bible, and that it might quite legitimately mean different things to different people. In any event, the starting point has to be people's current understandings – whether or not they happen to conform to the expectations of those already in the Church.

Different theological traditions will have their own ways of handling these particular challenges. But before we commit ourselves wholeheartedly to the search for New Testament ways of doing evangelism, we should think carefully about the most appropriate use to which we can put the Bible in Christian mission today. We can probably all agree that, to have integrity in their mission and message, the faith and practice of modern Christians must be continuous with that of Jesus and the earliest disciples. But that is not the same thing as merely trying to replicate their mission, and it certainly does not imply that we somehow need to take ourselves back into their world in order to be authentically 'Christian'. There are a few relevant considerations of methodology here. For example, not a single New Testament book was actually written for the purpose of providing its readers with models of evangelization. The book of Acts arguably comes close to this with the way it describes a variety of typical mission situations. Even here, though, it would be foolish not to recognize that there is an enormous cultural leap from life in the ancient Roman Empire to the complexities of modern Western culture. The mere fact that a particular methodology features in the New Testament does not mean we should – or could – apply it across the board in today's rather different world.

Even when it is possible to identify insights that seem relevant to contemporary circumstances, it is important to preserve the integrity of the various New Testament authors, and not do violence to their original intentions. In every case, they organized their materials for other purposes than those for which we might now wish to use them. In particular, we cannot be sure that the Bible writers included all they would have wished to say on a particular subject, had they been given the space and opportunity to do so. Every New Testament book was provoked by specific circumstances, and to a greater or lesser degree those circumstances influenced the selection of subject matter and the way it is handled.

In their enthusiasm, modern Christians often forget this, especially when dealing with the New Testament letters. Each of these is, in effect, only one half of the story. Reading a letter written by Paul, for example, is like eavesdropping on one side of a telephone conversation. We all know the challenges that presents! The amount of sense we can make of the overheard dialogue will depend on how well we know the person engaged in the call. If we know the people at both ends of the line, then we will have more chance of understanding the exchange than if we know only one of them. But even then we are unlikely to grasp what is being said with 100% accuracy. If that happens when we try to pick up half a conversation between people we know, and who live in the same world as we do, with similar cultural experience, then imagine the difficulties in spanning the centuries and trying to discern the nuances of what is now a non-existent half of a correspondence on theological issues between Paul and one of his churches![2]

Ordinary Bible readers are not the only ones who underestimate the difficulties. Professional theological scholars do the same, and their over-confident pronouncements on the nature of the circumstances addressed in some of the more complex New Testament books do nothing to encourage the sort of restraint that will serve us best in sharing faith with our contemporaries. Unfortunately, some of the New Testament books which look as if they could be most useful are also circumscribed by the most problems. Corinth, for example, is perhaps the nearest we come to a New Testament account of a church in something akin to a modern multicultural urban environment, yet it would be a bold person indeed who claimed to know with any precision exactly what was going on there at the time Paul was in correspondence with it. The same is true of the gospels. Like the New Testament letters, they were theological documents written to address particular needs. Their portraits of Jesus were specifically designed to present his message in a way that would be relevant to the concerns of their original recipients. That is why the New Testament contains not one single homogenized account of Jesus' life and teaching, but four different gospels – each one of them carefully crafted to meet the needs of different groups of people in the Roman Empire, with the aim of ensuring that the authentic voice of Jesus might be heard in diverse social and cultural contexts. This is not to say that the New Testament is of no use in today's evangelistic task. On the contrary, if we know how to ask the right questions it can have considerable value, which will be explored in some detail in later chapters. But we do need to acknowledge its limitations as well as its potential.

How then can we use the Bible? That depends what we want to use it for. In terms of evangelism, there are two ways of expressing that question. First, how may we use this remarkable book as itself a tool for evangelism? And then, how can we use it as a guide to help us identify appropriate models of evangelism that will reflect the central values of the gospel while also being culturally relevant to life in the new millennium?

THE BROADER PICTURE

Effective evangelism is not the same thing as persuading people to read the Bible. But that does not mean the Bible is irrelevant or useless in faith-sharing. As a matter of fact, if it is important to preserve our own continuity with Jesus, then we cannot do without the Bible, because (in spite of all its limitations) that is the only place where we can have any sort of access to knowledge of the teaching of Jesus and the lifestyles of the earliest churches. The Bible is a vital ingredient in the mixture that is successful evangelism. But it is only one ingredient, and not the whole mixture. At least three elements are involved in communicating Christian faith to people in today's world. Think of them as three different – though related – kinds of stories.

GOD'S STORY

First of all, both theologically and strategically, is God's story. Many Christians look out from the embattled cloisters of their church buildings and wring their hands in horror at what they see around them in today's world. 'Where is God?' they ask, and not a few conclude that God has somehow given up on our world, which is presumably why they then develop a faith that seems more concerned with the work of the devil and demons than about God and the Holy Spirit.

If that is our starting point, need we be surprised if evangelization never gets very far? It is a mistake to suppose that evangelization depends on Christians doing things for God. To imagine that God is somehow helpless, locked away in heaven with no capacity to do anything unless Christians set up church programmes, is to have a very impoverished – and maybe heretical – notion of who God truly is. The Bible emphasizes that this is God's world, and God is at work in it. Moreover, God sometimes works in the most unexpected ways. When the prophet Isaiah contemplated the plight of his people exiled in Babylon, he knew that God was at work in the great movements of world politics that would ultimately lead to their release and return to their homeland. Cyrus, the Persian emperor who overthrew the Babylonians and replaced their policy of transporting the peoples of occupied territories by a more humane approach, was so much in the centre of God's will that the prophet described him as God's 'messiah', the one anointed by the special grace of God's Spirit (Isaiah 45:1). Cyrus was not a Jew, of course, nor did he ever become a convert, but because he upheld values and standards that were central to the biblical faith, Isaiah had no hesitation in declaring that God was working through his empire in a very specific way.

It is not difficult to identify similar happenings in today's world, where many of the most remarkable changes of recent years obviously reflect the values of God's kingdom – things like the demise of totalitarian communism, as well as the rise of the new spiritual search in the West. The message is clear: God works not only through self-confessed Christians, but in many other ways through people of goodwill who (often without knowing it) share gospel values.

Those who accept the Bible's starting point – that people are made 'in God's image', and the whole creation is something of which God approves – will not be surprised by that. (See Genesis 1:1–31 and the repeated refrain that God regards the world as 'good'.) Jesus himself accepted this biblical faith in God as creator and sustainer of all things, and the way he used imagery from the world of nature conveys the clear message that God's activity can be discerned in it. Paul saw God at work not only in the world of nature (Colossians 1:15–20; Romans 8:19–23) but also in the world of other religions. On his arrival in Athens he was confronted with hundreds of altars to every deity imaginable. Nineteen centuries later, a Western missionary to Africa encountered similar scenes and dismissed them with the observation that 'When I carry my torch into the caves of Africa, I meet only filthy birds of darkness...'[3] Luke specifically records that Paul was 'deeply distressed to see that the city was full of idols' (Acts 17:16). But it was not Paul's style to denigrate and belittle the beliefs of others in this way, any more than it had been Jesus' approach before him (Luke 9:49–50). Far from condemning it all, Paul saw that God was at work even in this ostensibly hostile environment, and recognized an opportunity to share his own faith by identifying his Lord with the 'unknown god' of Athenian spirituality.

The Bible unhesitatingly affirms that God is constantly at work in the world in many ways, times and places. Evangelism is not about Christians working on God's behalf because God is powerless without them. Effective evangelism must start with recognizing where God is already at work, and getting alongside God in what is going on there. God's story, not ours, is the authentic starting point.

I learned this lesson personally in a striking way back in the 1980s, when I was Mission Convener of the Scottish Churches Council. In 1986 I was invited, along with the captains of Scottish industry and leaders from other walks of life, to a promotional presentation by a company which had been commissioned to organize a Garden Festival in the city of Glasgow as part of the urban renewal programme for British cities that was in full swing at the time. The event was to be held over a six-month period a couple of years later, and the message was simple: 'If you have a product to promote in 1988, do it at the Glasgow Garden Festival.' It so happened that we did have 'a product to promote': the Scottish churches had just agreed to celebrate 1988 as 'Year of the Bible'. Not long after, my partner and I found ourselves sitting with the chief executive of the Garden Festival company, asking if at some point in the year a small corner could be made available for the churches to celebrate this particular project. The conversation inevitably turned to the Bible. 'Why do you think people would be interested in the Bible anyway?' was the question; in response to which we enthusiastically pointed out the historical importance of the Bible in our culture, and the significance of its message for today.

The executive evidently got the message – or decided to call our bluff! At any rate, he commented that if the Bible was as important as we were apparently claiming, then a small event in a corner would hardly do it justice. As a result, we were offered the entire 120-acre site for one of the major Christian festivals: Pentecost Sunday. More than that, the company running the Garden Festival would finance the event! After all, they were paying entertainers on other days throughout the summer season, and to them Pentecost Sunday was just another day. There was a catch, of course: the Scottish Churches Council would have to come up with enough Christian artistes and performers with sufficiently varied skills to provide a balanced programme throughout the whole site for the whole day. That was quite a challenge, because it amounted to a total of well over 100 programme hours. However, not only did it all come to pass, but with an attendance in excess of 47,000 it turned out to be the largest single event to take place throughout the entire six months for which the Garden Festival was open – and in due course the Scottish Churches Council received a gold medal from a government agency to prove it! I learned a lot from that experience, not least that God is at work in the world – and probably moving well ahead of us – even before we do anything. The apparently unchristian world of Western culture is nothing like as hostile to the gospel as some Christians like to think. Why? Because this is God's world, and God is at work in it. 'Out of the mouths of infants…and of secular business people' (Psalm 8:2; Matthew 21:16).

BIBLE STORIES
Then there are the Bible stories – with their excitement, conviction and of course, their discontinuities and contradictions. Every Christian knows what might be called the main storyline of the Bible, which describes God's definitive actions in history. The creation, flood, promise to the people of Israel, the exodus, giving of the Law, the prophets, Jesus Christ, the gift of the Spirit and the life of the early Church – all these things are so central to the Bible's message that they have often been

called 'salvation history'. But every Bible reader also knows that these are not the only things in the Bible. There is a lot of other stuff in there as well, and it is not all such good news. Alongside the Sermon on the Mount are any number of blood-thirsty Old Testament heroes, many of whose exploits are so horrific they would be classed as criminals even in today's violent society. We would certainly find it hard to commend them as role models for serious searchers after spiritual truth. If our neighbours treated their families the way Abraham behaved with his wife and children, for example, we would all report him to the police – and unchurched citizens would do the same. The Bible has unquestionable strengths. It also has embarrassing weaknesses. It has the power to attract, and the ability to repel. Just as it is possible to play down the fact that God is at work in the world – and as a result end up with a fee-ble definition of evangelism that amounts to people doing a good turn for God – so it is possible to play down and ignore those parts of the Bible that might be said to be evangelistical-ly counter-productive. To use the Bible effectively and mean-ingfully, we should take account of all that.

You might be forgiven for supposing that up to this point sharing faith sounds like sharing theology: ideas about how God works in the world and notions about the Bible and its contents – all presented in a more or less impersonal, almost intellectual kind of way. We have been rather good at doing this in Western Christianity, but it has not led to effective com-munication of the gospel. If a purely cerebral, rational faith could change people, the Western Churches would not be where they are today. Living in Scotland, with our rich theo-logical and intellectual heritage, I am particularly conscious of this. Historically, we have had so much theology, and so many Bible teaching sermons (almost 500 years' worth since the Reformation alone!). Yet the fact is that theology and Bible reading and study seem to have made little effective difference to the moral and spiritual state of our nation. I have spent much of my life studying theology and preaching sermons, and I would not wish to deny that there can be a place for both these things. But we have to face the facts, however unpalatable they may be for our favourite theories and ideas. The faith of the Church has an objective content that needs to be communicated. That refers to what Christians corporately and historically believe. But the faith of the Church is also the faith of people. In that sense it is a subjective phenomenon: it finds its deepest meaning through what particular believers have discovered to be true in their own experience. For evangelism to be effective, we need more than just God's story and the Bible stories.

PERSONAL STORIES

So the third crucial element must be our own personal stories. The New Testament itself exhorts Christians to 'Be ready to give an account of the hope that is within you' (1 Peter 3:15). Effective evangelism happens, first, when Christians listen to other people's stories (their own experience, and the stories they recount as a way of making sense out of it all), and then continues as we share with others our own stories, reflecting our experience of life, thus enabling them to appreciate what we have discovered about the meaning of it all.

Jesus was an expert at this kind of communication. As the gospels depict him, his conversation typically had two main features: he asked questions in order to elicit other people's stories, and in response he told his own stories. When we preach sermons, or hand on ready-made summaries of Christian belief and theology, we inevitably present ourselves as experts. Doing it that way, it is all but impossible to avoid giving the impression that we are people who have it all together, people with no questions.

> Propositions are statements on a page; stories are events in a life. Doctrine is the material of texts; story is the stuff of life … Theology is a secondhand reflection of the Christ event; story is the unspeakable event's first voice.[4]

Telling stories demands personal honesty, accepting our weaknesses as well as our strengths. It is only when we reveal ourselves as weak and vulnerable that others will readily identify with us and be able to hear the invitation to join us in following Jesus. The truth is that we have something to share with others not because we are different, but precisely because we are no different. Yet we easily forget that, and 'evangelism' becomes little more than a statement of theological and doctrinal propositions.

Think of these three things as three circles. At the point where the circles intersect, that is where effective evangelism takes place.

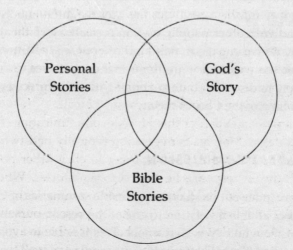

Notice, of course, that only a very small part of each circle intersects with any of the others. Not everything that God is doing in the world will of itself lead to people becoming disciples of Jesus Christ, though it may well extend the influence of God's kingdom. Not everything that is in the Bible will draw people to Christian commitment, though it may well contain valuable lessons as we try to discern God's will. And not every episode in our own stories will be evangelistically fruitful, though they will all be an intrinsic part of our self-understanding. But at the point where these three come together, exciting things can, and do, happen.

We could move these circles around and arrange them in a variety of ways, for their relationship is fluid and dynamic. At any given time, one circle might easily be more dominant than the others. When we look at the Bible through our perception of what God is doing in the world today, or through the spectacles of our own experience of life, we are likely to see its stories in new and enlightening ways. When we reverse the process and look at our own church life through the Bible, to enable it to inform and direct the way we interact both with God and with other people, we could easily be challenged to change. As we engage in this kind of open-ended interaction between these various ingredients in the mission of Christ, we are likely to discover some surprising models for the evangelistic calling of the Church today.

THE GREAT COMMISSION

The remainder of this chapter will explore some of the ramifications of all this in relation to one of the best-known mission texts of the whole New Testament. This is Matthew 28:16–20, the so-called 'Great Commission'. Its words are familiar:

Go therefore and make disciples of all nations, baptizing them in the name of the Father and of the Son and of the Holy Spirit, and teaching them to obey everything that I have commanded you. And remember, I am with you always, to the end of the age.

Coming as it does at the end of Matthew's account of the life and teaching of Jesus, it occupies a strategic place in this gospel. Some commentators find it a surprising way to conclude a gospel that in other respects can seem very Jewish. Perhaps Matthew was not so narrow-minded as he has sometimes been imagined to be. In any event, this narrative is not everyone's favourite Bible passage. Over the centuries, it has been used and abused for all sorts of disreputable purposes. In the hands of medieval European kings, it stirred the passions that led to the Crusades. In the thinking of the Conquistadores, it justified the forcible 'conversion' to Christianity of the native population of South America. And in the hands of the modern missionary movement in the eighteenth and nineteenth centuries, it moved European explorers not only to great personal sacrifice, but also on occasion to an unbridled nationalistic fervour that has led, with some justice, to the criticism that missionary endeavour was often just one aspect of Western imperialist ambitions.[5]

In the light of Christian history, it is not surprising that some people find this passage unhelpful in thinking about faith-sharing today. But it is strategically important in the New Testament. By placing it at the end of his gospel, Matthew effectively presents it as Jesus' last will and testament, his final instructions to the disciples who were to continue his message and ministry. Scholars have questioned whether Jesus himself would have spoken these precise words, with their careful use of a Trinitarian formula. Whatever the answer to that question, it is obvious that the disciples believed Jesus had commissioned them to continue his work; certainly, by the time Matthew put pen to paper towards the end of the first century, this vision was so obviously coming to fruition that it could not be questioned that it was the Lord's will for his Church. Moreover, when we look at it closely and compare it with the style of Jesus' own life, not to mention the motivation and achievements of his immediate followers, there are very good reasons for supposing that the understanding of mission presented here accurately reflects Jesus' distinctive attitude.

One thing that stands out is the sheer breadth of the definition of evangelism in this passage, incorporating at least three main concerns. First is the notion of proclamation, as the disciples are told: 'Go to all peoples everywhere'. Then is the idea of persuasion: 'make them my disciples'. Finally comes spiritual growth, for there is also included here the injunction to 'teach them to obey everything'. It is worth spending some time to look at these in turn.

PROCLAIMING THE MESSAGE

'Proclamation' is a term Christians often use to describe the evangelistic task. But the very use of such a word, with its overtones of someone who has a message delivering it to others who need it, and doing so in a somewhat triumphalist way, at once raises a question of method in relation to what we know of Jesus. Just exactly how is the good news to be shared with other people?

The New Testament provides several answers to that question, and the one given at the end of Matthew needs to be balanced with the others. But this one is distinctive enough to be worth pondering. Notice where Jesus starts. 'Go into all the world,' he says to the disciples. This is a startling emphasis for a religious teacher, who might perhaps have been expected to exhort other people to 'come in to the church.' Certainly within the Jewish context, Gentiles were always welcome to learn about Judaism by choosing to go into the synagogue, and becoming converts if they wished. But to go out and share the faith overtly with others would not have been part of the religious culture in which the disciples were raised.

Quite apart from that, there were other reasons why going out must have been the very last thing the disciples wanted to do at that point in time. There was a hostile world out there, which had little time for Jesus himself, and even less for them. By the time Matthew wrote his gospel, much of the Church was already suffering considerable persecution. But the seeds of it were there already in the weeks immediately following the first Easter. Jesus himself had been crucified, and the most obvious thing in the world would have been for his followers to lay low, at least for a while. But Jesus was clear and categorical. If God's Church is to do God's will, then God's people need to be mobilized. They need to share their faith with other people wherever they are. The needs of the world, not the concerns of the Church, are primary to an understanding of effective evangelism. The rest of the New Testament shows that this conviction was clearly a major key to the success of the early Church. They went out, taking their message to where other people were. They met them in the streets (Acts 2:1–42), the market places (Acts 18:1–3), the lecture halls (Acts 19:9–10), even on occasion in the sacred shrines of other religious traditions (Acts 3:11–26; 14:8–18).[6] When they worshipped they did not typically do it behind closed doors (Acts 2:46–47), and even the Eucharist was an opportunity for witness to unbelievers (1 Corinthians 11:26).

It is always easier – and certainly more comfortable – to meet other people on our territory than to venture to join them on theirs. It is considerably less threatening, because that way Christians can control what happens and ensure that no one says or does the 'wrong' thing at inconvenient times. But on this point the message of the New Testament is unequivocal: the Church is most true to its calling when its people are mobilized to look beyond themselves and out into the world. Evangelization is not about inviting the world to come into church buildings and look at us if they are interested. They are generally not.

None of this is likely to be completely new to readers of this book. Most people who have ever seriously contemplated the evangelistic imperative will be familiar with the need for the Church to 'go out', even if it is still true that whenever Christians think of mission they invariably adopt models of in-drag rather than out-reach. But here is a further question prompted by this text: how are we to go? The modern Church does not typically go from a position of military strength. That, we tell ourselves, is a regrettable feature of our past history that is now mercifully over. But it is still all too easy to espouse a cultural and personal imperialism which leads to a form of mission that can become a mere processing of people so they become like us; and so particular styles of dress, language or speaking are promoted, as if being Christian was a matter of being like we are. No doubt it is possible to understand this passage in an imperialistic way as saying, 'Go and conquer the world with the gospel.' It is, but only by ignoring its total context.

We read this New Testament story with the benefit of hindsight. We know as a matter of historical fact how this small, dispirited and disorganized band of people had in the course of less than a generation taken the message of Jesus not only to their own people, but to every major town and city in most of the known world of their day. To later Christians, they are heroes. But who were they really? How would any of us have responded to this great commission if we had been there? I think I know the answer to that question for myself, and it would have been fairly negative. 'But surely, Lord,' I might have said, 'you can't be serious. Just let us enjoy our own experience of your presence – keep to ourselves the little bit of happiness and meaning we have. There's a hostile world out there, you know, and we've already had enough trouble without deliberately looking for more.'

The text itself indicates that this is exactly how some of them did react. From the point of view of an evangelistic strategy, the most important statement in here is found not in the Great Commission *per se* but in one of the preceding verses: 'When they saw him, they worshipped him, *even though some of them doubted*' (Matthew 28:17). There is not much sign of imperialistic self-confidence here. This is not the militaristic clarion call of 'Onward Christian soldiers marching as to war'. On the contrary, Matthew depicts a group of people whose starting point is their own weakness – people with at least as much doubt as faith, who were prepared to go out onto other people's territory not to conquer it but with an overwhelming sense of their own inadequacy and vulnerability.

Throughout their evangelistic ministry, two things characterized these early disciples: commitment to Christ, and weakness in the face of the world. They did not share their faith from a position of strength, seeking to boss people into the Church like some kind of spiritual sergeant-major. They shared from a position of being in solidarity alongside other people, recognizing that they too had their weaknesses and doubts. To go out in this way was truly an act of faith for Christ's followers, committing themselves to something unknown and personally threatening. Remember, 'the medium is the message' – which in evangelistic terms means that 'Churches are free to choose the ways they consider best to announce the gospel to different people in different circumstances. But these options are never neutral. *Every methodology illustrates or betrays the gospel we announce*. In all communications of the gospel, power must be subordinate to love.'[7]

COMMUNICATING THE GOOD NEWS

What is the message? How are people going to be persuaded by it? We will come back to the actual content of the gospel later. Here we shall focus on its communication, though if the medium truly is the message (and that concept is not at all alien to the teaching of the New Testament), we can never entirely separate the two.

My daughter must have been about four at the time. The two of us were wandering around a park in one of our large cities. It was an autumn morning, with pale sunshine just beginning to penetrate the mist, and the smell of wood smoke was in the air. One minute we were laughing and chatting as we ran at top speed through piles of dead leaves, scattering them about and terrorizing nearby ducks and geese in the process. The next, we were deadly silent, looking for squirrels in the bare branches of the trees around us. As so often happens on such occasions, fun led to serious reflection, and as yet another pile of leaves went flying in all directions my daughter asked, 'Daddy, do you think God is at the bottom of everything?'

In the split second that it took me to decide exactly how to reply, our spiritual musing was interrupted by a commotion in the bush right next to where we were walking. Before I had time to realize what was going on, a middle-aged man dressed in a grey raincoat and clutching a tiny brown-backed book, jumped out directly in front of us and without further introduction fixed his piercing eyes on me. 'Tell me, young man,' he insistently demanded, 'are you saved?'

I remember being relieved that he was not the kind of person who actually wanted an answer to his question. His main purpose was to detain us for long enough to give me a quick summary of Peter's sermon on the day of Pentecost, and then to read a few New Testament passages about how I was 'living under law' when by taking his advice I could actually be 'living under grace'. With a final quick exhortation to 'Think about these things before it's too late', he disappeared with a flourish into the bushes from whence he had come – no doubt to materialize in some other part of the park where he would seek to evangelize other lost souls who were also wasting their time on trivialities, such as discussing the meaning of life with their children. Certainly, I couldn't help contrasting the two conversations. My daughter's response to this intrusion was interesting, if predictable: 'Daddy, what did that man want?' It was much harder to give a satisfactory answer to that question than to the first one she had asked!

We smile at that kind of story, but it is typical of so much that passes for evangelism in the modern Western Church. Imagine now a church on Sunday morning, full of people. 'Hundreds are being reached,' the church leaders tell themselves, as the earnest preacher at the front expounds the Bible. 'The teaching in our church is second to none,' they boast, though in truth they are only expressing admiration for their minister's remarkable ability to speak for 50 minutes without a break – for not too many of those present are moved by what they hear, and probably the church has had no new members for quite some time. Take a closer look at their faces, and you can begin to understand why. Many of them are bored to death. They like to give the impression that they are listening eagerly to every word of it, and some of them even look as if they are writing it all down for future contemplation. Mark you, the preacher is not fooled quite so easily. Many of them are writing next week's shopping list, while those who seem most engrossed in the pages of their Bibles are reading something quite different than the passage being expounded; a good half of the congregation are handing sweets round and trying to dispose of the wrappers without being seen. Many of them are wishing they were somewhere else. In desperation the preacher – who is a good and gifted person – concludes that these people, though they are in church, are closed to the gospel. For their part, the congregation wish it was all on the TV, so they could switch it off and get on with something more useful.

It sounds exaggerated? A survey of British churchgoers discovered that some 42% of them admitted to falling asleep in church. More than a third looked at their watch in church every Sunday, and an amazing 10% owned up to putting their watch to their ear and shaking it, because they thought it must have stopped. Though only 4% always wished they had stayed in bed on a Sunday morning, 67% said they often felt that way.[8]

What is happening? Probably there is a lot of talking, but no communicating. What the preacher and church leaders think is 'teaching' is not translating into learning. Yet no one has been taught until someone has learned something. Transmission of the message is just one small part of the total process of communication. It is only the first stage, and the easiest one. The others – communication and acceptance – are much more difficult to achieve. A great deal of so-called Christian evangelism is really just transmission of the message, but that is not the same thing as effective reception of it. There is an old definition of a lecture as 'a transfer of material from the professor's notes to the students' notes without it passing through the minds of either'. A lot of what Christians label 'evangelism' is just like that. We seem to imagine that people's heads are empty, and once we have learned the knack of prising the lids off them we can pour in the substance of the gospel, and our responsibility to communicate the faith has been fulfilled. But people are not like that:

Heads are neither open nor hollow. Heads have lids, screwed on tightly, and no amount of pouring can force ideas inside. Minds open only when their owners sense a need to open them. Even then, ideas must still filter through layers of experience, habit, prejudice, fear and suspicion. If ideas make it through at all, it's because feedback operates between speaker and listener.[9]

We all have filters. They are an indispensable part of who we are, and contain everything that we know and believe: our world view (basic values and beliefs about life); our experience and learning (those things we believe to be true); and our personality. We use our filters all the time to sort out information that comes our way. If we did not, we would soon be submerged by it. Think of what happens in your home when there is a commercial break on the TV. In a typical home, someone might go to the bathroom, another to the kitchen, others may engage in conversation. Very few will watch the commercials unless they have a specific interest in the products being offered. A lot of people react that way to anything connected with the Church. An earnest Christian couple knock on a door to evangelize the people who live behind it. A man answers, the callers announce they are from the local church, and what happens next? If the door is not closed immediately, there is a pretty good chance the man will call for the woman of the house. 'It's for you,' he will say, because his filters tell him that, though he probably knows next to nothing about Church, it is not something that relates to his life.

The same thing happens elsewhere. It is currently trendy for health care professionals to minister to the 'spiritual needs' of their patients, but more often than not the Church is perceived as totally irrelevant to this task because most people filter out 'Church' as being about joining an institution, whereas the spiritual search is something far more dynamic and relevant to ordinary people and the way they live. Our filters operate all the time, whether or not we are consciously aware of it. We can open them to varying degrees, depending on how we perceive the messages being presented to us. We can, and do, open them fully when we think the content of the communication is relevant for what we believe or need to have or know.

There are four elements in effective communication: the message (and the medium through which the message is channelled); the audience and their responses; the process of feedback; and the communicator, with his or her aspirations and intentions. The relation between these four is cyclical, and there is no 'right' place to begin the process of communication, though Christians generally start with their message. They have something to say, therefore they search for the best words with which to say it. Inevitably, starting at this point they tend to choose words that suit themselves. Christians are typically orientated towards ideas – either complex theological concepts, or something that looks much simpler but which in terms of communication still has inadequacies (an 'ABC of salvation'). The trouble is, most other people are somewhere else. Their starting point is not our message. I once heard someone complain that sermons were simply 'answers to questions no one is asking'. While I would not have thought of putting it quite like that, I immediately recognized what was being talked about, for I must have heard thousands of sermons that fitted that description: the only people who appreciate them are the ministers who preach them. Much of what we imagine is evangelism is just the same. Effective communication involves a lot more than merely presenting a message. This is nothing to do with the truth or otherwise of what our message is, for it is perfectly possible for a thing to be 100% true, and yet totally irrelevant.

When my daughter was small, like many young children she used to get up very early each morning. This was no problem, except at weekends when the rest of us were not too keen to be roused at five or six o'clock! She soon got the message, and developed the habit of taking herself off to watch the TV, so that when I rose somewhat later I knew exactly where to find her and what she would be doing. At that time, there were very few programmes shown in the early morning on British television. More often than not she would be watching a programme connected with the Open University. The scenario was entirely predictable. 'What is this all about?' I would ask. And the reply? 'I don't know.' What she was watching was 100% true – indeed, since it was usually some erudite professor exploring all conceivable angles on a subject, it sometimes seemed to me as if it could easily have been 150% true! There was certainly nothing wrong with what was being said. Quite the reverse. And there would be people out there for whom it all made perfect sense. But so far as my daughter was concerned, it was totally and absolutely irrelevant to her entire lifestyle and understanding.

Do you recognize the syndrome? Communication of the Christian message today is hampered not so much because we have an inadequate gospel, but because so often it is simply an irrelevant gospel. Those millions of people with a strong sense of serious spiritual search who appear to have no interest in the gospel, are not always rejecting the Christian faith. More often than not, they have no idea what it is. Christians think a message has been sent in their direction, but nothing has been received.[10]

To become the gospel – 'good news' – the Christian message has to speak to the needs of ordinary people. There is nothing profound or new in that observation. The very first generation of Christians knew it well. Reference has already been made to the New Testament gospels. But why do you suppose the early Church preserved four gospels instead of reducing it all to one comprehensive version of the life and teaching of Jesus? The answer is obvious. Each of the gospels was written as an evangelistic tool. Each is different, angled towards the needs of the various kinds of people for whom they were written. Moreover, the differences can in some instances be quite far-reaching. In the synoptic gospels of Matthew, Mark and Luke, the main subject of Jesus' teaching is presented as 'the kingdom of God'; in John, Jesus' teaching focuses on 'eternal life'. In the synoptics, Jesus' message is communicated through the use of story parables; in John the style is more elaborate (though still pictorial). Scholars have argued for centuries over which version more accurately represents Jesus as he really was. Maybe that is the wrong question, for surely this is an example of the flexibility with which the gospel needs to be presented to different audiences, in order that it might become 'good news' in relation to their practical needs, concerns and interests.

To impose a uniformity on the gospel, and force it into only one mould is to inhibit its effectiveness. In the first century, the adaptability of the Christian faith was its greatest strength, and the New Testament itself bears eloquent witness to how the situation and needs of those being addressed regularly determined the shape of the message. To stay the same, the gospel must change. Even where human needs are the same, different languages and cultures require that the message speaks with different accents and tones. We can all see how the needs of today's people are different from those of the first century. Most of us can appreciate that the needs of people in the two-thirds world are different from those of the West. But needs differ not just from one culture to another. Even in one town, different communities will have different starting points. Spiritual and cultural discernment will be a fundamental part of successful evangelization. To be true to the New Testament, the gospel needs to address these diverse needs with different emphases. This is one key reason why evangelism is more than just transmission of theological or doctrinal propositions. It is not, of course, the only one; in subsequent chapters we will explore others that are more specifically related to the content of the gospel message itself.

SPIRITUAL GROWTH

The third and final strand of the 'Great Commission' is what I have called the cultivation of spiritual growth and maturity. This is not the place to pursue this theme at length: it will form the major topic of the next chapter. But it is worth noting here that Matthew includes continued growth in faith as part and parcel of the task of evangelization. Jesus does not send the disciples out to gain converts for a cause, or members for a church. He instructs them to make more disciples – students, followers, learners – who are prepared to give all they have in order to follow their leader. He does not look for people to 'make decisions', but to open their lives to the power of the Spirit, so they may continue to be challenged by the good news. And by doing so, he clearly defines evangelism not as an event, but as a process. Grasping hold of that will have far-reaching implications for many areas of contemporary Church life.

CHAPTER 4

THE CALL TO FOLLOW CHRIST

Two questions are never far from the centre of any discussion of Christian faith: what is the gospel, and what does it mean to be a follower of Jesus Christ? You might think that after centuries of theological debate and exploration, at least the answers to such basic matters would be settled and clear-cut. But these questions are not as simple as they sound. Ask any group of Christians to explain or describe their own experience of faith, and you can guarantee that there will be almost as many answers as there are people. But they will probably fall neatly into one of two categories, typically distinguished by their divergent understandings of the nature of conversion.

TRADITIONAL UNDERSTANDINGS

What exactly do we mean by conversion? For some people, the very word 'conversion' can mean only one thing: an abrupt crisis in life, in which everything suddenly and totally changes. To be converted is like stepping from darkness into light; before this decisive moment, a person is not a Christian, after it they are left in no doubt that they are. Over the centuries, there have been several outstanding examples of experiences of this kind. In his *Confessions*, Augustine describes how, as he sat in a garden reading Romans 13:13–14 in the late summer of AD 386, 'in an instant, as I came to the end of the sentence, it was as though the light of faith flooded into my heart and all the darkness of doubt was dispelled.'[1] More than a thousand years later, as Martin Luther sat in the tower of his monastery in Wittenburg, this time reading Romans 1:17 (supplemented by, amongst others, the writings of Augustine), he too had a similar life-changing experience. Two hundred years after that, on 24 May 1738, John Wesley's heart was 'strangely warmed' in London's Aldersgate Street, as he listened to a reading from Luther's commentary on Romans.

These experiences were all different, of course. Augustine and Luther had both wrestled with the meaning of life and faith for a considerable time, while Wesley was already an Anglican priest, and indeed had led a mission to North America before his 'conversion'. But that has not prevented many modern Christians (particularly those with an interest in evangelism) from identifying the single episodic crisis turnaround as of the essence of being and becoming a Christian. What is more, the model for such experiences is traced back to the pages of the New Testament itself. The story of how God dramatically laid hold of Paul as he approached the city of Damascus, intent on persecuting the infant Church, has been viewed as an experience to be savoured and actively sought after (Acts 9:1–9, 22:6–11, 26:12–18; Galatians 1:11–17). Evangelists who work on this model of conversion skilfully steer their hearers to a point where they are compelled to make radical decisions about their own lives, inviting them to follow Christ by going out to the front of a large crusade meeting, or kneeling at the penitent form of a local mission hall. For many Christians, if 'conversion' means anything at all, then this is the only possible connotation it can have.

I remember visiting a large Presbyterian church in the USA. After the service, I was taken to the home of one of the pastoral staff to meet his family and share their lunch. To have a visiting preacher from Scotland, the heartland of Presbyterianism, was obviously a very significant experience for them, and the whole family, well scrubbed and dressed in their best clothes for the occasion, were lined up in the hallway to meet me. I have no idea whether I lived up to their expectations, but I shall never forget what happened next. The pastor went from one to another, and then came to the youngest child, a girl called Lucy who must have been about seven years old. 'And this is Lucy,' he said. As I greeted Lucy, I could hardly believe my ears as her dad continued, 'Of course, Lucy hasn't yet given her heart to the Lord Jesus – have you, Lucy? – but we're all praying for her. Who knows, maybe your visit will help her decide for Christ.'

Well, how do you follow that in conversation with a seven-year-old? You might be forgiven for imagining that this child must have been some kind of uncontrollable monster who was virulently anti-Church and unchristian – though in truth she was as well behaved a youngster as I have ever come across. As we walked along the beach together later that day, Lucy revealed herself to be a girl who knew her Bible, who loved Jesus, and who was probably far more disciplined in her prayer life than I have ever been. I knew what was going on, of course, because this was not the first time I had met people like her father. So far as he was concerned she was a little pagan; he knew that to be true because she had not yet adopted certain patterns of response to Christ which he was able to recognize and affirm as authentic. I did momentarily reflect that it was a strange family in which someone who was such an intense believer could manage to raise such a miserable sinner as he thought his daughter to be. I never asked that question, of course, for I knew what the answer would be: Lucy had never come to a point of decision at which she 'gave her heart to the Lord', or got herself 'born again', and so by definition she was totally outside the grace and love of God.

During the same trip, I heard an evangelist speaking on TV about New Agers who believed in reincarnation. 'I don't care how often you've been born,' he ranted, 'if you've not been born again, then God has no time for you!' More recently, I was guest speaker at a week-long ecumenical Bible convention, and towards the end of the week I was cornered by an earnest woman who wanted to express appreciation for what I had been saying and doing. 'You're certainly different from other ministers,' she said, something with which I could not quarrel, and which I took to be a compliment (though that was probably not her intention). 'I can see you *really* love the Lord,' she continued, 'and God is *really* using you...but—' (as she lowered her voice to a whisper, I sensed the punch-line was coming) 'are you *really* born again?' I knew what she was after, and I must confess that only served to ensure my response was more evasive than it might otherwise have been! Unless I could relate how I had come from a life of great sin to a life of fanatical faith in Christ, preferably as a result of some unbelievably striking, if not bizarre, crisis, then she found it hard to accept that I could possibly be, as she put it, a 'real Christian'. This is a very popular way of understanding the nature of the gospel, and hence discipleship and evangelism. I freely admit that, historically, it is Christians with this sort of outlook who have kept alive the evangelistic vision of the modern Church, though I also suspect that many of their 'converts' slipped out through the back door of the church as fast as they entered at the front. Still, for generations when mainline Christians were occupied with other concerns (generally the internal affairs of the Church itself), people seeking a 'born-again' experience were often the only ones calling the unchurched to faith. Moreover, I would be the first to accept that some people do have such dramatic experiences of God. But it is a serious mistake to universalize these into a model that everyone must follow, and to do so is likely to be highly damaging to the evangelistic enterprise.

BASIC QUESTIONS

The overwhelming majority of today's Christians do not have an understanding of God that is dominated by a dramatic crisis leading to major changes in their life. Many have grown up among other Christians, and never really found themselves rejecting faith in any profound way. Of course, they have had questions, and have frequently had to struggle to hold onto their trust in God. But they have never been against God in any fundamental way: as they have gone through life they have simply grown into a deeper understanding. Instead of experiencing a sudden U-turn, God seems to have kept these people in a straight line from childhood through to adult commitment, by means of Christian nurture in home and church. As a result, they find themselves embarrassed and confused when people call them 'unchristian', just because they are unable to identify a time when they were 'born again'. It is alien to their own experience, and as a result they are easily turned off by a concept of evangelism which for them seems to be focused in the wrong place.

A major survey of British churches in the 1980s discovered that 'the actual word "evangelism" seems to be disliked by some as having a hard-sell connotation'.[2] Most Christians do not see faith as a commodity to be marketed, and while they would not deny the reality of dramatic experiences in the lives of those who have them, they would certainly wish to add that there is more to discipleship (and, consequently, evangelism) than that. If our holistic understanding of the 'Great Commission' is correct, they could claim to be following the example of Jesus in this.

It could be argued that the reason so many modern Christians have hesitations about this model of evangelism and conversion is because they have too little contact with those who are truly unchurched, and these are the people who are more likely to have crisis conversion experiences. There is no doubt that if the Church is to grow, it will need to gain converts from outside. But equally, there is no evidence that such people will typically meet God through crisis conversion experiences.

Finding Faith Today is one of the most exhaustive studies ever conducted of the faith journeys of recent converts. Out of a broadly-based sample of 511 people who had made a 'public profession of faith' in the previous 12 months, 69% described their coming to faith as 'gradual'. Moreover, even in churches describing themselves as 'evangelical', and therefore probably with a heritage that would tend to predispose them to assume the crisis model of conversion as the norm, only 37% claimed to have had this kind of dramatic conversion, while the rest (63%) described their faith journey as a gradual progression.[3] The report comments:

> The gradual process is the way in which the majority of people discover God and the average time taken is about four years: models of evangelism which can help people along the pathway are needed.[4]

The simplistic view of conversion as a one-off, dramatic crisis experience must also be modified in the light of the teaching of the New Testament. Consider Paul himself. Whatever it was that happened on the Damascus road, it was part of his ongoing experience of God. It would be wrong to imagine that before this occasion Paul was a complete unbeliever. As a Pharisee, how could he have been? He certainly believed in God, lived within the parameters of a biblical morality, and expected the coming of the Messiah. These continued to be central pillars of his Christian faith, with the exception that he now identified Jesus of Nazareth as the Messiah. In terms of his own lifestyle, he was neither spiritually nor morally bankrupt at the point of his 'conversion'. Paul was not actively seeking deliverance from a threadbare Jewish spirituality that had proved unworkable; the popular picture of a weary, guilt-ridden Paul, trudging up the Damascus road full of doubts and self-pity, is a fiction.

Many of Paul's most fervent admirers have popularized this image, not least Martin Luther who experienced exactly that kind of release from his own guilt-ridden conscience. We need not question the reality of the spiritual experience of those who have such a life-changing escape from the bondage of personal guilt. But the mere fact that some of them found new direction through reading Paul does not mean Paul himself must have been like them. Reading Paul through the spectacles of his admirers is a dangerous business, and has frequently misrepresented both his personality (as dominated by guilt) and his theology (as dominated by sin and the concept of an angry God).[5] Paul never saw it that way. Looking back to his pre-conversion past, he described himself not as a guilt-ridden and defeated wretch, but as a self-confident, spiritually satisfied enthusiast (Philippians 3:4–6). He was as sure as anyone could be that he was right, and that he was doing the will of God. The real challenge of the Damascus road was that he discovered he was wrong, and that is why his conversion affected every part of his being and his theology had a place for personal needs, not to mention a social dimension and cosmic and ecological implications.[6] Conversion in the New Testament is not the spiritual equivalent of a trip to the religious supermarket in search of a new experience. It is far richer – and more challenging – than that.[7]

What then is conversion? Wherever we look in the New Testament, one thing seems clear: *change* is always very near the centre of the gospel. No one ever meets Jesus and stays the same! At the beginning of his gospel, Mark summed it up in the familiar slogan, 'Repent and believe in the good news'

(1:14). This was the message of Jesus in a nutshell, and it contains two elements: doing (repent) and thinking (believe). There is an emotive, intuitive element, combined with a rational or reflective element. Faith links together an objective and a subjective component. Both are important, though not the same.[8] This model of faith, with these two elements held together, should undergird all our modern methodologies for evangelism. It reflects the fact that deeds and words – actions and thoughts – were at the centre of Jesus' own evangelizing strategy. Disciples are committed to both; bearing witness to both will make more disciples, and advance the kingdom of God.

It is worth emphasizing this because a lack of balance on this point has been the cause of some of the most tragic – and unnecessary – divisions of twentieth century Church life. I refer, of course, to the division between the 'doers' and the 'believers', the social activists and the 'preachers of the gospel', the so-called liberals and the card-carrying evangelicals. The social activists need to remember that without the proclamation of a message about Jesus, then there is little difference between Christian do-gooders and their secular counterparts. And the proclaimers need to remember that doing good is neither an optional extra, nor something that should be used as a carrot to attract people to the 'real thing' (preaching). It is the real thing.[9] At least, it was for Jesus, who spent a good deal more time doing than speaking, and in whose ministry the deeds generally preceded any words (which, when they were used at all, were often in response to questions that people asked about what he did).

This dynamic interplay between doing and thinking, repenting and believing, the affective and the cognitive, the right brain and the left brain, also functions as a model for discipleship. What was Jesus actually demanding of people? What did he mean when he asked for 'repentance'? What did he expect people to do? Certainly, a good deal more than marching to the front of a crowded crusade meeting and praying a prayer of commitment. More, even, than reading their Bible, praying and being a faithful member of their local church. Many studies of this Greek word 'repentance' (*metanoia*) describe it in terms of someone travelling along a road, and suddenly realizing they are heading in the wrong direction. As a result, they need to do a U-turn. We might also, more accurately, think of it in terms of someone climbing a mountain with friends, and becoming aware that others have found a better track, as a consequence of which they are making faster and more satisfactory progress. Such climbers know where they want to be, but are unsure of precisely how to get there. It needs someone on the higher track to show them the way and invite them to join it. In terms of the spiritual journey, that is what Jesus' call to repentance is all about: changing direction, but to a place that in your heart of hearts you knew you always wanted to be. Naturally, doing this means that a person's whole lifestyle and values undergo a considerable change, so as to reflect the claims of God's kingdom. There is no shortage of New Testament examples of the demand for such radical and far-reaching discipleship, nor of those who were prepared to accept it, as well as of those who were unwilling to pay the price. 'Repentance' in this sense is a holistic notion. It affects everything a person is and does. No area of human behaviour is excluded.

Jesus also called people to 'believe'. Alongside demands for changed behaviour and lifestyles, the gospels contain a lot of theology, mostly open-ended theology designed to get people to ask questions rather than to present them with safe, ready-made answers. Think of the way the key terms of the gospels are open to so many understandings – phrases like 'the kingdom of God', or 'the Son of Man'. Even now, scholars are still debating the precise nuances of such teachings within the context of first-century Palestine. Maybe we shall never exhaust their significance, because Jesus actually intended it all to be somewhat indeterminate.

Parables are used in the same way: there is never only one 'authorized' understanding of what they mean. Jesus was intent on creating a space in which people would be free to reflect on the significance of his message for their own lives. Once a space has been created, then the rest is up to God. The early Church was able to hold together a vast and diverse spectrum of opinion, ranging from those conservative Pharisees who were part of the church in Jerusalem, to the liberal Paul and his mystical converts in Corinth. But whatever the specific outcome, once a person has met Jesus, the way they see things and understand and interpret them is radically challenged and changed. Belief is important, but it is not the whole of the gospel. Theology and doctrine are part of the total package, but getting them sorted out is not necessarily the first step in the journey of faith; for many people in the postmodern world, it is likely to be the last.

PETER'S CONVERSION AS A BIBLICAL MODEL

If we now focus on a particular New Testament example, we may begin to see how all this works in practice, and what difference it should make to the evangelistic calling of the Church today. Next to Jesus, Peter is one of the most accessible characters in the gospel stories.[10] We know more about him than any other disciple, and his story obviously fascinated those early Christians who preserved it orally, and finally wrote it down. Here, we have space only to skim through some key aspects of his story. But as we do so, bear in mind that, as well as the relationship between doing and thinking, discipleship always seems to involve challenge and change;

ask, therefore, at which points Peter was most truly and profoundly challenged to change. I believe that Peter's conversion to Christ is one of the foremost models of faith in the whole New Testament, and one that is of crucial importance today – especially for Western Christians who find themselves needing to share the gospel with successful people who apparently can manage their lives without God.

We can trace six stages in the discipleship of Peter, each one leading on naturally from the other.

1 EARLY LIFE
'I BELIEVE IN GOD'

Peter was brought up as a Jew, so there was probably never a time in his life when God did not feature. He always believed something, and long before he encountered Jesus he would have some kind of faith understanding that had developed from his childhood. When Jesus had particular lessons he wanted the disciples to learn, he later chose children as their teachers – something that surprised the adults, but enabled Jesus to affirm his belief that children reared within a believing context were not pagans, and had a faith to share, however simply it may be expressed at that stage of their life (Mark 9:33–37, 10:13–16).[11] That was the starting point for Peter's journey into discipleship.

2 CALL TO DISCIPLESHIP (MARK 1:14–20)
'JESUS SEEMS A GOOD GUY'

I hesitate to call this story Peter's 'conversion', though on a common understanding of the term that is undoubtedly what it was. Before this encounter on the shore of Lake Galilee, he was not a follower of Jesus; after it, he was. Could there be a more profound about-turn than that? By any standards, whatever it was that happened to Peter and his brother Andrew on that day was remarkable and life-changing. So what actually did take place? At first sight, it might look a bit like a classic crisis encounter along the lines of what has traditionally been promoted in fundamentalist and evangelical Church circles. It certainly happened at a time in Peter's life when decisions tend to be made in those terms. For he was probably no more than a teenager – maybe even an adolescent – and at that point in life where we typically characterize and articulate things in terms of decision-making that will affect the whole future course of our existence.

Because of the crucial importance of this story, it will be worthwhile pausing to notice in more detail some of the things that were involved here. First of all, Peter was called to change direction: 'Come and follow me,' said Jesus. In his mind's eye, Peter no doubt had a picture of what it meant to be successful. His life seemed to be running in well-defined directions. His father and grandfather had done it all before him, and he was building for his future on the social and economic successes of previous generations. He knew where he'd come from, and where he expected to go to. Yet Jesus says, 'Leave all that, you come with me!' 'You? Who are you?' Peter might reasonably have asked. There is more than a good chance that at the time Jesus was unemployed. As a local builder in the town of Nazareth, his business will almost certainly have had its share of the many lucrative contracts that were awarded in connection with the rebuilding of the nearby city of Sepphoris, but the project was completed not long before Jesus began his public ministry. It is tempting to think that he, and thousands of others, would be thrown out of work at that time.[12]

Whether or not that is so, Peter must certainly have contrasted his own secure lifestyle with that of Jesus, who apparently had no regular home, and no prospects. Everything he knew about Jesus told him that he was not being offered fulfilment in life in the terms he had seen it before. He was not being called to join with the rich and powerful, but with the poor and the marginalized. It would mean a radical upheaval of all his social norms. Yet here was Jesus with this grand vision of God's kingdom, and Peter recognized he was being presented with something that was big enough and good enough for it to be worth giving his life for it. 'As his disciples, we announce his solidarity with all the downtrodden and marginalized ... those who announce Jesus as the servant King ... are invited to enter with him daily in identification and participation with the poor of the earth.'[13]

Jesus also challenged Peter to change his priorities. Mark comments that 'at once they left their nets and went with him' (Mark 1:18). Can you imagine all the things they might have done first? But following Jesus meant that he must come first. To follow him meant things that had previously been of great importance now took a different place. Security, prosperity and a comfortable lifestyle were no longer of all-consuming importance. This must have been one of the more liberating aspects of being a disciple. Instead of being caught up in a life continually under pressure, Peter was offered a different direction. Leaving the nets was not a negative move, taking the easy way out by hiding from the harsh realities of life. It meant taking a new, positive and challenging direction in life and faith. The basic call of the gospel is to follow Jesus!

Furthermore, Jesus invited Peter to reassess the purpose of his life. 'What are you here for?' Jesus asked, to which the reply was, 'Catching fish – the same as everybody else.' The difference that Jesus makes is encapsulated in his call to 'Follow me and I will teach you to fish for people' (Mark 1:17). This takes us to the core of the challenge to discipleship. Peter needed to learn that discipleship is not a once-for-all thing, but an ongoing process. 'I will teach you,' Jesus offered. But learning something about another person is not purely a cerebral affair. Obviously, facts and information are involved, but that is not the whole story, and in personal terms it is unlikely to be the first priority. When two people fall in love, their feelings are far more important than factual information about their partner. Things like a person's height, hair, eye colour – even age – are not high on the list of things that one needs to know in a relationship. There, 'knowledge' is an altogether more personal thing, as you experience this other person, share yourself with them and discover things that probably can't easily be put into words anyway. Western Christianity has too easily specialized in knowledge of theological and dogmatic propositions about Jesus, without creating space for disciples to 'know' him more closely. Peter made that mistake, and sometimes his grasp of the facts ran ahead of his personal knowledge. For him, the development of spiritual intimacy was ultimately to be one of the most threatening aspects of discipleship. Notice, though, that Jesus' purpose is not to teach disciples purely so they can know a lot. What they have learned of him (and, no doubt, themselves) they are to share with others. These people were already good at catching fish: now they are to trawl for people.

So, we might say, Peter became Christianized. He became a disciple of Jesus Christ. His direction, his priorities and his purpose were all challenged – and he responded. He was converted. But was he? Certainly not by some modern definitions. From the standpoint of twentieth-century evangelistic strategies, what is missing from this story is at least as significant as what is included. We look to this story in vain for evidence of personal guilt, confession of sin, prayers of commitment, forgiveness, acceptance of theological dogmas, admission to the life of the Church and all the other signs of commitment that have so often been identified as an indispensable part of 'the conversion experience'. Jesus demanded none of these, which would no doubt make him a very poor evangelist in the eyes of many today, for after all Peter only responded to the invitation Jesus gave him.[14] Of course, no one would seriously go along with that – would they? It seems that, according to Jesus, conversion is a much more complex business than many of his modern followers have allowed it to be; it begins with the simple invitation to 'Follow me'. As we move on to subsequent episodes in the life of Peter, and unpack some of the other elements that were involved in his faith commitment, we will find ourselves forced to grapple with the possibility that by focusing on one single crisis experience, modern evangelism has trivialized the gospel. Could it be that we fail to reach successful and satisfied people not because our message is too hard, but because it is not demanding enough?

3   CONVERSION OF THE MIND (MARK 8:27–30)
'I NEED TO THINK THIS THROUGH'
Like the others who accepted Jesus' call, Peter spent much time in the presence of Jesus, watching what he did, hearing what he said and discovering some new things about himself. As Peter got to know Jesus better, other challenges began to emerge which he needed to integrate with his life experience and which demanded some response.

Initially, Peter had committed himself to Jesus in the impulsive way that young people often do when confronted by charismatic figures. A young fisherman from rural Galilee instinctively recognized that Jesus was somebody new and different, apparently enjoying a more immediate relationship to God than many of the other rabbis who were around at the time, and certainly more open to sharing it with ordinary people. Peter knew he would have an instant rapport with this person and so he was attracted. But as he got to know Jesus better, he began to understand that he was more than just a trendy radical. For one thing, Jesus' trendiness was obviously somewhat different from that of most wandering charismatic teachers of the time. His message was not really related to the political aspirations of his people, suffering as they were under Roman domination. Nor was Jesus very forthright in describing his own mission. The enigmatic term 'Son of Man' was his favourite title for himself, but no one had a very clear idea what that was supposed to mean (although its very mystique only served to emphasize Jesus' distinctiveness). As a result, Peter was forced to think. Who could this Jesus really be?

As he reflected on that question, he began to reach new conclusions that broke the mould of his previous thought-patterns in a very big way. Mark highlights this by placing the conversion of Peter's mind at Caesarea Philippi. It was home to a shrine dedicated to the Greek god Pan, and also boasted a great marble temple built in honour of the Emperor Augustus. An appropriate place, therefore, for Peter to reflect on the significance of Jesus in relation to other competing religious traditions. When challenged by Jesus' question, 'Who do people say that I am?' Peter's answer was unequivocal: 'You are the Messiah'; in Matthew's version of the story, he adds, 'the Son of the Living God' (Matthew 16:13–20; Mark 8:29). For a Jew, there could hardly have been two more explosive concepts than these! His entire theology was blown apart – and remade.

The same thing frequently happens among young adults today, when as students they begin to think things through for themselves, questioning and clarifying the values of their parents. Peter never went to university, but he did leave home, and he spent time learning from Jesus. It was a time for talking things through, thinking new thoughts and – as often happens at this stage of life and faith – crystallizing them into hard-and-fast faith formulations, which sometimes manifests itself in an abrasive attitude towards others. New understandings

seem clear beyond doubt, though appreciating all their implications may take much longer. This comes out quite obviously
in the experience of Peter, who in theological and intellectual
terms maybe got the words right, but had no idea what they
meant in relation to his own emotions or personal commitments. In fact, when Jesus went on to explain what the words
really meant, Peter found himself unable to handle it. His will
was in tune with Jesus, and he knew he really wanted to follow him: that was the lesson of Mark 1:16–20. His mind was in
tune with Jesus, and he was able to acknowledge him for who
he truly was: that was the lesson of Mark 8:27–30. But his emotions were somewhere else altogether, and at this time of clear
intellectual challenge and change, he also found himself given
a severe rebuke by Jesus (Mark 8:33). He was still struggling to
discover how to accept himself with his imperfections, yet be
free to express his love for Christ.

4   FEELINGS IN CRISIS (JOHN 18:15–27, 21:1–23)
'CAN I REALLY LOVE HIM THIS MUCH?'

Peter continues to play a major part in all the gospel traditions, living uneasily with the tension between motivational
and intellectual commitment, yet somehow unable to handle
his own feelings. This tension is only resolved towards the
end of the gospel story, in an episode that was so significant
for his spiritual journey that it features in all four gospels.

Peter's uncertain emotional commitment to Jesus eventually surfaced in the unexpected circumstances of the high
priest's garden, after Jesus had been arrested and was about to
face trial for his life. This was a different situation from many
of those Peter had previously faced. Here, merely using the
right form of words to describe his belief in Jesus was not
going to be enough. It was not so much that his theology was
wrong or inadequate, just that theological formulations can

never be the whole picture. In Peter's case, he was caught off guard by a simple question asked in a courtyard by an insignificant servant. If she had asked, 'Do you think this man might be the messiah?', Peter would have known the answer to that question, for he had sorted it out long before. Instead, she was more direct and personal, but for that very reason her question was a lot more threatening: 'You are one of this man's friends, aren't you?' (Matthew 26:69–75; Mark 14:66–72; Luke 22:54–62; John 18:15–27). Peter was not yet ready to handle a question couched in personal terms like that. A theological question would undoubtedly have been a lot easier. But this was different, for it impinged on Peter's internal spiritual search, and touched chords deep down in his psyche. It brought to the surface all sorts of uncertainties and hesitations that he had not yet felt able to handle. It revealed that though his basic life orientation – and his thinking – had undergone the sort of fundamental change we might call conversion, there were other areas of his personality that still remained fundamentally untouched by the gospel: his emotions.

This is a stage of faith which many modern Christians – especially Westerners, and men in particular – find especially threatening. A lot of people are much happier with rational, cerebral, theological beliefs than they are with something that will touch their emotions. As a result, they never face up to this kind of challenge, but are content to sit on the spiritual sidelines. Instead of following through the painful process of allowing the deepest recesses of their person to be challenged and changed by the gospel, they prefer to stick with a cerebral, 'left-brained' understanding of faith.

How did Peter break through this tough challenge? We might debate which is the most appropriate New Testament passage to use to answer that question. In the context of Luke's gospel, it could well be the experience of the day of Pentecost (Acts 2:1–42). In the fourth gospel, which I have chosen to follow here, it is a post-resurrection appearance of Jesus to Peter (John 21:1–23). Either way, it is only resolved as Peter allowed himself to be radically changed from the inside out. And the resolution of the problem was no less painful than his initial discomfort at realizing what he had done when he denied he knew Jesus. In the story in John 21 Jesus invites Peter to make emotional commitments that, up to this point, he had been either unable or unwilling to make. Notice that Jesus did not cover the old ground again. His message this time was not, 'Come and follow me'; Peter had already demonstrated his willingness to do that. Nor was it a test for theological soundness to discover if he still believed all the right things; Peter could have handled those questions. Instead, Jesus posed a question that Peter was much less comfortable with: 'Do you love me?' He tried desperately to avoid answering it, because it was challenging a whole area of his being that needed to be changed. But as he was able to respond to this renewed call to conversion, he found personal healing and fresh courage that moved him in a new and exciting direction. In due course, in the experience of the earliest Church, Peter's wholehearted commitment of his emotions to Christ was matched by the presence of the Spirit, and the next time he was challenged he was ready to go to prison (Acts 3:1–4:4). He had finally made it in his faith pilgrimage! Or had he?

5 WORLDVIEW CONVERSION (ACTS 10:1–48)
'WHO IS GOD, WHO AM I, WHAT IS IT ALL ABOUT?'
How much of a person needs to change in order to be a follower of Jesus? All Christians recognize the essentially personal elements of morality and relationships that are included in conversion. But what about the gospel and the public world? What about the big issues, the way we see the world? These are crucial questions for today, and the answers that Christians

give will radically affect the progress and credibility of the Church well into the new century. How does the good news relate to our culture? It is not a coincidence that this question came to Peter as soon as he got involved with the business of evangelization. By taking seriously the call to share the Christian message with others, he found his most deeply cherished preconceptions about human existence were taken apart – and restructured.

Like all of us, Peter was part of a very specific culture. In his case, he made sense of things by thinking of the world in terms of relations between Jews and non-Jews (Gentiles). He was so confident that this reflected the ultimate truth of how things actually were that, though he was willing to share the message of Jesus with Gentiles, he felt it would only work if they could all be made into Jews first. Other people in his day thought in similar ways, though the terminology was different. Educated Romans, for example, made sense out of the world by thinking of themselves as a cut above the unsophisticated and brutish 'barbarians' who lived on the fringes of the Empire, while their entire economic and social system was based on maintaining the distinctions between slaves and free people, women and men, and so on.

Peter was challenged on this one when he received a call from the home of Cornelius, a Roman centurion (Acts 10:1–48). He immediately found himself in a turmoil, and it was a painful business to extricate himself from it. To him, everything about Cornelius was wrong: he was the wrong race, in the wrong sort of job, asking the wrong sort of questions. He could not possibly be the kind of person for whom the gospel was intended. Now what was Peter's problem? It is easy to describe him as naive, bigoted or just plain stupid. But the real nub of the matter was that he had not fully worked out what it meant to be a Christian. Back by the shores of Galilee, he had been prepared to turn around and follow Jesus. Subsequently, his thinking and his emotions had been challenged. In fact, his entire lifestyle had changed at so many points that it felt as if he had literally given up all he had to follow Jesus. But there was one bit of his life that was a 'no-go' area for the gospel. 'You cannot change the way things are,' said Peter, and so the whole framework of cultural, political, economic and racial assumptions on which he had based his life was still unchallenged by his faith in Christ and, therefore, fundamentally unconverted.

He found himself learning some painful and difficult lessons. He was forced to admit that many of the things he thought were just 'the way the world is', were not that at all: they were a time-bound, cultural view of things. He also had to learn that the Christian gospel must challenge the cultural assumptions on which people live. Disciples cannot keep Jesus shut up in one little compartment of life. It may be possible to be a part-time Baptist or Anglican (or Catholic, Presbyterian, Methodist, Pentecostal or whatever), but being part of God's kingdom is a commitment that enfolds the whole of life. Evangelization is not just about private religious experience, it is concerned with the communication of a message that claims to be the absolute truth in all areas of life. For Peter, at least, this was the most fundamental conversion of all. This time, his entire worldview was being challenged. His personal commitment to Jesus was in no doubt, but he still operated on cultural and political assumptions that at bottom were – so far – untouched by his faith in Christ. The story ostensibly tells of Cornelius's conversion. But if you ask who was the one in this episode to undergo the most traumatic challenge to change, then it certainly was not Cornelius! 'The call to conversion should begin with the repentance of those who do the calling, who issue the invitation.'[15] The relevance of all this to the evangelization of today's world hardly needs to be highlighted.

6 'SHARING MYSELF AND MY FAITH'

The rest of Peter's story is less accessible to us because of the nature of our sources in the New Testament. No doubt, like many modern Christians, his faith development did not proceed unhindered in a straight line from simple beginnings to maturity. There would be times when he went back and questioned his intellectual commitment to Christ. There would be other occasions when he was forced to redefine the depth of his emotional conversion. And we know for certain that he found it hard to accept the challenge to his worldview that was involved in following Christ. Long after the Cornelius incident, he was in conflict with Paul over the same questions (Galatians 2:11–14), and as late as the mid-50s he was still sufficiently narrow in his outlook for some legalists in Corinth to claim him as their patron. (See 1 Corinthians 1:12; though they may have been using his name without his permission or encouragement.) Following Christ is often like that, as we move in and out of different stages of faith at different points in life. In workshops, I have often used a child's toy 'slinky' spring as a visual image of faith development, observing that progress from one end of the spring to the other often feels like going round in circles, but nevertheless there is still a progression forwards from one end to the other.

Certainly, in Peter's case there was no doubt about his fundamental hopes and aspirations. He joined with enthusiasm in the evangelistic calling of the Church, first in Galilee, then in Antioch, and afterwards travelling through much of the Empire before arriving in Rome, where his commitment met the ultimate challenge, and he did not flinch from giving his life for the Christ he loved so much. Through much turmoil, many blind alleys and not a few mistakes, Peter still turns out to be a powerful role model for all subsequent generations. Or, more exactly, it is precisely *because* of the turmoil, the blind alleys and the mistakes that his willingness to give all he had for Christ seems so encouraging to others. For is not this the stuff out of which discipleship is made, and in the midst of which the concept of conversion takes a form that is anchored in the everyday experience of real people?

SIGNPOSTS FOR FAITH-SHARING

In chapter 2, we considered the nature of postmodern culture, and in particular the kind of opportunities now presented for inviting people to follow Jesus. One of the key themes that emerged from that discussion was the importance attached by today's spiritual searchers to personal formation, growth and transformation. Viewed in that light, and understood from a perspective of personal faith development, the Bible stories of disciples like Peter assume a new significance – not only as relevant models of conversion, but also of how Christians might effectively share their own faith journeys with those who as yet do not follow Jesus. By way of identifying some of the key considerations here, let us return to our initial questions. What was going on here? If you like, at what point did Peter become a 'real' Christian? When was he truly converted? Three comments might help to give direction to such enquiries.

Firstly, we should note that in the course of the years of his life to which we have access in the New Testament, Peter was growing up. Probably he was little more than a teenager when he first met Jesus, and the narratives all indicate ways in which he was growing: physically, spiritually, morally and personally. Growth in all these areas was running parallel. People respond to God in different ways at different stages of growth. Not just in terms of physical growth, as we mature from childhood, through adolescence, to adulthood – but in personal growth continuing through the whole of life. We are all persons in the process of becoming somebody, and sensitivity to where people are at in their personal maturity will be an integral part of responsible evangelization. 'The response of faith is to present as much as one knows of oneself to as much as one knows of God.'[16] There is an appropriate response to God for different stages of life. When my daughter was about 18 months old, I remember her looking me in the eyes and saying, 'I love you, daddy' – and then adding, 'I love Jesus too.' That was an appropriate response to God for a child of that age. Of course, she expresses her faith differently now, and no doubt when she is as old as I am she will have different responses again. To insist on processing people so they all look like peas in a pod is not the gospel. People do not have experiences – they are experiences. Wherever we look in the gospels, awareness of this was always Jesus' starting point. That alone is a good enough reason for us to take it seriously.

Secondly, crisis points played a key role in Peter's experience. I remember my friend Raymond Fung, one-time Evangelism Secretary to the World Council of Churches, drawing my attention to the Chinese character for 'crisis'. It is actually two characters (wee-gee), which together mean 'a dangerous opportunity'. People are at their most vulnerable during a crisis, yet at that time they are also most open to change:

the impetus for movement is frequently an event or experience in our lives over which we have little control ... a health crisis, change in relationships, models of others we want to emulate, a teacher, reaching personal limits, deep questions about oneself, being hurt, responding to others' needs, experiencing God in a new way, telling your own story to another, loss of a relationship, death, developing a quiet time, losing truths once held dear, longing for God ... at that moment in our journey we have a choice. We can choose to plunge ahead not being afraid of change, or we can turn back by blocking our feelings and not dealing with the issue. This can be a critical time.[17]

If the Church is to fulfil its evangelistic calling, then it needs people who are sensitively aware of the crisis points, both in their own lives and in the experience of others.

Thirdly, notice how often other people played a key role in Peter's decisions to change. Crisis points by themselves do sometimes lead to faith experiences, and a significant number of people seem to find themselves drawn to Christ at such times without any specific contact with a church or Christians.[18] But more often, it is other people who are instrumental in facilitating the spiritual quest. Jesus himself played a key role in Peter's faith story, gently challenging and setting up signposts to send him off in new directions. This is a skill we must explore further in a later chapter. But sometimes, it was other people who were not necessarily disciples themselves. The servant in the high priest's garden, and the searching Cornelius, both played a significant part in Peter's personal journey of faith.

This chapter has deliberately focused on a particular New Testament example of conversion in all its multifaceted diversity. But the same conclusions could be reached by different routes. In reflecting on the experience of Peter, I have frequently been impressed with the way in which it parallels many of the findings of Christian educators who have explored the meaning of faith from the perspective of developmental psychology. I am thinking in particular of the work of James Fowler. Taking his cue from Erik Erikson's identification of eight distinct stages in human development, from cradle to grave, Fowler pinpointed what he called six 'stages of faith'. The precise nature of these stages is open to a good deal of debate, and Fowler and others have refined the model many times since the idea was first put forward.[19] One version to which I find myself particular attracted (maybe because it reflects my own spiritual journey fairly closely) is that proposed by Janet Hagberg and Robert Guelich in their book *The Critical Journey*. This is not the place in which to engage in an extensive comparison of these various understandings of the nature of faith and conversion, but it is striking how easy it is to place the New Testament model of Peter alongside these others, and the appendix indicates how this can be done.

In terms of practical evangelization, the most striking conclusion is that the New Testament, the experience of the majority of Christian people, and contemporary developmental thinking all converge in suggesting that conversion to Christ is not a single event, it is a process. But there are many events in the process. By having a sensitive awareness of those events and this process, first of all in our own lives, today's Christians can begin to develop models of faith-sharing that will avoid some of the mistakes of the past, at the same time as we formulate new evangelizing models that will affirm the spiritual search of our culture and create new ways for people to respond to the call to follow Jesus. In the process, I believe we will also uncover relevant ways of sharing the good news about Jesus with those successful people who say, 'I have no need for God: my life is okay without religion.'

CHAPTER 5

THE CALL TO WORSHIP

There has often been resistance to seeing worship as evangelism. Writing back in 1965 Donald McGavran, the founding father of the church growth movement, drew a strong distinction between the two. 'Worship is good,' he wrote, 'but worship is worship. It is not evangelism.'[1] McGavran subsequently modified this strident statement a little, but the notion is still widely accepted in one form or another. In *The Logic of Evangelism*, Professor William Abraham also differentiates evangelism from worship.[2] And at parish level, as the churches of the early 1990s searched for an instant formula for evangelistic success, much attention focused on what came to be known as 'seeker-friendly' services. Here too a good deal of emphasis was placed on the notion that, to be 'seeker-friendly' to today's spiritual pilgrims, worship must be given a low profile, if not locked firmly in the closet. Indeed, many are now claiming that worship is something that suits Christians, but alienates those who are not yet committed. As a result of this philosophy, thousands of churches are experimenting with a form of evangelism which specifically excludes the experience of worship as being, at best, irrelevant to the whole business of calling women and men to faith in Jesus Christ, and, at worst, as an alienating experience that might actually prevent people from following Christ.

These ideas, and others like them, are undoubtedly trendy, at least in certain evangelical circles. But they should not be accepted without close scrutiny. Paul wrote of the importance in his own ministry of being prepared to 'become all things to all people, that I might by all means save some' (1 Corinthians 9:22), and that is a sentiment with which I find myself in complete agreement. There are many places in church life where we need to be more adventurous, and faith-sharing is certainly one of them. In particular, I would say we need to be more creative in exploring how faith can be shared not in church buildings (where Christians feel comfortable), but in the spaces and places where other people feel safe (and Christians may feel more vulnerable). At the same time, however, Christian evangelization is not concerned with marketing and packaging a commodity that is to be bought and sold in the supermarket of faiths. The spiritual journey – conversion – is about people being caught up into the presence of God, and responding in ways that will move them on towards that total commitment to Christ which, according to the New Testament, is at the heart of discipleship. Worship plays a key role in that kind of faith journey. Other types of experience (in particular, left-brained, cognitive perceptions of faith) may well point people in that direction, but they are not an end in themselves. Effective evangelism and renewed worship are inextricably linked. You cannot have one without the other, and to try and do so will lead to serious imbalance. Churches that are unprepared to face up to the challenge of renewal in worship will easily turn evangelism into just another marketing exercise. Churches that focus exclusively on their own internal spirituality will easily become introverted and irrelevant to the needs of the world. But put the two together, and you have an exceedingly powerful, and faith-enhancing, combination. Keeping them apart may be easier – and it certainly reflects the reductionist approach of traditional Western thinking. The widespread dissatisfaction in our culture with this way of understanding things is in itself a good enough reason for asking if the separation of evangelism from worship does not owe more to cultural conformity than to spiritual integrity.

THE 'MCDONALDIZATION' OF SPIRITUALITY?

Could it be that the Church's evident embarrassment with its worship is actually just one further evidence of that secularization of the Church and of Christian belief, already hinted at in chapter 2? One of the most penetrating recent analyses of Western culture is sociologist George Ritzer's book *The McDonaldization of Society*.[3] He locates the prime cause of our present malaise in the way that rational systems have come to dominate the way we live ('McDonaldization': because the service of fast-food is one of the most accessible models of this trend). Put in a nutshell, the Enlightenment-inspired process of rationalization, which identified the highest human good with efficiency, predictability, quantification and control – while it has not all been bad news – has led to a devaluing of the human spirit and a heightening of the personal alienation that in any case seems to be an inescapable part of the universal human condition. The development of rational systems to control and organize every aspect of existence is leading to the breakdown of community, and the very systems that were created to enhance the quality of life are having the opposite effect: 'it tends to become a dehumanizing system that may become antihuman or even destructive to human beings'.[4] And so – to give a trivial, though telling, example – people are desperately trying to reinvent simplicity, as small shopping outlets multiply with the aim of doing things 'the way granny used to do them', and even large commercial organizations get in on the act with 'home-made' products that range from 'traditional' ice cream to personal hygiene products made with 'pure' ingredients like baking soda.

In everyday life, people have generally managed to live in some kind of uneasy truce with all this. Work is becoming increasingly dominated and dictated by bureaucratic systems and controls, which marginalize people's basic creativity, but workers still put up with it because they need the money. Likewise, lonely people still go to fast-food restaurants that are designed to minimize contact with other people because, in the end, they can be served quickly and hopefully move on to engage with other more interesting things. Patients who are dissatisfied with the mechanistic approach of healthcare professionals still keep going back to them because, on balance, that is the cheapest option. But when it comes to the Church, a different set of factors enter the picture. Everyone needs an income, food and healthcare – but does everyone need the Church? Especially if the Church is presenting those same values of efficiency, predictability, quantification and control that seem to be creating so many discontinuities in the rest of life? It would require a longer and more detailed study than is possible here to explore this in depth, but one does not need even to be cynical about the Church to see how these four highly prized objectives do seem to be reflected in so much of what goes on.

Is efficiency manifested in the promulgation of over-simplified theologies which need to have an answer for everything, and leave people no freedom to reflect for themselves – nor, arguably, space for the Spirit of God to work? Is everything so quantified and calculated in the Church that there is no time for people to establish meaningful patterns of community, because it all has to happen within the parameters of 'services'? Are our forms of 'worship', whether formal or informal, so predictable and resistant to change that we are unable to engage with a spirituality that is more concerned with the content, and less with the packaging? And does the way we define ministry in terms of 'authority' not owe more to considerations of power and control than to empowering people to be whole and equipping them for their own ministry? These are not questions about Church structures *per se*, nor are they an implied criticism of liturgy, ritual, or other established features of Church life.

Churches of all traditions can be dehumanizing places. I remember a conversation with a minister's spouse, who commented: 'I sometimes feel like screaming in church. I just have to get out before I go mad.' That person was neither mentally disturbed, nor spiritually uncommitted, but found that what went on in church – and especially, what passed for 'worship' – was so antithetical to the spiritual search that in order to find God she was being forced to the fringes even of her own congregation. Nor is her experience at all untypical. I have lost count of the number of clergy from whom I have heard similar sentiments in recent years – not a few admitting that they would never go to church if they were not paid to do so! Surprisingly, Ritzer's study says almost nothing about the Church, but his description of the wider disaffection of our culture voices precisely how many would describe their experiences of Church:

> Human beings, equipped with a wider array of skills and abilities, are asked to perform a limited number of highly simplified tasks over and over. Instead of expressing their human abilities…people are forced to deny their humanity and act in a robot-like manner.[5]

Since being human is to be made in God's image, spaces that do not allow people to express their humanity – even religious spaces – are ultimately contrary to the gospel. Shirley Maclaine puts her finger on the same problem when she reports a conversation with a channelled spirit entity named 'John', who comments: 'Your religions teach religion – not spirituality.'⁶ Surveys of people who leave the Church have consistently identified exactly the same concerns.⁷ If that is true of those who leave the Church, it is also true of those who choose not to join it. We can no longer afford to ignore the unpalatable fact that what we now do is part of the problem, and doing more of the same – even in a more trendy or jazzed-up fashion – will not therefore be part of the resolution of the problem. To put it a different way, for those to whom the Church's rationalized ways of operation are meaningless and irrelevant, where are the spaces in which they can explore the spiritual equivalent of Ben and Jerry's ice cream or Arm and Hammer cosmetics? Without a radical addressing of that kind of question, and an accompanying redefinition of what we mean by worship, there will be no effective re-evangelization of the West.

Such redefinition will need to begin by a return to our roots in the New Testament, for it is undeniable that worship and evangelism are inextricably linked together in its pages. Worship was absolutely central to the life of the early Church, and was a major factor in the rapid growth of the earliest Christian community from an insignificant group of Galilean peasants to become a movement that shook the Roman Empire to its foundations. When John's gospel depicts Jesus speaking of how God's glory in the Church would be recognized by those outside, and attract them to the gospel (John 17:1–26), it was not just wishful thinking, but a reflection of what had actually happened in the Church by the time the fourth gospel was written. Moreover, wherever the Church is growing today, worship is at the centre. In world terms, those Western churches that appear to be growing without a renewal of worship are the exceptions that prove the rule.⁸ On a global scale, more people are attracted to discipleship by worship than by any other single factor, including most of the things to which we conventionally attach the label 'evangelism'. Moreover, worship has led to remarkable Church growth in many countries where any kind of overt Christian evangelizing activity is forbidden. China is a classic example, where for decades the Church has grown underground as Christians have worshipped, and as their non-Christian friends have been drawn into a context where there was a sense of the presence of God.[9]

But it happens in other places too. A Roman Catholic bishop whom I know was visiting an Islamic country, where Christian evangelism was officially forbidden. The only thing the Church could do was worship – and they did. At the end of a Eucharistic celebration, a group of Muslim men made their way to the front of the church. Not knowing what was going to happen next, my friend assumed the worst, and thought their presence could only mean one thing: trouble. In fact, they said they had been so impressed by the unspoken message they had received merely by watching what went on, and appreciating for the first time the true meaning of the bread and the wine, and the good news that lay behind it all, that they wanted to know more about the Christian faith. They were not drawn to Christ by an evangelistic sermon, still less by an apologetic lecture – for they had heard neither. All that happened was they sensed the presence of God in the worship, and knew it was for them.

That kind of thing happens all the time all over the world. Why does it take us by surprise, when the New Testament itself describes the Eucharist as 'proclamation', that is, witness? In 1 Corinthians 11:26, Paul uses an unusual Greek word (*katangello*) when he says that in the Eucharist 'You *proclaim* the Lord's death…' Elsewhere in the New Testament the same word is used of proclaiming the gospel (Philippians 1:17; Colossians 1:28). The significance of the experience of authentic worship for faith has always been tacitly recognized in our creedal statements. The old Scots Catechism asks, 'Why was I created?', and responds with, 'I was created in order to worship God...' Much modern psychology has reached the same conclusion, namely that a sense of mystery, discovered and expressed through something like worship, is basic to the human condition. This is a constant thread that runs through much of the thinking of Carl Jung, for instance, and explains the popularity of mystical experiences among spiritual searchers in the Western world today.[10]

There is also an obvious theological reason for linking worship and evangelism. We have already noticed how Matthew's 'Great Commission' identifies spiritual growth as part of the evangelistic task of the Church, while our discussion of conversion pointed in the same direction. If discipleship is a holistic call, encompassing the whole of life, then evangelization needs to have the same quality. If scripture, theology, history and the experience of the world Church today all seem to bring evangelism and worship together, then we need very strong and compelling reasons for separating them, even (or especially) if we do it as some kind of marketing device to make the gospel 'seeker friendly'.

WHAT IS WORSHIP?

One of the most outstanding and genuinely original books of recent years is *The Isaiah Vision*, by Raymond Fung. He identifies three elements that are central to effective evangelism: partnership with the world for peace and justice, the invitation to worship, and the invitation to discipleship. Though he uses completely different terminology, and has travelled by a very different route to arrive at the same conclusion, his comments bear a striking similarity to those already made by using the model of 'McDonaldization'. As he looks at the interplay between worship and evangelization, he suggests that Western churches have a problem with understanding how worship can be evangelism, because they have a basic problem with their worship.

> To some Christians, the idea of inviting our...partners and friends to worship with us is highly problematic. It could be embarrassing. The worship services in many of our churches are often either so uninspiring and clannish, or so unintelligent and unintelligible – or both – that we'd rather not invite others. If that is the case, we have a real problem on our hands...How can we have the kind of worship to which we are not embarrassed to bring our partners and friends? Indeed, how can we have the kind of worship that may expose others to an experience of God?"

At a time when there seems little consensus on what worship actually is, or on what worship is supposed to accomplish, we need to start with some basic questions. What exactly do we mean by 'worship'? By way of exploring that question, come on a quick trip around three churches. Like me, you have probably visited them before, and doubtless noticed some of the same things as I have. The descriptions that follow are caricatures, of course. They are deliberately exaggerated (though not much), in order to highlight some distinctive trends. But, like all good cartoons, they are only overstating what is already there in real life.

Even to someone who has never been inside a church building before, the first one would probably feel vaguely familiar territory. In essence, it is an auditorium, not too different from a theatre or cinema. Certainly, everything happens up at the front, where the key players operate as if taking part in some kind of theatrical performance. I remember once leading a training course for people whose job was to welcome visitors to their church services. Part of the group exercises we engaged in was to identify the different types of people who might arrive at the church door, and to think about their likely impressions. One wit described the scene as he imagined an anthropologist doing research into human behaviour would perceive it: 'People standing up, kneeling down, closing their eyes, singing, going to sleep, paying money, eating sweets, and throttling children.' He was deliberately being cynical, of course, but he gave an accurate enough account of the behaviour that was labelled 'worship' in that particular church. In this sort of worship, the only person who really matters is the minister. If there was nobody there to carry through this role, then 'worship' could not happen: it would have to be called off. In recent years, some churches have modified this pattern slightly by trying to move away from the idea of a spiritual prima donna 'conducting a service' on behalf of the others, but they then typically replace the solo performance with a kind of variety show, in which other people move on and off stage basically to go through the same routines as the minister would have done single-handed in other circumstances.

This model of 'worship' is most likely to be encountered, on the one hand, in highly sacramentalist churches, and on the other (at the opposite end of the theological spectrum) in highly evangelical congregations. Apart from the concerns about control already mentioned, this pattern of worship conveys some interesting messages about the perceived nature of worship itself. To put it somewhat simplistically, if we adopt a theatrical model for worship, in which everything is in the hands of experts of one sort or another, merely acting as performers to an audience, then people will respond accordingly. They will see Church as a show, and assume that once they have paid for it they have no further responsibility. They are quite likely to pick up the message that, whatever 'worship' truly is, it is something that happens exclusively between individuals and God. For many attenders at such services, the clergy almost embody God, and the whole language of the building and the service gives the impression that worship is oriented in only one dimension, namely the vertical. There is nothing horizontal, no sense that interaction with other people might play a significant part in it all. If people in this church inadvertently make physical contact with others (or do so at the 'wrong' points in the liturgy), they will back off very quickly and apologize as if they had committed an unmentionable sin. Which, in a way, they have, for they are not there to have dealings with other people, only with God. And even that is likely to be a one-way communication, as they spend most of the time sitting passively and listening to whatever is said from pulpit or altar.

Church number two is quite different. Almost the exact opposite, you might say. Many things will be tolerated here under the guise of 'worship'. To the casual visitor the whole thing might seem to be out of control, as if almost anything could take place (though in truth there is probably a very strong control mechanism). There is just one thing that seems consistent and characterizes everything else, and that is the necessity for the worshippers to lift their hands in the air in order to make anything happen at all. This is the sort of church where you can easily imagine a vote being taken by people putting their hands down instead of up. I remember visiting a church like this in California, which had an amazing building, including a whole series of fans on the ceiling to help keep the congregation cool during the hottest part of the summer. My attention was drawn to these fans because the lower sections of the stems fixing them to the ceiling were bright and shiny by comparison with the parts nearest the ceiling which had a much duller appearance. By way of making small talk, I commented on this to the pastor who was showing me round. 'Oh yes,' he said, 'we did that to improve the quality of our praise.' On seeing my bemused look, he went on to explain that these people could do nothing without their hands held high, and in order to encourage them at least to think about why they were doing it, the church leadership had decided to lower the fans to just a little above head height! People can easily do things out of habit in worship, whether it be sitting in serried ranks watching a theatrical-style production from an accomplished ministerial performer, or whether it be in the allegedly more relaxed atmosphere of the kind of church where everything significant happens an arm's length above the heads of the worshippers.

Church number three tries to have the best of all possible worlds by combining practices from the other two. Historically, its people have come from a background where worship was always on the theatrical model, but they would like to learn something from a more exuberant style of worship, and even to incorporate some aspects of it alongside their own traditions. Their worship service typically begins in what seems to be a very traditional mode, but then part-way through the proceedings a balding man who has been forty-something for as long as anyone can remember, and who obviously regards himself as extraordinarily trendy, appears from the transept and says, 'Now let's have a time of *real* worship.' This is the cue for guitars, drums, and other noisy instruments to be dragged out, and a group of musicians (who might easily be the most talented people to do anything through the whole service) then lead 'worship' for ten or fifteen minutes. Here, 'worship' seems to mean singing a particular style of modern praise chorus to the accompaniment of a lot of noisy music. The noisier the better, for it may well be accompanied by much vigorous hand-clapping by the congregation, though there is little, if any, arm-raising in this kind of church. If *this* is worship, then I wonder what had been happening before – and what happens after it? Because typically, the drums and guitars are stacked away again, and the service then continues in the same dreary format as it had before all this started.

As I said, these are caricatures, though most of us will recognize ourselves in them. And not everything about them is bad. Take the theatrical model, for example. The theatre can have a very powerful influence on the lives of those who go to it. My previous description focused on some of the potentially negative aspects of a theatrical-style worship. But there is such a thing as good theatre. Reflect for a moment, though, on what it is that makes for good theatre. It is when it moves from being a mere spectacle that is observed, to engaging with the audience. Theatre moves up a gear when it grabs the attention and the audience get involved. The New Testament gives a similar image of meaningful worship. There, worship is a shared experience, in which everyone has a part, which takes place where people are (rather than up-front on a stage or altar), and has space for all types and ages of people. Like other aspects of the gospel, worship is intended to be a holistic experience, which engages and uses all the gifts, talents and insights of the whole people of God (and that means more than just the full-time clergy, though it quite definitely includes them too).

There are many ways to define worship. My definition would be simple: worship is all that I am, responding to all that God is. You can unpack that in several different ways. Individually, of course, with the emphasis on 'all that *I* am'. Who am I as a person? First and foremost, I am a body: I have a physical dimension. I understand things by touching, seeing, smelling them. I am also a mind, with the capacity to think and reflect on the meaning of things. Then I have feelings and emotions, and relationships which encapsulate yet other dimensions of my complex being. If worship is to engage the whole of myself as an individual, then it will somehow need to include all these facets of the person that I am, and facilitate their response to God.

We can also think of this definition of worship in a corporate dimension. For when people meet together for worship, they are not alone. They meet in the company of others. Who are these others? What would it mean for worship to start from a recognition of 'all that *we* are' together? In any congregation that is even vaguely representative of the whole community, there will be children, young people, older people, women, men, single people, divorced people, married people, blended families, different ethnic backgrounds, various educational backgrounds, people with jobs, people with no jobs... the possibilities are as endless as the variety of humankind. What would worship need to be like in order to facilitate all these different people responding to God in ways that are meaningful and relevant to them?

Then, of course, God is in there. God is the centre of all worship, and worship would not be worship unless it focused on 'all that God is'. But what do we mean by 'God'? That is a big question, and God would not be God without being bigger than anything we can possibly comprehend. But both the Bible and Christian theology provide us with a few signposts. One of the central confessions of Christian belief is that 'the Word became flesh' (John 1:14). We undermine the heart of the faith if we try and put it all back into words again. Whatever else might be included, belief in the incarnation centres on the conviction that God became a person. If worship is about responding to all that God is, then relating to persons is going to be a basic part of it, for the whole of humanity is made 'in God's image' (Genesis 1:27).

EVANGELIZING WORSHIP

Worship is fundamental to the Christian life. If worship is a central part of the gospel, and if evangelization is about communicating the whole gospel, then clearly there can be no effective evangelism without authentic worship. Responding to the gospel is about responding to God, and the context in which this most readily takes place is worship. Maybe that all sounds somewhat idealistic, for obviously not everything to which we attach the label 'worship' has a spin-off in effective evangelization. Churches are worshipping all the time, yet their numbers still continue to decline throughout the Western world. But the opposite is also true. Churches in other parts of the world are worshipping all the time – and their numbers are growing, as their worship attracts people to the reality of God in their midst. 'Worship is our way to God and at the same time our celebration of the love of God. The key to authentic worship is the presence of authentic worshippers.'[12]

What sort of worship, then, will be evangelizing? It would be easy to answer that question by providing a blueprint indicating how such worship might work out in a particular context. To do so would limit the usefulness of this discussion, for the precise nature of the things people do in worship is culturally relative. But whatever is done should certainly facilitate a holistic response to God. In chapter 2, reference was made to the fact that discipleship ought to engage heart, soul, mind and strength (Mark 12:29–31), and on that minimal definition worship should therefore encompass at least the emotions, thinking and body, as well as having a mystical element to it. If it is to go further, and reflect 'all that we are', then the checklist would soon grow. In keeping with the purpose of this book, however, we will concentrate on the general attitudes that might inform and inspire evangelizing worship.

1 WORSHIP IS A LIFESTYLE

Mention worship to most Christians today, and they immediately think of services and meetings – events of some kind. People can, and do, worship meaningfully in church services, but to identify the two is a distortion of the nature of worship.

It was Martin Luther who coined the phrase, *Laborare est orare*, 'work is worship'. The early Church would certainly have agreed with him. In the early chapters of Acts, their entire lifestyle is fundamental to the fact that 'day by day the Lord added to their group those who were being saved' (Acts 2:47). The way they related to each other, the style of their meals, their use of material goods: all these things, and others besides, were crucial to their life of evangelization, witness – and worship. The dynamic evangelistic impact of such lifestyles is frequently mentioned in Paul's letters (for exam ple, 1 Thessalonians 1:2–10). Everything they did was very public. There were no closed doors in the Church, and that was one of the things that distinguished them both from their Jewish heritage, and from the many competing sects of the Hellenistic world. Elsewhere, worship was an event which drew people in to sacred spaces (temples) at sacred times (religious festivals), and where scrupulous attention was given to excluding those deemed to be disqualified from participation. This meant that in the Jerusalem temple, Gentiles were largely kept out of the most significant places; in the synagogue, women and children were strictly separated from the men; and in the many Hellenistic mystery religions, only initiates were allowed full access, because by definition everything was kept secret and hidden from outsiders. But for the earliest Christians, worship was the reverse of all this. Instead of being an activity requiring withdrawal from the world, the experience of worship opened them out to the needs and concerns of the world.

This no doubt explains why Christian worship generally took place in people's homes (Romans 16:3–16, for instance, lists several 'home churches' that collectively constituted the Christian community in that city). The typical Roman villa was both the workplace and the home. Worship and evangelism happened where people lived and worked, and both of them grew naturally out of the relationships of everyday life.[13] This inevitably opened up the Church's worship to all sorts of people, for Christians lived and worked alongside those who were not yet believers. Their worship needed to display an uncommon degree of integrity, for home is the one place where it is impossible to carry on some sort of act. People are most truly themselves when they are at home.

Much contemporary worship – whether by accident or design – is exclusive, and caters for those who are already in the Church. The New Testament implies that worship in the early Church was an inclusive activity, open to anyone who cared to join it, not just to be a spectator but a participant. Acts describes the Jerusalem Christians worshipping in the street as well as in one another's homes, while Paul took it for granted that unbelievers would be wandering in and out of the worship in the church at Corinth (1 Corinthians 14:25). His description of the setting in which the Eucharist was celebrated is especially instructive in this regard. In 1 Corinthians 11:23–34, he was seeking to correct abuses of the occasion caused, among other things, by rich and prosperous people holding their dinner parties in one corner of the room while poorer people could only sit and watch them. He did not counsel them to abolish this almost festive atmosphere, but instead to correct the injustices and imbalances that were occurring.

New Testament worship also seems to have involved all generations. Children were taken for granted as part of the Church. Modern theological debates about baptism have tended to obscure the sociological fact that the whole structure of the early Church was family based. If a child belonged in a family, then she or he belonged to the Church. This is never spelled out categorically simply because it was taken for granted. Nor was it ever a cause of controversy, which explains why it is never formally discussed in any of the New

Testament letters (all of which were *ad hoc* responses to particular debates and questions which arose in specific contexts).

The pattern of worship in these early Christian communities explains why no one felt it necessary to establish a Christian temple as an alternative either to the Jerusalem temple, or
the various shrines of other religious traditions. Christians did
eventually find themselves conforming to the religious expectations of their pagan neighbours, but this was not the original
pattern, and stemmed more from cultural pressures than from
the central values of the gospel.

2 WORSHIP IS INTERACTIVE

Nowadays, it is common to talk of worship as something to be
'conducted' by the clergy or other recognized leaders. Again,
this practice did not characterize the life of the early Church.
In Corinth, Paul was faced with the problem of what looked
like too much participation in worship, as different people
within the congregation insisted on doing their own thing –
and all doing it at the same time, in competition with one
another. This was clearly unsatisfactory, but Paul did not tackle it by insisting they should all be silent while one or two
authorized people conducted worship on their behalf. That
would have been relatively easy, and in practical terms could
well have resolved the problem. But Paul knew that to do so
would also have undermined some fundamental aspects of
the gospel itself.

So instead of silencing the whole orchestra, he adopted the
more difficult course of defining the role of various players,
and helping them to get the music in such an order that the
end-product would be a harmonious expression of praise to
God. In what must be one of the most perceptive essays on
worship and ministry in the early Church ever to be written,
Ernst Käsemann correctly noted that

> the diversity of charismatic functions is normative even
> for the ministry of preaching; all ... are bearers of the
> Word of God and contribute to the edification of the com-
> munity. Even the apostle is, as Paul is always emphasiz-
> ing, only one charismatic among many ...[14]

An insufficient recognition of the importance of this will create a spiritually unhealthy dependency culture in the Church.
Whether we realize it or not, people are being taught that
being the Church is something somebody else does for them.
We will not make effective evangelists that way! It is unrealistic to suppose that people who are not allowed to play a role in
the safe environment of the Church will suddenly be able to
share their faith in the world outside.

Paul makes exactly the same point more subtly – and more
theologically – in his discussion of how the Eucharist should
be celebrated. 'Do this ...,' he writes (twice, in 1 Corinthians
11:24–25), in each case using the *plural* form of the Greek verb
for 'do' (*poieite*). For many Christians today, worship is a noun,
but for Paul and his contemporaries it was very definitely a
verb: a plural verb, as well, because it was to engage the whole
Christian community together. No doubt this helps to explain
why worship came to be described as 'liturgy'. The Greek
word *leitourgia* described the various jobs different citizens
carried out in the ideal city state. These were the things for
which they had responsibility and for which they were
equipped by their natural gifts and talents. The doing of all
these things in harmony with others was what kept the community working properly. Paul's use of the 'body of Christ'
image in 1 Corinthians 12:1–31 is a near-perfect application of
that into the Church context – with one exception. In the Greek
city-states, citizens could be forced to play a particular role
whether or not they wished to do so. Paul, by contrast, always
emphasizes the free and loving service of Christians in

response to God's grace. In the New Testament sense, this is what liturgy should be. A 'service' is literally Christians 'serving' one another, as they respond to the greatness and goodness of God. This at once puts a question mark against a theatrical model of worship. If worship is to be service of one another, then by definition this is not something that can happen from the front, regardless of whether it is clergy or lay people who do it. It will take the whole of God's people even to begin to reflect the whole of God's glory to the whole community, and the idea that one or two people can approximate to that – even if they do claim to be expressing themselves on behalf of others – is foreign to scripture. If we cannot be open with one another in church, how can we be open in sharing faith with other people outside it? And if clergy will not be open, weak and vulnerable, why should they expect others to exhibit these characteristics?

One of my saddest memories is of a minister with a close relative who had been saved from a disaster in which other people lost their lives, and who insisted that no mention should be made of this in a service, because he would be embarrassed to be prayed for. He himself had never shown any hesitation about praying for other people – and whether or not he realized it, he was sending out signals saying that he had no needs. He did, of course, but by repressing them and keeping everything 'in control' he presumably found it less personally threatening. But in the early Church, 'Let us pray' meant just that (as it does in many churches in the two-thirds world today), not 'You sit still while I pray on your behalf'. Many church leaders wrestle with this, but they frequently give confusing signals, by saying they want others to be 'more involved' in worship, but then never creating any opportunities for them to do so with integrity.

3   WORSHIP IS DIFFERENT FROM TEACHING

The relationship between what the Church thinks is 'teaching' and what the New Testament identifies as worship takes us into a potential minefield, because an over-emphasis on teaching and intellectual learning is a familiar Western obsession whose influence extends far beyond the boundaries of the Church. It takes us back to the Enlightenment again, and its stranglehold on the expectations and understandings of Western Christianity, particularly the rationalist view that the only things worth knowing are things you can think about. This may well be one key reason why so many churches are on the decline today. It seems to be fashionable to say that our Western churches have become very middle-class, but that analysis misses the more fundamental issue. It is more accurate to say that the churches have become very bookish, and mainly appeal to people who think and process information in particular ways, and those people (at least in the past) have tended to belong to the middle-classes – though even that is much less true today than it once was. Nevertheless, that legacy is still very much with us.

In worship workshops with churches of many different denominational and theological traditions, I have often used the Honey and Mumford *Learning Skills Questionnaire* as a means of helping people come to terms with what this means both for their worship and their evangelization. Honey and Mumford identify four different learning styles, the Activist, Pragmatist, Reflector, and Theorist.[15] I can almost guarantee that any church in the West selected at random will have a substantial preponderance of people who are either reflectors or theorists (most probably the latter). At a time when the numbers of people who prefer these learning styles are declining in the general population (even among the educated middle classes), this is bound to be bad news for the Church's ability to reach other types of people. In so many churches, worship has become a very cerebral activity. Any minister who doubts that could do worse than reflect on how much time is spent on preparation for the various elements of Sunday worship. That will help to identify where our priorities lie, and is likely to be a salutary and challenging experience. It certainly has been for me.

It is a mistake to confuse worship with teaching, and trying to do both at once is likely to mean that we do neither very well, for they are fundamentally different things. The root of the problem was identified in a previous chapter, namely our insistence that being a Christian is basically a cognitive experience, and so everything needs to be in words all the time. I need to affirm here that there is nothing wrong with words and thinking, and our fundamental problem is one of balance. But the point needs to be emphasized so strongly simply because so many of us have a lop-sided understanding here, and this imbalance affects both the nurture of those who are in the Church and the evangelization of those who are not. Sometimes our cerebral bias comes out in simple, even trivial ways. For instance, Christians do not always appreciate how alien things like hard-backed hymn books and Bibles can be to the average person in the street, who in everyday life probably never handles any literature other than a tabloid newspaper and takes in most of their learning from the TV or computer screen. More often, it affects the way we present the gospel itself. It is not unusual to hear it said that children need to achieve 'years of understanding and/or discretion' in order to make satisfactory faith commitments. Though it might be dressed up to look like theology, that is not essentially a spiritual or theological statement at all. To link faith to a particular level of intellectual attainment or development is a secular rationalist sentiment (and it is, of course, bad news for anyone called to minister to the mentally impaired). This cerebral emphasis has also led to an over-emphasis on the importance of sermons, of children going to Sunday *Schools*, with a consequent assumption that the assimilation of facts and information is of the essence of Christian commitment. Within the Protestant tradition, this all goes back to the Reformation with its insistence on the centrality of 'the word', and it has often been embodied in the stones of church buildings, which are constructed like lecture halls. Their silent message is that people are there to sit and listen, and in many churches it is physically impossible to do anything else.

As I reflect on all this, I find myself challenged – not least because I have spent much of my life thinking, writing about theology and preaching sermons. It would be convenient if these questions would go away, or could be dismissed as spurious and misguided. But there are at least three pressing reasons why we should take them seriously.

First is an evangelistic concern. Whether we like it or not, it is a simple fact that a cerebral and cognitive approach to faith does not attract ordinary people. When people describe church worship as 'boring' they are not necessarily expressing spiritual preferences. How can they be when all the evidence shows there are far more people who are self-consciously engaged in the spiritual search today than ever before? Rather, they are saying, 'This is not my way of doing things – and therefore if this is what Christianity is about, then it's not for me.'

There is also a concern about communication, and the obvious fact that much of what we think is 'teaching' is not getting through anyway. I never cease to be surprised at the numbers of ministers who tell me they have been faithfully teaching their people for years, and yet at the same time bemoan how untaught they are! If that seems to be happening, then no matter what we think has been going on, it obviously was not teaching, because no one has been taught until someone has learned something. And we do not learn all we need to know just by listening. Remember the Chinese proverb: 'I hear – I forget, I see – I understand, I do – I remember.'

In *Finding Faith Today*, John Finney found that many people 'clearly received the gospel at a non-cerebral level – through human relationships and pastoral care, through mystery, and emotions'. He went on to comment that we need 'means of evangelism which do not rely so heavily upon the communication of a verbal message', and asked, 'Is too much of our evangelizing excessively verbose and aimed only at the intellect?'[16] If mystery and the emotions are part of the ways in which people come to faith, then renewed worship is likely to play a significant part in evangelism. But for worship to be released to do that, we need to recognize that making teaching central is more likely to hinder than to help. American churches generally accept this by holding teaching classes for all ages separately from worship. At least, that is their theory, though in practice 'worship' often turns out to be much the same as teaching, the only difference being the number of hymns and prayers that might be included.

There is also a theological issue involved here. William Abraham comments that 'we need to abandon the image of proclamation that is so prevalent in the modern Protestant tradition. That image, represented by the solid, tripartite sermon, usually read from a manuscript, is a culturally relative phenomenon.'[17] Walter Wink goes further, and argues that the kind of sermons to which Abraham refers are yet another classic example of how the Church has unthinkingly adopted the values of secular modernity as part of its own worldview:

There is in the sermon no feedback, no opportunity to find out where people are, or how the text is finding them out. The sermon tends to foster a binary form of left-brain response, a yes/no, I agree/disagree mode of passive assent or dissent, without provoking genuine thought or responsiveness. It perpetuates the clergy/laity split and the authoritarian image of the preacher as the sole dispenser of God's word ...The Reformation ostensibly gave the Bible back to the people, only to see it spirited away once again by professional clergy and, later, by biblical scholars with their labyrinthine scientific apparatus.[18]

It would not be difficult to take that statement and turn it into the kind of checklist we used in chapter 2 to highlight the differences between today's culture and the values of modernity and Enlightenment which preceded it. And it would be obvious on which side the traditional sermon falls. It is almost a paradigm of modernity. If anyone doubts that, they should take a look around at some of our church buildings. One of the most extraordinary church buildings I have ever visited was exported stone by stone from Glasgow to Jamaica in the early decades of the nineteenth century. Now standing on a hilltop not far from Montego Bay, it features a magnificent and huge pulpit – in design terms, a hybrid between a ship's bridge and a medieval minstrel's gallery. My partner who was with me suggested I go and stand in it to have a photograph taken – which turned out to be impossible, because there was no direct access to the pulpit from within the church sanctuary. Whoever stood in the pulpit could only enter by a specially constructed clergy door that was outside the building altogether. If ever there was a classic example of the over-emphasis of a cognitive model of 'teaching' under the influence of the Western imperialist vision, this must be it – for not only does the pulpit's design imply that the preacher is almost in the place of God, but its inaccessibility also served (at least in its historical origins) to separate the white clergy from the (mostly black) congregation. Whoever designed that church was clearly strongly influenced by the values of modernity (and hardly at all by the New Testament!).

Without question, though, the New Testament paints a very different picture. There, the 'ministry of the word', that has historically been so important to some traditions, could never merely mean teaching the contents of an ancient book. If the concept of 'ministry of the word' is to have any theological integrity, it must imply learning about *the* Word – God's Word – Christ himself. And the way in which 'the Word became flesh' should be a model to modern Christians seeking to encourage others in their faith journeys. The centrality of the incarnation as a model for faith-sharing was touched on in chapter 2, and it is also relevant here. Notwithstanding the sentiments of some of the best-loved Christmas carols, the incarnation is not about how 'God became a man'. At the heart of the gospel is the fact that 'God became a child', and that makes a world of difference to the models that Christ's disciples are called to adopt in both sharing and celebrating their faith.

The original 12 disciples found it hard to understand why Jesus was not a powerful conqueror, an expert who had everything together, and who simply told people how it was. They struggled not only with the ultimate evidence of his apparent weakness (the cross), but also with his insistence on telling stories and leaving people with personal space to decide for themselves how to respond to his message. This was not their image of how God should work. But it was the medium God chose, and the fourth gospel exhorts its readers to follow God's example in the ways they share their faith (John 20:21). This should also be the model for modern Christians as they seek to evangelize. There is something intrinsically incompatible between the openness of Jesus' style and the way many modern Christians present themselves as 'experts'. Unlike the nineteenth-century exporters of church buildings to the non-western world – and, sadly, some of today's clergy – Jesus did not place himself 'six feet above contradiction', either literally or metaphorically. He was open to listening to other people, and engaging them in dialogue. We find the same model in other early Christian leaders. In Acts 20:7–12, Luke describes Paul's meeting with the Christians in Troas. As a matter of fact, it is the only description anywhere in the New Testament of anything approximating to a church service (as distinct from theoretical advice about worship, of the sort given, for example, in 1 Corinthians 14:26–40). Most readers think the significant thing about it was that Paul spoke until midnight and the unfortunate Eutychus fell asleep. But what is really interesting here is the way Paul's 'preaching' is described. The NRSV says 'Paul was holding a discussion with them' (Acts 20:7). The Greek verb used is *dialegomai* – the root from which we get the English word 'dialogue'. Paul was 'dialoguing' with these people, listening as well as speaking (which no doubt explains why he was able to sustain it for so long). Then later, after the Eucharist had been celebrated, he 'continued to converse' in a more informal way until daybreak (Acts 20:11).

A few years ago, I read through all the New Testament gospels trying to identify Jesus' style of evangelization, hoping to find some guidelines that could be useful today. I was surprised that none of his messages could with certainty be identified with the sort of monologues that dominate much modern worship, and those cases where there could reasonably be some discussion of such a possibility turned out to be fewer than the fingers of one hand, even ignoring altogether any questions of duplicate accounts or shared traditions between the various gospels. Jesus' weakness and vulnerability is striking, and evangelists who wish to be as successful as he was should take a leaf from his book. We have something to share with others not because we are different, still less because we are experts and know it all, but because we are no different. We struggle with the same things as everyone else. We share the same tensions of joy and anger, success and failure, expectancy and frustration. But however threatening the chaos might be, we also meet God in it all – and that is really good news (for us as well as for others).

Teaching and learning can most usefully take place in a context that is not worship, but that does not mean spoken communication is wholly inappropriate in worship. After all, if worship is a holistic thing, then that will include verbal messages, albeit combined with many other less cognitive activities. In the context of evangelism, it is worth noting that Christians who are continually criticized in sermons by preachers who pretend they have no problems of their own will not make good evangelists. It takes no skill to overload people with guilt and induce a very low self-esteem. But unless people feel good about themselves and their churches they will never share their faith with others. The same goes for those who come to worship unsure of their faith status: they are likely to be looking for compassion and community, not commitment and challenge. People need to be lifted up, encouraged, enthused and inspired to think it might be worth following Christ – and while there will always be exceptions, the best way to do that is more likely to be through sharing our own stories with one another, than through complex analytical expositions of scripture. That was the style Jesus adopted, and as with so many other things we could do worse than follow his example.

4 WORSHIP ENGAGES ALL THE SENSES

By the time we reach the age of five, we have already learned more than half of all that we will ever need to know. So think of how a baby learns and discovers things about the world. Eating and tasting seem to be favourite starting points: babies put everything into their mouths, and no matter how much their parents try to discourage it, it will make little difference.

Touching and feeling are quite important too; eventually we get round to understanding things by thinking. It was Kierkegaard who said that you have to live life forwards, and reflect on it backwards: at the end of life, you can perhaps begin to articulate what it has all been about, but at the time you make sense of it in a different way. Now compare this with how we respond to God! Again, our Western culture generally warns us off anything to do with the senses. Time and again, we convince ourselves that so far as God is concerned, people cannot trust their feelings: they can only trust theology or the Bible. But why? We trust our feelings everywhere else in life. As a matter of fact, most of us make most of our major life decisions on the basis of our feelings. If we go to buy a car, then the crucial thing is whether it feels right. If we feel happy driving it, we buy it. If not, then regardless of its theoretical specification, we are likely to leave it at the showroom. When we fall in love, the same thing happens, and we decide to form permanent relationships for no other reason than because it feels right. Relating to God is different from relating to a human partner, but it cannot be that different, and if worship truly is all that I am, responding to all that God is, then there is no way that the emotions and feelings can be excluded.

The fact that children were part and parcel of the Church in New Testament times should warn us against supposing that its worship was centred around cerebral and cognitive activities. If we take seriously the fact that there is an appropriate response to God for different people at different ages and stages of life, we need to accept that some people may never feel the urge to express their faith in theological abstractions, though for others that may easily be a growth point. How many things are there in the average church's worship to engage an individual's total personality? How is the body, and all its senses, engaged in responding to God? How are the emotions caught up, not to mention our human relationships and intuitions? What physical, visible, tangible symbols do we have to direct us to the God whom we come to worship? If the answer is none, then why are we surprised when our churches appeal to only one sort of person, namely those who are able to think and imagine internally in mental abstractions? One of the major reasons for the rapid growth of alternative and non-Christian forms of spirituality in recent years is the need felt by many people for some kind of hands-on symbols, rituals, and experiences that will hold out the promise of putting them in tune with the mystery that is God.

There are also a few theological considerations here. If God is really and truly incarnated into our world, then that means Christians should respond to God with all their senses. How do you think Jesus understood and responded to God as a child? If, as the creeds affirm, he was truly and fully divine from the beginning, then that must say something significant about the range and style of our own possibilities.[19] We are impoverished if everything has to be put into words. In human relationships, words are frequently inappropriate or inadequate – so why suppose that words alone could ever be big enough to convey the totality of God's kingdom? When John the Baptist sent to Jesus wanting to know whether or not he was the Messiah, the response he got was surprisingly non-verbal: 'Go back and tell John what you have seen and heard: the blind receive their sight, the lame walk, the lepers are cleansed, the deaf hear, the dead are raised, the poor have good news brought to them' (Luke 7:22). If worship only addresses our minds, we will be spiritually handicapped – and people who are seriously looking for meaning and direction in life will likely go somewhere else. Contrasting the rising popularity of therapy with the demise of Christianity, one writer identifies the reason in the fact that Christianity is concerned with

dwelling intellectually upon the dogma, with a consequent lack of therapeutic, by which I mean the lack of
any real body of ideas and practices to help people
change. The near total absence of practical aids to human
psychological and spiritual growth within Christianity
left a vacuum which psychotherapy had to fill, based
upon principles which it had to discover for itself.[20]

Exploring the non-rational side of ourselves in a context of
worship may at least begin to redress the balance.

5   WORSHIP ENGAGES WITH CULTURE

In both Old and New Testaments, worship was the one point
at which the culture of the day was most strikingly affirmed,
and challenged. In the worship of ancient Israel, mythological
stories of monsters and dragons could be rewritten to become
hymns in praise of Israel's own God (for example, Psalm
74:12–17). In the New Testament, baptism (a familiar practice
in Judaism as well as Hellenistic mystery cults) was utilized
and given a new meaning. The familiar was taken up and
transcended. In a very real sense, it was converted! Raymond
Fung writes that worship 'must embrace the everyday concerns of the worshippers. They need to know that the things
they care about from Monday to Saturday, God also cares
about.' At the same time as such worship

embraces the cares and concerns of our mundane living, it
does not deal with them primarily on the level of human
relationships, economics or politics. We do not use the
occasion to indulge in our own political preferences. We
meet to reaffirm our faith in the sovereignty of our great
and compassionate God 'who is able to keep us from
falling, and to present us faultless before the presence of

his glory with exceeding joy'. Such worship is authentic and, for that very reason, truly evangelistic.[21]

It is precisely because Christians are contextualizing their faith within the culture and customs of their own heritage that worship has such a powerful evangelizing dynamic in the world church today.

The patterns of worship followed by Western churches evolved at a time when that was happening in our own culture. Three hundred years ago, most people spent their entire lives in the same community. They travelled only short distances, if at all, and the inhabitants of any particular community not only lived alongside each other, they also worked together and met one another socially every day of the week. What then took place in church on Sundays was a real celebration of their community life, and an opportunity to bless and celebrate what they had done together on the other six days of the week. The kind of services that developed were appropriate expressions of worship for this type of close-knit community. Today, however, that has all gone.[22] The average church does not reflect the life of a recognizable community, because people now travel more and work at a distance from where they live. Even churches which operate within defined parish boundaries are likely to be a 'gathered church' in this sociological sense. As a result, Christians find themselves saddled with patterns of celebration that no longer reflect contemporary culture and lifestyles, which as a result are unable effectively to challenge and transform them. Instead of Sunday worship blessing and celebrating the activities of the rest of the week, what happens in church is radically different from everyday life, even as it is lived by those who belong to the church! Today's churches may first need to build community before it can be celebrated. This chapter has highlighted the holistic nature of true worship, as something that should engage the whole of God's people using the whole of their faculties to respond to the greatness of God. Since most of us are already quite good at engaging our minds in worship, we will probably need to work hard at identifying appropriate ways of engaging our bodies and our emotions. In their book *Megatrends 2000*, sociologists John Naisbett and Patricia Aburdene confirm that this is in any case one of the major concerns of our culture, and they predict that interest in the creative and visual arts will take over from involvement in sport as a major leisure activity of the next decade.[23] This is a significant cultural peg on which evangelizing worship can quite easily be hung by those with spiritual vision.

The *Epistle to Diognetus*, a second-century apologetic explaining and commending Christianity, lays considerable emphasis on the fact that Christians were fully a part of the culture of the time: 'The difference between Christians and the rest of humankind is not a matter of nationality, or language, or customs. Christians do not live apart in separate cities of their own, speak any special dialect, nor practise any eccentric way of life.' The anonymous author goes on to affirm, however, that they do 'have some features that are remarkable', foremost among them the fact that 'for them, any foreign country is a motherland, and any motherland is a foreign country.'[24] Striking the right balance between accepting the secular community as our 'motherland', and yet questioning its values as part of 'a foreign country' is both demanding and essential for any effective evangelization. Part of the challenge involves accepting the ethos of our culture. Some years ago I wrote an article for a popular magazine under the title *Real Churches have Organs*, in which I discussed the unease some have in utilizing culturally appropriate musical instruments in the context of worship. It obviously struck chords with many readers, and produced the largest postbag I have ever had. Considering some of the (to me) more interesting things I have written on other topics, that in itself probably says something about the points at which many churches find themselves wrestling with culture. It somehow seems easier to live with what Michael Marshall aptly calls 'the claustrophobia of religiosity', than it is to interact creatively with culturally appropriate ways of doing things.[25]

It is not just in terms of the content of services that we need to think through our culture more profoundly. What about the times at which Christians meet for worship? One of the reasons why more people went to church in previous generations is that what the church did fitted their overall lifestyle more closely than tends to be the case today. The times at which churches met on late Sunday mornings related to an agricultural economy in which farmers needed to structure their day around the milking times of cows. Then when gas lighting was invented, churches started to meet on Sunday evenings, though not too late because in those early days technology was insufficiently advanced to guarantee the reliability of safe lighting, either in church buildings or in the street. In any case, with no cars and little organized public transport people needed to allow plenty of time to walk home. And so began the hallowed traditions – still followed in many churches – of meeting each Sunday at 11am and 6.30pm. A friend of mine was invited to preach at a church whose services were at 11.10am and 6.10pm, and thinking these were somewhat curious times he asked why. The answer was simple: people used to catch the train to the church, and it arrived at the nearby station five minutes past each hour. The rail track to that particular town had been inoperational since the 1930s, yet the church still continued to meet at times convenient for rail travellers half a century earlier! When we compare the Sunday habits of Christians with the demands faced by other people, it is not hard to see why so many simply cannot fit church into their schedule. Many people find that Sunday is the only time available for a whole variety of significant tasks. They visit relatives, do the shopping, engage in recreational activities of one sort and another, and spend time just being together. To be relevant, the church needs to take account of all this, instead of sticking with outmoded habits which not only sideline those not in the church, but also impose an enormous load of guilt on their own members, whose lifestyle also requires them to do these things on Sundays, and somehow fit church in as well. Churches could do worse than take a fresh look at all this, and some might even want to ask if Sunday really is the best time to meet anyway.

Our culture also has a spirituality of its own, expressed most obviously in the thinking we now identify as the New Age, but also more widely. Most Christians have been programmed to think that God always works in neatly definable ways in people's lives. Different Christians will have different ideas of what those ways are, depending on their own traditions: they know a person is on a 'real' spiritual search when they look and sound the same as them. But God's Spirit does not always operate like that, and many Christians are unable to perceive where God is at work because of their own limited expectations. One of the great ironies of our time is the way that the Western churches are declining at the same time as the sense of spiritual search in the community is increasing in intensity and fervour. When we begin to see the world the way God sees it, we might be able to accept other people's starting points, and welcome them into the worshipping community.

It is easy to dismiss all this as peripheral to the business of evangelization. But to do so is a mistake – and the experience of growing churches all over the world shows it to be. It is unrealistic – and certainly theologically and biblically heterodox – to separate the renewal of worship from the evangelistic task. This may well be the key question to which the Western churches need to address themselves today. What happens in worship could well turn out to be the single most influential factor in our success – or failure – as evangelists.

Sigmund Freud once saw a patient who tried to convince him she had a happy marriage, while all the time she was slipping her wedding ring on and off her finger. When real problems later surfaced, he remembered this and realized that her unconscious body language conveyed a more accurate message than the words she used. Much evangelization seems to be like this. Christians are trying to convince others of the truth of their message, while in terms of their own experience of worship they are slipping the ring on and off their fingers. Renewed worship will not only attract outsiders. It will also equip and empower those who are already committed to Christ.

There are plenty of resources available within the Christian tradition to enable worship to become truly evangelizing, empowering people to respond in the totality of their being to all that God is. Historically, different sections of the Church have highlighted different details, as if they were the complete picture. One of the encouraging outcomes of today's increased ecumenical awareness is the appreciation that different traditions can enrich one another, learn from one another, and together move to a new position. Historically, the sacramental understanding of worship has emphasized signs, symbols, ikons, and so on, and in its own way has focused on the noncognitive side of worship. But it has generally played down the importance of learning and beliefs, and as a result has often degenerated into empty ritual. The evangelical tradition, on the other hand, has majored on the importance of theological understanding, and the centrality of preaching. It has minimized the significance of feelings, and all too often has produced an arid and narrow Biblicism, confusing scriptural knowledge with love of God. As a consequence, it lacks the power to challenge or transform the will and redeem the emotions. The charismatic approach has unhesitatingly gone for the need of people to be moved and healed by worship – often to the neglect of any serious reflection on the meaning of faith. As a result, it can become little more than a form of subjective personal therapy. Each one of these traditions has identified some things that are central to the concept of evangelizing worship. But the potential richness of worship only becomes apparent when all three combine. One of the greatest Old Testament characters, Isaiah, was called to be a prophet through such an experience, and the account of his call specifically identifies the characteristics of sacramental, evangelical and charismatic worship as having a part to play (Isaiah 6:1–8). Authentic worship still inspires the prophetic vision and attracts people to follow Christ, because it opens new windows onto God's glory and goodness, and provides a holistic context in which the whole of the human personality can begin to respond to everything that God is. And that, surely, is what evangelism is all about.

CHAPTER 6

THE CALL TO BE CHURCH

Once congregations begin to realize the need for sharing their faith with other people, they are easily fired up with visionary enthusiasm. As we consider the development of various international movements for evangelization throughout the twentieth century, there is no shortage of rhetoric to encourage us to think big as we contemplate the evangelistic task. Back in 1910, John Mott enthused the Edinburgh International Missionary Conference with his talk of 'the evangelization of the world in this generation'. Eighty years later, the sloganizing was still going on, as the Lausanne II International Congress on World Evangelization met in Manila, under a banner which spoke confidently of how they would equip 'the whole Church to take the whole gospel to the whole world'.[1]

There are several biblical passages which can provide inspiration for this kind of grand vision. When Paul gave an account of his own ministry to the court of Herod Agrippa II, he spoke in the same style (Acts 26:16–18), and by any standards his achievements were remarkable. For the striking language he used to explain the nature of his evangelistic calling was matched by his ability in being able to deliver the goods. Paul was perhaps the most successful Christian evangelist there has ever been. In less than a generation he travelled the length and breadth of the Mediterranean world, establishing growing and active Christian communities wherever he went.

He and others of his generation not only spoke of changing the world with the gospel: they quite literally did that.

So what was their secret? Paul, of course, was always conscious that he was only a messenger, and that it was the power of the Spirit which really brought a change to the lives of those whom he met. It is easy for us to look back with rose-tinted spectacles, knowing as we do that Paul's enterprise was successful. But in reality, things were no easier for him than they had been for Jesus a generation earlier. As he considered the many hardships he had to endure, he described himself as a 'common clay pot', just a temporary container for the renewing power of God, which was the real source of his success (2 Corinthians 4:7). Running throughout the story of these earliest Christian communities is the conviction that the great expansion of the Church was the work of God. In chapter 2 it was suggested that what God is doing in the world must always be primary in our thinking on evangelism: 'God's Story', as it was called there. The first Christians knew that. They were such unlikely people to change the world, it was obvious that if anything was going to happen, it would not be through their own efforts. But they began with the certain knowledge that because God was at work, literally anything could happen. That undoubtedly gave a cutting edge to their witness to faith in Jesus Christ, and is absolutely foundational for understanding their success.

PLANNING FOR MISSION

At the same time, however, they never made the mistake of thinking that even heavenly visions could come to fruition by themselves, without some hard thinking and incisive planning. Paul is a classic example of a mission strategist, and the careful design and planning of his own work shines through both in the book of Acts and in his own writings. There is no question that Paul was excited by the possibility of spreading the gospel through the whole of the Mediterranean basin in his own lifetime. He was a fanatic in the true sense of the word! But he also knew that for this vision to become reality, he would need to give careful thought as to how it could be done. The great visionary and idealistic aims were important: they would motivate him to the very end of his days. But bringing them to fruition required him to identify a series of specific goals, and then to develop strategies that would enable him to achieve what he wanted to do. Appreciation of this is going to be important for Paul's modern-day successors. Most of us tend to be good on ideals and aims, and not so good on goals and strategy. This is often for the best reasons, of course: we feel the urgency of the task, and in the face of enormous need we assume that time spent in prayerful planning will be time wasted. Why waste time praying, reading books (the Bible included), attending workshops and conferences, listening to the experience of other Christians, when we could be out there getting on with the job? It is tempting to think that way. But it is the pathway to personal frustration, institutional disintegration and spiritual ineffectiveness. If that had been Paul's attitude, the chances are he would have worn himself to a standstill in no time at all, and ended his life in despair with the task still uncompleted. As it was, he knew the value for evangelism of listening, as well as speaking: listening to God, to other Christians, and to the unchurched culture in which he ministered. Because he understood the importance of that, we are still in awe of his achievements 2000 years later. These are skills that today's evangelists must also learn to excel in.

There can be no question that Paul's meeting with the risen Jesus on the Damascus road was a crucial turning point in his life. It challenged his personal priorities, not to mention his theology, and according to all the accounts, he was specifically conscious on that occasion of receiving a call to evangelize the world (Acts 9:15; 22:15; 26:16–20; Galatians 1:11–12, 15–16). By the time his sight had been restored, he knew for certain that his life would never be the same again, and it would be spent in sharing the good news about Jesus. Within a few days of his arrival in Damascus, that was exactly what he was doing, in the streets and the synagogues and anywhere else that people would listen. He had all the verve and energy of a new convert, and a burning desire to spread his message far and wide. His commitment and enthusiasm were at a high point. Surely, he must have been tempted to launch out immediately in pursuance of the missionary task that was to be his life's work. In fact, Paul did the exact opposite. In the short term, he withdrew from public life and went off into the desert near Damascus to work through his new experience, and no doubt, to reflect on the best way of approaching the enormous task that now lay before him (Galatians 1:17). Even after that, Paul eased himself into it only slowly. It was three full years before he had any contacts with the original church back in Jerusalem, and it was another 14 years after that when he found himself heading to Jerusalem as part of an official delegation from the church in Antioch.[2] At that time, Paul had only recently arrived there, having been brought to that Syrian city just a year or so earlier to facilitate the work of this largely Gentile congregation. There is a good deal of disagreement as to how these time periods of three and 14 years relate to each other, but there is no question that it was well over a decade after his Damascus road experience before Paul had the opportunity to put his strategy for evangelism into operation.[3]

In describing Paul's planning procedure, a few technical terms have been used and it will be worthwhile unpacking them a little. First of all, Paul had a great visionary aim. That was what motivated and inspired him: the grand vision. But then by way of fulfilling this grand vision he set up a series of specific goals. These were particular tasks that were not themselves the grand vision, but which would all contribute to the implementation of the broader mission statement. Then he adopted a series of strategies in order to move towards the achievement of those goals: the detailed things that would need to happen to get from A to B. For a simple example of this, we might think of how towards the end of his missionary travels Paul took a collection to help the church in Jerusalem. He knew the Jerusalem church was suffering financial hardship, and he had this great idea that all the Gentile churches he had established in Greece and Asia Minor could send a gift to them as an expression of love and solidarity. At the back of his mind there was also the hope that such an act of generosity would help to smooth over the problems that some Jewish believers felt about accepting Gentiles directly into the church without insisting they should all become Jews first (Romans 15:25–28). This was definitely the grand vision: a sharing of resources, and the strengthening of worldwide Church unity. It is the sort of vision that is easy to dream about for a long time (give or take a few details, it is an ideal that the world Church today still strives for). But before such a dream can become reality, specific goals need to be set. Paul did that. He set a goal that was specific in terms of its objective (he would personally take the collection to Jerusalem), and also in terms of its time-scale: he would be there by the day of Pentecost (Acts 20:16). When the Day of Pentecost came, Paul was able to know for sure whether or not he had made it. To maximise the chances of success, however, he also needed an appropriate strategy. And so he set specific targets for members of the churches as they gave their contributions (1 Corinthians 16:1–4), and during the process he arranged for reports showing how it was going (2 Corinthians 8:16–24). He also seems to have delegated other people to co-ordinate the effort in churches with which he himself had no immediate physical contact, and Troas was the central collection point where they all met up before proceeding to Jerusalem (Acts 20:4–6), no doubt because that was a regular embarkation point for the sea passage that could get them to Palestine by the deadline date. But in the midst of all this planning, the grand vision had not been displaced: it continued to inspire people to give, and they often did so beyond their means and disregarding the urgency of their own needs (2 Corinthians 8:1–5).[4]

Paul used exactly the same planning process in his evangelistic work. He had to, because it was going to be an uphill struggle to spread the Christian message right across the Mediterranean world in the course of his lifetime. He was realistic about the opposition he would face, and the built-in barriers to the gospel that the Roman Empire presented. Potentially, racism could have been an enormous problem. Though Jewish people contributed a great deal to the economic success of the empire, they were still the objects of suspicion, if not hatred, by those who held the reins of power.[5] The possibility of class conflict also loomed large, because to be faithful to Jesus his followers needed to be open to all sorts of people, including slaves – and that would immediately place the Church in situations of potential confrontation with the economic system of the day. Quite apart from social barriers of this kind, the Empire was a very pluralistic culture, with many religious faiths competing for attention. Under the onslaught of philosophical speculations, the old religions of Greece and Rome had lost their power to attract, but philosophy had not taken their place in the popular imagination. As a result, there was a great spiritual vacuum at the heart of the Empire, and religious practices of all kinds were rushing in to try and fill it.[6] Moreover, within this marketplace of faiths the Church was less well organized than most of its competitors. By comparison with the population of the Empire, its numbers were small, it had no real structure, few if any full-time professional Christian workers, and those it did have were (with only few exceptions) generally not the kind of people who were naturally equipped to make a big impact on society.

Paul was not operating in some privileged situation. The challenges facing him were no easier than those faced by the Church today. Indeed, there are some striking sociological similarities between the world of the first century and the postmodern context of today – which might well help to explain why some popular ancient spiritualities such as Gnosticism are currently making an unexpected comeback. If anything, though, the circumstances of Paul's day were even more complex and demanding. In the light of that, how then did he manage to make such extraordinary progress? First, he made the effort to understand the culture in which he operated, its strengths as well as its weaknesses. He was also prepared to use his culture, and exploit to the full the opportunities it gave him in terms of his mission. But then he also addressed his message quite specifically to the needs of his culture, whether they were moral and spiritual or social and economic.

Once he began to understand his culture, he soon realized that in terms of the successful completion of his mission, he had a lot going for him. There was the universal use of the Greek language, for instance. Ever since the time of Alexander the Great (333–323 BC), Greek had been the international language of the Mediterranean world. That meant Paul, as a native Greek speaker, could travel anywhere in the Roman Empire and be easily understood. Moreover, it meant he could write in Greek to people in distant cities, and his letters could be read without the need for translation.[7] Even the spiritual vacuum of his day presented creative opportunities, for the collapse of traditional Western religious traditions was accompanied by an increasing curiosity about religions originating in the East. In terms of the Empire, that meant the faiths of Palestine (Judaism and Christianity), as well as esoteric cults from places like Egypt and Persia. So the real question over which Paul had to strategize was how best to organize his own itinerary in such a way that he would achieve maximum geographical coverage with his message.

Paul's route was never haphazard. He can rightly be described as a frontier evangelist, yet he never visited a geographical frontier himself. He could have spent months, even years, trekking through uncharted territory, or picking his way laboriously across country paths to reach remote places. He did neither of these things. Instead, he took advantage of the major highways the Romans had built across their Empire. Combined with regular sea routes, they gave ready access to all the major centres of population, and these were the places Paul visited. Trade and distribution were organized on a provincial basis, and the capital cities of the Roman provinces were crucial hubs of communication, for Paul as for the many merchants who were constantly on the move. Paul made a conscious decision to go in person to those places that were easy to reach, and would be key centres of communication. He knew that he could never personally take the gospel to every person throughout the Empire. But if he was able to establish enthusiastic groups of Christians in the capital cities, then they in turn could spread the good news into more remote areas. Moreover, visitors from rural districts were always travelling into their nearest urban centre, to sell their goods in exchange for things they needed back home. If these people were reached with the gospel, then they would take their faith back to their own people. At least one of the churches to which Paul subsequently wrote a New Testament letter (Colossae) was the product of this strategy, and had been evangelized by Epaphras, one of Paul's converts in Ephesus, which was the capital of the province of Asia. But there would be others, and it is likely that many of the people Paul identifies as his co-workers were engaged in this sort of church planting exercise.

MISSION AND LOCAL CULTURE

Martin Luther once observed that 'If you preach the gospel in all aspects with the exception of the issues which deal specifically with your time, you are not preaching the gospel at all.'[8] For Paul, doing this effectively involved three things.

BUILDING BRIDGES

As Paul reflected on the need for persuasive communication, he never made the mistake of thinking that one person was pretty much the same as another. This is one of the factors to which we need to give urgent attention today. Modern Christians tend to assume that the gospel can be articulated in exactly the same way no matter to whom we are trying to communicate. Naturally enough, we unconsciously imagine that everyone is like us, and so we angle our message and our strategy towards a particular kind of person. Of course, people like us (whoever we are – for all ethnic groups and strands of society tend to make the same assumption) need to hear the gospel. But there are specific issues that need to be addressed in different cultures. The key issues change from one generation to another, and the questions of people today are quite different from the questions of people in our grandparents' generation. They will also be different for different groups within the community. We have already identified some of today's leading questions in chapter 2, but it will not do simply to adopt someone else's understanding: we need to be ready to listen to the actual people we meet, and formulate our message accordingly.

Take just two examples from the New Testament, both of them documented in Acts 14. When Paul got to the city of Iconium in the southern part of the Roman province of Galatia, he found there a large Jewish population (Acts 14:1–7). Most of the cities he visited had significant Jewish communities. For these people, the Hebrew scriptures were their rule of life, and the synagogue was the focal point of their community. Like Jews everywhere, they were looking forward to the fulfilment of the ancient promises, and eagerly awaiting the appearance of the Messiah who would usher in God's kingdom. With people like this, Paul had a head start. Their culture had already raised all the questions to which Paul thought he knew the answers. And they were asking those questions in terms with which Paul was familiar, for he too came from a Jewish background in a great Hellenistic city. They did not always accept what he said, but the content of Paul's message was in no doubt: Jesus as the Messiah for whom they were waiting. The synagogues were also a good place to contact non-Jewish people, especially the upper classes. Many thinking Gentile people were attracted to the Jewish faith, partly because of its ancient roots, partly also because it offered them a more structured moral framework than their own *laissez-faire* society provided. Some of them accepted the Jewish faith, and became full proselytes by being circumcised and keeping the whole of the Old Testament Law. Others were referred to as 'God fearers', sharing the religious values of Judaism but unwilling to take upon themselves the burden of keeping the Law. Wherever there was a synagogue, Paul always headed there first. Not only did he meet people like himself (and, like us, he felt more at home with his own sort), but he was also likely to meet significant people in the Gentile community. Paul knew well enough that the gospel had a special place for the poor and marginalized. But he also recognized the importance of reaching the decision-makers and property owners. The synagogue was a good place to start doing that.

The city of Lystra was just to the south-west of Iconium, but it was a totally different sort of place. It was geographically off the beaten track, and was also a Roman colony: a place that had been settled by Roman citizens, mostly veterans from the imperial army. Their colony was established about 6 BC at the instigation of the emperor Augustus, who wanted to consolidate his power in the province of Galatia. There would be a minimal Jewish population in a place like this, and quite different ways of looking at things. They certainly had no deep interest in the Old Testament, and it is a fair guess that most of them would have absolutely no knowledge of it at all. Nor (unlike the people whom Paul later met in Athens, Acts 17:16–34) did they have any acquaintance with the theories of the Greek philosophical schools. Their spirituality was altogether more straightforward, and centred on devotion to the traditional Greek pantheon, which provided them with different gods and goddesses to be honoured at particular points in life, without anyone needing to pay much attention to dogma or theology. People like this were not going to be attracted by a sermon on the identity of the Messiah (that would have meant nothing to them), nor by an apologetic lecture on philosophical themes (that would have been over their heads). The thing that spoke to them was the healing of a man who was lame, as a result of which Paul had an opportunity to tell them more of the Christian faith (Acts 14:8–20).

There is much that we could learn from these (and other) stories of Paul's evangelizing strategy. We need to remember that culture is not a national characteristic, but a local phenomenon. Even in the same town, there will be several different cultures, each with their own questions and potential entry points for the gospel. Many churches assume that geography is a useful way of defining culture. This is the basis on which the parish structure originated, and it can easily mean that a single church might find itself with two or three (even more) quite distinct cultures within a single parish. If churches are to relate to them all, they will need to be far more flexible than is typically the case, and a good deal more open to adopting different styles for different types of people. They will also need to beware of the tyranny of 'the good idea', by which I mean a strategy that works well in somebody else's parish. What is a good idea in one church is neither more nor less than that: a good idea for that one church. It is unlikely to be an effective strategy for another church, because there will be distinctive cultural factors that have contributed to its success in that particular place, and other cultural factors that will tend to undermine its usefulness in a different place. This is why it makes more sense for us to share our attitudes to evangelism, rather than our blueprints. It might seem easier to pick up a ready-made plan from somewhere else, but in the long run it is likely to lead to frustration and bewilderment, as we invest a lot of time, energy and money, and still reap very meagre results. To be sensitive to the needs of the actual people to whom we minister will take more effort (and, I daresay, more spiritual discernment), but that is the only way to anchor the gospel in our own culture.

BEING AVAILABLE

We have previously noted the importance of effective two-way communication in the evangelistic task. Like Jesus, Paul exemplifies this in the way he seeks to get alongside people. If evangelism is to be successful, we must start where people are, not just in terms of place, but also in terms of their own thinking and understanding. In the earlier discussion of conversion we saw how Paul has been misunderstood as a result of being viewed through the experience of Martin Luther. But this is not the only distortion in modern perceptions of Paul. A false image of Paul has been created in the likeness of nineteenth-century Western imperialism, and he has been unjustly caricatured as the ultimate exponent of an oppressive and unappealing style of evangelization.[9] It is undeniable that some of the worst excesses of Protestant missions in the last 200 years have claimed to find their inspiration in Paul, perceiving him as an abrasive retailer, purveying a prepackaged religious product wherever he could find consumers gullible enough to buy it. This is, at best, a one-sided view of Paul, if not a complete misunderstanding of all that he stood for. The book of Acts and Paul's letters speak with a common voice at this point. Paul was not motivated by the mentality of the enterprise culture, driven by the desire for successful empire-building. On the contrary, his style of faith-sharing was so relaxed that he was constantly surprised at the extraordinary results it produced – something to which the thanksgiving sections of his letters frequently testify.

Paul's method was not a form of megaphone diplomacy, nor was it based on authoritarian principles, and he always spoke *with* people rather than *at* them. Whether in the synagogue or, as at Ephesus, in a hired lecture hall, Paul was always open to challenge and debate (Acts 19:8–10), and when he describes his own evangelistic procedures in 1 Thessalonians 2:1–12, he goes to some lengths to emphasize that he was not interested in bullying people to make them accept his message. Paul can on occasion use military metaphors, but when he writes of evangelization he uses the language of the nursery, not of the battlefield. His concept of sharing of the gospel began from the expectation that he would need first to share himself (1 Thessalonians 2:5–12). By so doing, he created a space in which other people could also be themselves, and decide without coercion how and when to respond to the challenge of the gospel. Paul adopted the same open-ended approach with his converts, and it is obvious that many of the profound heartaches that emerge in his letters stemmed from his practice of allowing and encouraging converts to develop their own sense of spiritual maturity, rather than imposing a ready-made framework on them.[10] We desperately need to learn from Paul at this point.

THINKING CREATIVELY

In terms of his own expectations, Paul always thought positively. Because he began from the premise that God is at work anyway, he was able to expect things to happen – and so he knew it was worth taking the risk of challenging people to follow Jesus. Like Jesus, Paul was able to challenge people effectively, because he was doing it from alongside them, and from a position of personal vulnerability and openness, rather than a position of strength. His model was not a sergeant-major, trying to boss people into the kingdom, but 'a nurse, tenderly caring for her own children' (1 Thessalonians 2:7). Does this indicate part of the reason for our own ineffectiveness? Could it be that we often get no results because we never ask for anything? Maybe even that we are not in a credible position from which we could invite others to discipleship? Are we content to allow people to circulate on the fringes of the Church without looking for specific commitments? And are we unable to challenge without threatening them, because we are not ourselves prepared to be open to their needs and questions?

Stagnating churches are often the victims of their own attitudes. They always think negatively. Someone shares a new insight or idea, and before they have even finished explaining it, a dozen people will have thought of 50 good reasons why it won't work. We can be defeated by ourselves, long before we start to engage with others! We think small because we have small expectations of God. Paul could think big because he knew he was in the service of a big God. William Carey got it right with his slogan, 'Attempt great things for God – expect great things from God'.

These then were the factors that led to Paul's establishment of strong, growing churches, which had mission at their heart. They were churches that grew naturally, as people were attracted to what they found in them. They were churches that had no need to recruit evangelists to lead missions: that only makes sense in a church where mission is an event. These churches were more concerned to develop people whose whole lifestyle would be directed towards the activity of mission. Here, evangelism was a natural part of the pastoral process, and every member of the congregation was mobilized for the task of sharing the good news. That is how Jesus expected it to be. The new command: 'that you love one another' encouraged his followers to believe that 'by this everyone will know that you are my disciples' (John 13:34–35).

> Jesus made it absolutely clear that Christians who love one another in unity are capable of proving to the world the divine nature of Christian fellowship and the deity of Jesus Christ … The new command is a missionary command. The command to love one another is not a domestic policy of the church. It is its foreign policy.[11]

We have already seen how taking evangelization seriously will have far-reaching implications for the way we worship. It will also place new constraints on the way we structure our church communities.

THE CHURCH IN THE COMMUNITY

The church at Antioch was certainly one of the most outstandingly successful missionary churches mentioned in the New

Testament, 'the cradle of Christianity'.[12] This was the first place where significant numbers of Gentiles became Christians, as the gospel was presented in culturally appropriate ways. It was here too that the followers of Jesus were first given the name 'Christians' (Acts 11:26). Moreover, Antioch was Paul's home church, the congregation from whom he received all his inspiration, and much of his support. It will be worthwhile to reflect on some of the characteristics of this church.[13]

OPEN TO ONE ANOTHER – AND TO THE WORLD

We saw in the previous chapter how worship is something that all God's people are called on to do together. The church in Antioch appears to have been structured along similar lines, with a plural and diverse leadership. In Acts 13:1, five people are listed as leaders in this church, and they are an interestingly diverse bunch: 'Barnabas, Simeon who was called Niger, Lucius of Cyrene, Manaen a member of the court of Herod the ruler, and Saul'. Barnabas we know to have been a landowner from Cyprus (Acts 4:36–37). Simeon is described as 'Niger', which most likely means he was an African. Manaen was quite probably a childhood companion of Herod Antipas. We know nothing of Lucius, and then there was Saul, a fairly well-off Hellenistic Jew. They obviously were not all from the same social class or educational and racial background. Nor were they the only leaders in the church. Two more are named in Acts 15:32, but who knows how many there were in total? This looks very much the sort of church which led Ernst Käsemann to claim that in the New Testament 'all the baptized are 'office-bearers'…[which] seems to be as good as saying that really none of them are.'[14] It is also consistent with the way in which Paul – as an apostle – was easily able to accept the ministry even of his own converts. Consider, for example, the way he describes his Philippian converts as 'partners', rather than subordinates, emphasizing that they have had this status right from the very first day when they came to faith (Philippians 1:3–6).

Historically, the churches with which most of us are familiar have tended to be run like business organizations or governments, with a management structure that starts at the top and extends downwards. In this kind of organization, decisions are taken by those who are in charge. Policy is determined in relationship to the way they perceive the needs of the structure, and the fewer people who take part in the decision-making process, the more smoothly things appear to run. At the time of the industrial revolution, most businesses operated this way. In the work-place it led to a mechanistic structure, in which workers were treated as if they were replaceable machine-parts, rather than as individuals with any worthwhile personal insights or objectives. Churches are not the same as commercial enterprises. They are voluntary service organizations, which people choose to join, or not to join as the case may be. Here, the top-down style of leadership tends to have a different outcome. Unlike workers, church members cannot be ordered to carry out certain tasks, and as a result most of the real work ends up being done by those who are in charge.[15] Of course, all that is changing today.

> The mechanistic, reductionist Enlightenment paradigm
> that has dominated the school, work place, church and
> mission for the last 250 years is breaking down. The full
> shape of the new paradigm is not yet clear. It is likely to
> be biological rather than mechanical, relational rather
> than individualistic, systemic rather than reductionistic,
> and integrated as opposed to dichotomistic. This means
> we need new kinds of leaders, thinking about the world
> in new ways ...[16]

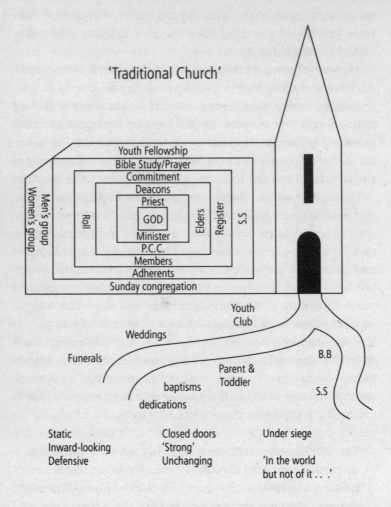

'Traditional Church'

Youth Fellowship
Bible Study/Prayer
Commitment
Deacons
Priest
GOD
Minister
P.C.C.
Members
Adherents
Sunday congregation

Men's group
Women's group

Roll
Elders
Register
S.S

Youth
Club

Weddings

Funerals

B.B

Parent &
Toddler

baptisms

S.S

dedications

Static	Closed doors	Under siege
Inward-looking	'Strong'	
Defensive	Unchanging	'In the world
		but not of it . . .'

In this new atmosphere, the balance of responsibility has shift-ed, and management strategists might talk of an organization belonging to its 'stakeholders', that is 'all those inside or out-side an organization who are directly affected by what it does'.[17] In industrial terms, 'stakeholders' might include such groups as employees, suppliers, investors, consumers, the government, and so on. The objectives of a corporation conceived in this way would be 'not to serve any one of its stakeholder groups to the exclusion of any of the others. *It is to serve all of them by increasing their ability to pursue their objectives more efficiently and effectively.*'[18]

This raises two significant questions for the Church, both of them related to the Church's place in the community and ultimately, therefore, to its mission. Who are the leaders? Who are the stakeholders? To take leaders first, there is no doubt that closed church structures of the kind where the leaders' main role is to take all the decisions about what needs to be done, and then carry them through themselves, will tend to stymie effective mobilization of human resources. Because of the rapid changes in our culture, this structure is becoming less and less capable of doing anything at all, but inasmuch as it can still be made to work, it is geared up for maintenance and not for mission. It is virtually impossible for a church organized this way to be a church with mission at the centre.

It is not so long ago that people expected to find their own worth through paid employment. This is no longer an option, partly as a result of rising unemployment, partly through increased dissatisfaction with a materialist worldview. There is already evidence of the adoption of 'designer lifestyles', as people put work lower down their personal agenda, and rate personal fulfilment correspondingly higher. Over the next few years, change in this direction is likely to accelerate very quickly.[19] As people look around for ways to maximise their usefulness, they will increasingly want to belong, to be a part of things, to have a contribution to make. If they have no opportunity to do so, then much of the corporate energy of the Church will be taken up with its own internal tensions. Leaders who continue to hold onto the old 'top-down' style will increasingly find themselves feeling like the cork in a well-shaken bottle of champagne – and the fewer people there are in the cork, the greater the tensions are likely to be. Unfortunately, there is always the danger that the cork will be blown out, probably blown apart, and the precious contents of the bottle wasted. At the same time as old-style leaders find it tougher to hold on, other Christians who are committed to the Church will find themselves facing increasing pressures as they wrestle with irreconcilable tensions between the gospel, with its promise of new life (which matches their personal aspirations), and their experience of ecclesiastical structures which seem to have the opposite effect. Some of them may leave: it is not hard to resign from a group where there are no real relationships of mutual acceptance and affirmation. At the same time, unchurched people who are engaged in the spiritual search are likely to look in from the outside to such churches, and see what they offer as irrelevant to their own primary desire to make as much of their life as they possibly can, by being useful to others as well as to themselves. In terms of evangelism, the difference between the traditional model and the stakeholder model is the difference between a church still trying to package and market a religious product which people may take if they want (they typically don't), and offering the gospel – which will change us as well as them. The one battens down the hatches, seeing itself as a faithful remnant under siege, possibly even regarding itself as 'strong' because it refuses to change. But this kind of inward-looking and defensive church will never evangelize. The other might be regarded as doctrinally 'weak' because it networks into the community, its structures are flexible, and it is geared towards building bridges to people who are not yet believers. But it takes seriously the challenge of Jesus' question, 'Who are my friends?' (Matthew 12:46–50) – and is effective in reaching people with the good news.

So much for the church's leaders. But who do we mean by the 'stakeholders' in the church? The answer to that would vary from one congregation to another. But people in my list would be God, the members of the church, their friends and relatives, youth groups, Sunday Schools, clergy, lay leaders, people's work contacts, those who attend the church, groups such as parent and toddler groups, and the general public. Though he has not used the same terminology, Raymond Fung has pointed the way to how such a model of church can be evangelizing, by entering into partnerships with people of goodwill in the community, and on that basis being accountable to the 'stakeholders' and bearing witness to 'the hope that is within us' (1 Peter 3:15).[20] The way this might work would be for a church to identify the other people working in the same community, with a concern to meet the needs of the same people. Many of these people will be working with a vision statement that is at least amenable to Christian values, if not based on them: the 'Isaiah Vision' (see Isaiah 65:17–25) in Raymond Fung's definition. Adopting this model, a church might identify people such as dentists, lawyers, social workers, shop owners and managers – or whoever seem to be the 'movers and shakers' in the community – and approach them to offer the services of the church and enquire how Christians can begin to meet the needs of the people, as these others perceive them to be from where they are looking. The church can then enter into partnerships with others, in which these others immediately become 'stakeholders' in what the church is doing, and the church becomes a 'stakeholder' in what they are doing.[21]

Some years ago, my wife was appointed to chair a committee in our own church, to identify appropriate ways of using our building (a large city centre facility). She decided to adopt this approach, to see if it would work. The first person she spoke to was the manager of the shopping mall just across the road from the church. He was surprised to see her, because no one from any church had ever approached him before. But he understood well enough what was being offered, and in no time at all had produced a list of projects for the church to follow through. The agenda he came up with could have taken two or three years to work through – and other interest groups also produced their ideas of where the church's ministry might integrate with the community's needs. All in all, the opportunities that were identified could easily have represented a ten-year plan for the church. Once a church is prepared to welcome such people as 'stakeholders' in its own organization, this relationship is quite likely to develop into a two-way stakeholding commitment, as others working to serve the community also open their structures to whatever contribution the church can make. It was no surprise to me that in due course the manager of the shopping mall invited the church to take its message into his space, in the form of singers, dancers and musicians during Advent. It is one thing to invite others to come onto our territory to hear the gospel: that is what we normally do, and very few come. But being ourselves invited onto other people's territory is much more important. When Jesus sent out the 70, it was not to invite people to come to them, but themselves to be invited in (Luke 10:1–12).

Once this kind of two-way acceptance and trust takes off, the church will find itself swamped with opportunities to minister to all sorts of people within the community. But it will need to be prepared to accept people as they are, and not to bring any hidden agendas to such collaborative enterprises. The church that thinks about adopting this approach may feel intimidated at first, but be assured you will have no shortage of opportunities presented to you. The greatest restriction you are likely to find will not be the invitations coming from the community, but the inbred suspicion, hostility and tunnel vision that unfortunately pervades so many of our churches.

In this approach to evangelism, ministry is not something that is delegated by the leaders to other people. It is about all

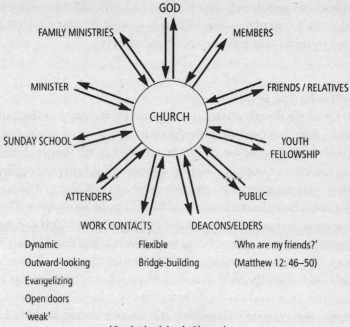

Dynamic   Flexible   'Who are my friends?'
Outward-looking   Bridge-building   (Matthew 12: 46–50)
Evangelizing
Open doors
'weak'

'Stakeholder' Church

of God's people sharing in the ministry of Christ wherever they are, forming partnerships with others in the community, and then inviting them to follow Jesus. And because there is no way all this can be done exclusively by clergy, the hallmark of this church will be

> a radical distribution of power to the laity. At the present the laity exists to serve the clergy's program. The clergy will be important, but the heroes of the twenty-first century will be laity…these, fully empowered by the church, will make the difference.[22]

Don't allow mention of the new century in that quotation to undermine the fact that this vision has ancient roots. To empower ourselves to face the future, we could do worse than look back – to places like 1 Corinthians 12, Ephesians 4:11–12, and indeed to the ministry of Jesus himself.

OPEN TO THE SPIRIT

If all God's people are set free to exercise ministry in the name of Christ, then by definition the church will see an explosion of diverse ministries, for its effectiveness will no longer depend on the gifts of only one or two people who, however brilliant they may be, cannot be equally good at everything. The need for the whole church to be mobilized should be obvious. Theologically, it must take the whole of the people of God to reflect the whole of the glory of God to the world. But there is also the simple practical consideration that unless we are all sharing our faith then the vast majority of people will never hear the gospel: 'In a world where the number of people who have no opportunity to know the story of Jesus is growing steadily, *how necessary it is to multiply the witnessing vocation of the church!*'[23]

Open leadership encourages both the development and the expression of diverse gifts. It leaves room for people to be free to be themselves. As we approach the twenty-first century, there will be more people looking for more places to belong – not just those who opt for part-time working, but also those who are in retirement, and still want to be useful to someone. A church that is open to accept what such people have to offer, and actively facilitate their offerings, can expect to have no shortage of opportunity for effective evangelism.

The book of Acts specifically mentions 'prophecy and teaching' in the church at Antioch (Acts 13:1). But no doubt other gifts of the Spirit were also being used there. Some believe that when Paul described the ideal church in 1 Corinthians 12, he was looking back to what he had experienced in Antioch (it certainly did not reflect what he had learned from Corinth!). The two ministries mentioned here by Luke – teaching and prophecy – are representative of the two major aspects of charismatic endowments as we find them described in the New Testament. Teaching emphasizes the importance of the rational understanding and presentation of the faith. This was something that Barnabas and Paul evidently specialized in, for they had spent a whole year teaching the church in Antioch (Acts 11:26). We have generally emphasized teaching to the exclusion of almost everything else, particularly in the Reformed tradition, but also more widely. We should not lose sight of the importance of thinking about our faith by allowing ourselves to be stampeded into irrationalism by the general move in that direction within Western culture. We do, however, need to give urgent attention to the most appropriate ways of facilitating useful learning among Christ's followers, and that might involve the sacrifice of a few of our sacred cows. But we must not spend so much time and effort on the rational side of faith that we ignore other dimensions that are of equal importance. The church in Antioch gave teaching an honoured place, but it was also open to the non-rational and the supernatural, exemplified by the mention here of 'prophecy', which is no doubt singled out as just one example of the kind of numinous or mystical gifts that were important in the life of this church. Both aspects of ministry are important for evangelism. Teaching can (if we are lucky) change the way we think. Only the experience of spiritual power can change the way we are. Earlier chapters have drawn attention to the fact that this is what today's spiritual searchers are looking for. We need to be ready to engage constructively with that search.

The church in Antioch was not afraid of real transformation. They expected something to happen, and so they were not surprised when, as they were 'worshipping and fasting', God spoke (Acts 13:2). When people worship, something happens: worship really is a verb, after all! The one thing most of us need more than any other is to have a renewed awareness of the Spirit of God at work in our midst. So often, church life is routine and commonplace, and we are content for it to be so. It is worth observing, though, what happens when the church is truly open to the Spirit. The work of the Spirit among these people in Antioch certainly made a difference to their own life and witness. But it did not inspire them to think only of themselves, still less to become mere specialists in personal devotions. In Acts 11:27–30 we see how spiritual renewal led directly to social concern, as the church sent Barnabas and Paul to take practical assistance to the church in Jerusalem, which was having a hard time as a result of famine. And in Acts 13:2, attentiveness to what the Spirit was saying led to a move forward in evangelization whose repercussions were to be worldwide. This kind of church is not inward-looking, but outward-looking. The Christians of Antioch found themselves fired with a new vision for the needs of the world, and filled with a new power to meet them – and both stemmed from their sensitivity to the work of the Spirit.

OPEN FOR MISSION

'God works in mysterious ways' say the words of an old hymn, and that just about sums up what happened next in Antioch. Saul and Barnabas were their very best workers. The idea that they might be sent out somewhere else must have seemed crazy, even if it was the order of an inspired prophet (Acts 13:2–3). But the obedience of the Church to that injunction was the start of the wider mission work of Paul, arguably the most successful evangelistic outreach there has ever been. As Paul's work proceeded, he sought to establish churches along the lines of the one he knew best back in Antioch. In particular, he always trusted his converts, allowed for their natural diversity in both temperament and outlook, and as a result established a whole network of churches with mission at their centre. As far as evangelism is concerned, one of the most important books ever written on Paul was Roland Allen's slim volume *Missionary Methods – St Paul's or Ours?*[24] He spent part of his life as a missionary in China, though his thinking was largely ignored until he was long dead, perhaps because he came from the Anglo-Catholic tradition and as a consequence was held in suspicion by the conservative evangelicals who did most to foster evangelism in the middle years of the twentieth century. But he has come into his own more recently, not least because of the way he anchors his observations into solid exegesis of Paul's own letters and the book of Acts. His work is challenging, not least to our present denominational structures, but as Lesslie Newbigin observes in the foreword to a recent reissue of his book, 'Quietly but insistently it has continued to challenge the accepted assumptions of churches and missions, and slowly but steadily the number of those who found themselves compelled to listen has increased...this quiet voice has a strange relevance and immediacy to the problems of the Church in our day.'[25]

What was Allen saying that is so revolutionary? His understanding of Paul's method centres round five main features. First of all, Paul refused to transplant the law and customs of the Judean church into the Roman provinces where he worked. In other words, he knew that the gospel must be translated into the culture of different peoples. But as a result, he was often persecuted, especially by the Jews. Secondly, he refused to set up a central administration. At the time, the Jerusalem church was probably trying to establish itself as the headquarters of the international Christian movement. Paul resisted that: there is only one mention in any of our sources of a time when he acceded to the wishes of the Jerusalem leaders, and on that occasion the narrative makes clear that he only went along with it at the request of other people (Acts 15:1–35). Paul knew well enough that his converts needed to be trusted and given responsibility for their own faith if they were to be useful evangelists.

Allowing others to take responsibility for themselves is a thread running through the other characteristics Allen identified. He notes that Paul declined to establish tests for orthodoxy. He was much happier to deal with cases of deviance as they arose rather than laying down rules in advance. He resisted the temptation to predict what *might* happen, preferring to act on what did happen. That way, he left himself space to be able to learn even from those with whom he disagreed. He also did not insist on every church being the same. If an issue arose and was dealt with, Paul *did* not then apply the judgment to all the other churches. The diversity of church styles in the first century was staggering compared with the conformity in the modern church, where one congregation can look pretty much the same as any other, even of a different tradition.[26] But that was what gave the gospel its universal appeal. Finally, Paul encouraged churches to deal with matters of discipline corporately, instead of delegating decisions to leaders – as evidenced most strikingly in 1 Corinthians 5:1–13, where Paul (in an injunction clearly addressed to the whole congregation, not just to leaders) offers advice about dealing with a man who was cohabiting with his step-mother.

A PLACE TO BELONG

What does all this amount to? To put it simply, people need to belong. It is a basic human need.[27] If a church cannot fulfil the relational needs of its own members, then it will never be relevant to its community. A church that tries to fit people into slots in its own pre-determined structures, rather than making space for people to exercise their own gifts and talents, cannot evangelize and will not grow. If the need to belong is not fulfilled, then those who are already in the church are likely to withdraw, lose their sense of purpose and commitment, maybe even become resentful, cynical and critical of others. It sounds too easy to say that the church should be people-centred rather than programme-centred. But it needs to be said, for a church that finds difficulty creating space for people will find it hard to leave space for God. Without space for both people and God, we are unlikely to commend the gospel to others.[28]

In a sermon preached on 4 February 1968 in Ebenezer Baptist Church, Atlanta, Martin Luther King eloquently described the kind of church that will be evangelizing in today's world:

> ...the church is the one place where a doctor ought to forget he's a doctor. The church is the one place where a PhD ought to forget that he's a PhD. The church is the one place that a schoolteacher ought to forget the degree she has behind her name. The church is the one place where the lawyer ought to forget that he's a lawyer. And any church that violates the 'whosoever will, let him come' doctrine is a dead, cold church, and nothing but a little social club with a thin veneer of religiosity... It's the one place where everybody should be the same standing before a common master and savior. And a recognition grows out of this – that all men are brothers because they are children of a common father.

That kind of church could easily commend the gospel to today's spiritual searchers.

CHAPTER 7

REDEFINING THE FAITH

Just about the only constant thing in today's culture is that things are changing all the time! Values and expectations that were once taken for granted are being questioned and reshaped with increasing frequency, and the Church inevitably finds itself caught up in the rush to keep up with the times. Often, however, Christians have great difficulty trying to sort out which things need to be discarded, and which things are worth retaining, perhaps in some modified form. Some find it easier to do nothing. Or, rather, to do what seems like nothing. For in reality, we are all changing all the time – whether we recognize it or not. The real choice facing the Church is whether we will allow the world to change us (and it will – in accordance with its own standards and values), or whether we are prepared to take risky initiatives that might enable us to become the God-driven force that ultimately will change the world.[1]

To take initiatives for effective change, we must give urgent attention to two things in particular. One priority must be for us to tackle our inherited allegiance to forms of thinking and ways of being that are locked into a culture that is now being discarded. In other words, we must work out what it means to be Christian in a postmodern context. At the same time, how-ever, this question itself needs to be set in the perspective of another, larger question: what does it mean to be faithful to the gospel in this new situation? What are the spiritual values we need to rediscover and emphasize in our generation in order to communicate the gospel of Christ in a way that will be both effective as communication and loyal to the message of Jesus? Some of the communication issues have already been explored in previous chapters. Here I want to focus on a few of the larger theological issues related to the task of articulating the call of Christian discipleship in today's world.

Historically, a culturally-facilitated discovery and re-emphasis of particular expressions of faith has often been at the cutting edge of renewal within the life of the Church. For example, at the time of the Protestant Reformation, the problem of personal guilt was a major issue affecting many people in Europe. In that context, Martin Luther discovered – or, to be more precise, recovered, for it had been there all along – the biblical answer to this burden, and his discovery changed the face of the continent. A century ago, in the time of the great Victorian evangelists, many people were terrified by death and what might follow it in 'eternity'. The Bible's answer to that question became a major theme in many of the hymns written at the time. Today the lyrics of people like Sankey sound sugary and sentimental, but in their day they led to a significant expansion of Christian witness. Those two quite different examples highlight the way in which particular aspects of Christian belief have been more relevant to people's felt needs at some times than at others. But other examples could be cited where new understandings of the Bible have led to society being challenged to change in quite radical ways. The question of slavery was one such, where the particular cultural circumstances of the seventeenth and eighteenth centuries created a space in which the radical nature of Jesus' message (and that of Paul) could be truly appreciated for the first time, and Christians whose forebears had for centuries lived quite happily with slavery now became militant in their fight to get rid of it. Ironically, in the light of the situation in which we now find ourselves, one of the catalysts for such rediscovery was the secular Enlightenment notion of 'the rights of man' – just another indication (if more were needed) that, whatever its flaws, the Enlightenment has not all been bad news. Nearer to our own time, the wider cultural awareness of the equality of women and men has created opportunities for a re-examination of long-held assumptions about the Bible's teaching, and some surprising new insights have emerged as a result.[2] I fully expect that the growing concern for the plight of the world's children will also open the door for new insights into the biblical teaching on this subject, that will in due course lead to the kind of liberation for children and their ministry in the Church that we have already seen to a limited extent with women in ministry.[3] It is in this context of ongoing historical development and cultural change that the time is now ripe for what I have called a redefinition of the faith. This will not be a redefinition that devalues and discards all that has gone before. Rather it will be motivated by asking what are the elements of Christian belief that we now need to rediscover and emphasize in new ways in order to call people into effective discipleship in the cultural circumstances in which we find ourselves. In the process, some things will inevitably need to be laid on one side – especially those that are more clearly rooted in the uncritical acceptance of previous cultural fashions than in scriptural theological positions. But for the most part, my redefinition is not offering a polarization between the past and the future. Think of what we now have as a glass that is half-full of water. Most of what is in the glass is good, wholesome and profitable – at least for those who are already church members. The problem is not so much with the half that is full, but the half that is empty, and it is that empty half that needs to engage our attention, for the filling of that space will be one of the things that will make a major difference to Christian life and witness in the new century.

In identifying those things that we now need to re-discover and emphasize in a new way, we might do worse than begin from the felt needs of today's people. Undoubtedly, the great need of people all over the world is to find personal fulfilment and a sense of meaning in life. A key question for many is just this: how can I become the best person I could possibly be? A major influencing factor in this is a fresh awareness of the possibilities of a more holistic style of living, which is the other side of the coin of increasing scepticism about the exclusive use of rational categories as the only, or the best way to make sense of life. It is instructive, for instance, that in his study of the faith journeys of recent converts in English churches, John Finney discovered that virtually all of them defined the Christian life in relational terms – with God, with other people and with themselves – rather than in terms of specific beliefs in theological or doctrinal propositions.[4] The way we define Christian faith needs to address those concerns. At the same time, discipleship is an experience of challenge and change, as we saw in our study of Peter's faith pilgrimage. We also need to identify the questions that might be the right ones for this point in time, that will reflect the gospel challenge as well as affirming and lifting up those who are hurting.

THE BIBLE

I want to begin with the Bible, firstly because I believe that any authentic Christian theology must take its starting point there, and secondly because the Bible is close to the heartbeat of fast-growing churches in all parts of the world today. As ordinary people – often newly-literate people – come face to face with its message, they find themselves propelled in life-changing new directions that influence not just personal religious beliefs but, in many places, the whole political and social structure.[5] By contrast, in the Christian heartlands of Europe, the Bible has been consistently studied and preached for 500 years or more – and it seems to have exactly the opposite effect. Instead of being inspired to passionate fervour by its message, people appear to be turned off by it – and that goes for church members just as much as for non-Christians. Why? This is an urgent question for Western Christians, and there are many legitimate ways of addressing it. The symptoms of this evident unease have already surfaced in several forms in earlier chapters. A basic part of the challenge is how to relate the Bible to other aspects of people's normal life experience. This comes from two directions: how can we read the Bible, and how can we relate our own experience of faith to what we find in it, in such a way that on the basis of our understandings we can then stimulate and facilitate other people's faith pilgrimages?[6]

The diagram illustrates clearly enough where much – if not most – traditional Bible exposition begins. On the one hand, there are the issues and questions of contemporary society. Of course, these things usually present themselves not as abstractions, but in specific contexts, as the problems of particular people in particular times and places. The received wisdom encourages the reader to reason from the particular to the universal, and then attempt to tackle broad, general principles rather than the specific examples we all face day by day. We then face the difficulty of how to bring the Bible, which also is mostly a book of personal stories, alongside these abstracted principles. So we go through the same process with the Bible, discarding the story form in the effort to extrapolate from it a collection of notions that can be labelled 'biblical principles'. The interpreter then tries to bring these 'biblical principles'

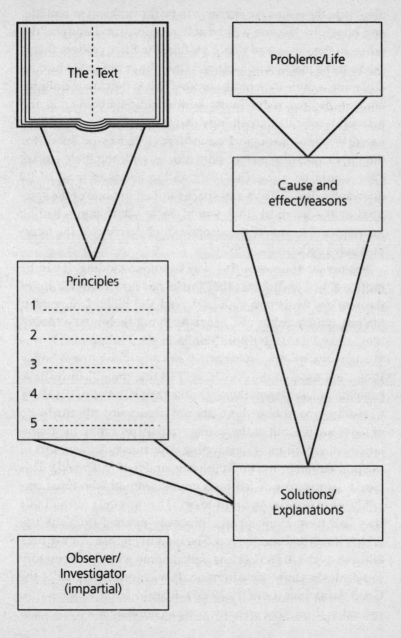

The Text

Problems/Life

Cause and effect/reasons

Principles

1 _____

2 _____

3 _____

4 _____

5 _____

Solutions/
Explanations

Observer/
Investigator
(impartial)

alongside the issues we perceive to be the problem in real life, and hopefully the one will be able to inform and address the other. In the process of doing all this, the Bible readers themselves stand in splendid isolation from the entire procedure, as if playing a game by remote control. This is the classic Enlightenment-inspired reductionist hermeneutic embodied in the historical–critical methodology that for generations has dominated Western theological education.[7] It leaves no space for the interaction of personal faith stories with the Bible stories (that would be 'subjective') nor, in the hands of most of its exponents, does it leave any space for the intrusion of the spiritual or the mystical (that would be to allow non-scientific assumptions to violate the supposed 'objectivity' of the interpretative process).[8]

For people trained in this way of understanding, it can be quite a shock to discover that this is not how the majority of the world's Christians typically read the Bible. I remember visiting with a group of Christians living on Smokey Mountain, a huge garbage tip in Manila in the Philippines. It was about as challenging an experience as any white Anglo-Saxon Protestant male could ever have. For one thing, I must have been the oldest person there. Unlike the churches in the West, Christian groups elsewhere are not predominantly made up of older people, but of the young – partly reflecting the population balance in most developing countries (just over 40% of the population of the Philippines is under 15 years old). This particular group was led by a young woman who must certainly have been in her mid-teens. The only bits of the Bible they had were a few scraps (probably rescued from the tip) which she proceeded to read. She read in English, for my benefit, and as she did so I at least felt at home with the Bible story to which she drew our attention. It was Jesus' parable of the Good Samaritan (Luke 10:29–37). I could see it was new for several of them, though to me it was a familiar story. I thought

I knew all there was to know about it, and when the group leader asked the question, 'Now who are you in this story?' I took it for granted that I knew the answer to that as well. At least, I knew who I would like to be. That was easy. I recognized the possibility that I might be the priest or the Levite, who passed by the wounded man and left him on the roadside. I knew I would really like to be the Samaritan, who did good by taking the robbers' victim to a place of safety – though in my heart of hearts I had the sneaking suspicion that (in common with many Western people) maybe I was more like the innkeeper, who would do good but only when someone else paid him for it. Anyway, when we were given the opportunity to share our thoughts with one another, I had no difficulty knowing what I was going to say. It was just as well that I was not invited to speak first, for I soon realized that I was responding quite differently from everyone else who was there. For them, there were no agonizing choices as they sought to identify with the characters in the story. They all knew precisely who they were: the person beaten up and left for dead by the roadside. I realized in an instant what was happening. Though I had debated within myself who I might be, in reality my options were strictly limited because I had taken it for granted that, whoever I was, I would be one of the authority figures in this story. It simply never occurred to me that I might be poor and powerless like the man on the roadside. As I realized what I had done, I could hardly believe it. I thought of myself as globally aware and politically correct – yet, even surrounded by the sights and smells of such obvious poverty, I still unconsciously read into this Bible story the imperialistic assumptions of my culture, assuming that if I was in there at all, then I would have to be in control of somebody.

Poor people in the two-thirds world are not the only ones who look at the Bible in a different way from traditional Western Christians. People in our own culture also have a lot of challenging questions, and we do not always know how to use the Bible in addressing them. I remember being invited to give one of the keynote addresses at a large annual Christian teaching event in the UK. My subject was to be Abraham – and I had a pretty good idea what the organizers wanted me to say about him. Was he not a man of great faith, the founder of the people of God, and commended in the New Testament as a role-model for Christian believers? Of course. But as I read his story more closely in the light of the realities of life in Britain today, that all seemed a million miles away. For Abraham was also a man who without hesitation encouraged the king of Egypt to have sex with his wife Sarah, when he thought it would save his own skin (Genesis 12:10–20). He was a man who chose another sexual partner when the same Sarah failed to deliver him a son (Genesis 16:1–4). He was a man who, when Sarah eventually did have a child, deliberately engineered tensions between his two partners and their sons (Genesis 21:8–14), and who generally engaged in domestic abuse and violence of a most horrific sort. Reading the Bible 20 years ago, I don't suppose I would have noticed much of that. But in today's world, these are key issues. If this is the kind of role model the Bible gives us, then who needs the Bible? As I struggled with this particular passage, one of the few things that was completely clear to me was that a historical–critical exegesis of the passage was unlikely to yield many answers.[9] What I needed was a more intuitive understanding of the tensions in Abraham's family – and of how God somehow could be found in the middle of so much exploitation and suffering. At the time, I had only recently been experimenting with mask-making as an aid to the exploration of personal spirituality. To cut a long story short, I made a series of masks of the various characters who feature in the Abraham story, first imagining and then reproducing in plaster on my own face the expressions of Sarah, Hagar, Ishmael, Isaac – and Abraham – as at different points in the story they came to terms with the dynamics of their home life and relationships.[10] The result was stunning. Abraham genuinely wanted to serve God – there was no doubt of that. But his faith was so self-centred that he was incapable of seeing what he was doing to those around him. And the good news was that, far from being a model of morality to be followed by today's Christians, Abraham's imperfections were a mirror in which we could see our own struggles, and discern God's loving presence even in all this mess – as the God of Abraham actually turned out to be on the side of those whom he abused and victimized.[11] As I delivered that address I was well aware that I was looking at this familiar story not only from a different angle, but in a way that could be potentially disturbing for some of my hearers. Some were disturbed – and as a matter of fact, I have never been invited back to that particular Christian event from that day to this! But for many more Christians, who for the first time saw their own life stories mirrored in scripture (and that included violent people like Abraham, as well as his victims) it created a new space for them to address deeply-hidden wounds, and to move on to claim the healing which the Bible also seemed to offer them.

Now what was I doing with the Abraham story? Certainly not what I had been trained to do. Instead of using the reductionist models of the Enlightenment, I consciously adopted the new ways of reading the Bible that I had learned from Christians in the two-thirds world.[12] Instead of distancing myself from the text, pretending that the feelings and experience of people today were irrelevant, I actually began with them, and instead of working forward from Bible times worked backwards from today's world, and then addressed questions to the Bible text in the light of contemporary life. Our typical approach has been to use the Bible as a window, through which we might gain some insight into the world of

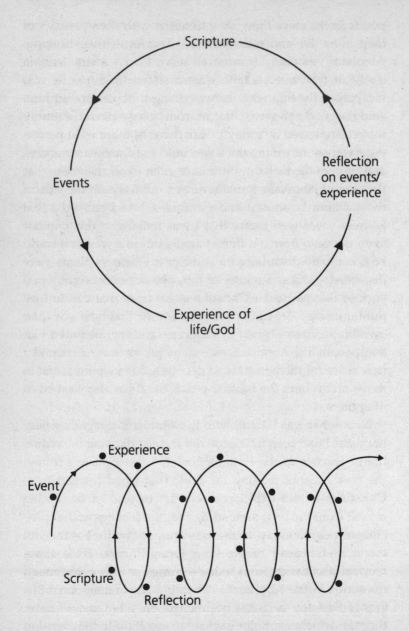

which it speaks. The only problem is that very few people can then make the leap back from that ancient world and apply what they learn to life in today's world. As a result, Bible study easily becomes a history lesson. It will be more helpful if we think of the Bible as a two-way mirror. We can see through it and back into its world. But we consciously allow the reality of our own world to be reflected in there, and use what we can see as a way of asking the Bible new – and relevant – questions. This way, we can expect to learn something about what God might be saying to us now, as well as what God said in ancient times to other people. 'We bring our experience *to* the Bible, we draw new insights *from* the Bible, we go back to our own situation *with* the Bible, and see it all in a new way.'[13] When you look at the Bible through the eyes of ordinary people, expect some surprises! And particularly when you open yourself to the kind of 'emotional exegesis' represented by mask-making, expect to be challenged yourself. But be assured that some exciting things are likely to happen when people realize that the Bible does after all relate to *the way* they feel, as well as to their mental processes. Incidentally, far from being a late twentieth-century idea, this was the way Jesus used his own Hebrew scriptures. Luke 24:13–35 (to which we will return in the next chapter) is one of the more striking examples.[14]

THE ENVIRONMENT

Not entirely unrelated to the way we use the Bible is the fact that many sensitive people are rejecting Christianity because they see it as having no relevant theology of the environment. An article written by Lynn White Jr back in 1967 has been quoted so often, it hardly seems necessary to repeat it here. But it is worth reflecting on what he wrote, for it is an opinion widely shared today not only by card-carrying activists in the environmental movement, but by many others:

> Christianity in absolute contrast to ancient paganism and Asia's religions...not only established a dualism of man [sic] and nature but also insisted that it is God's will that man exploit nature...Christianity bears a huge burden of guilt...We shall continue to have a worsening ecological crisis until we reject the Christian axiom that nature has no reason for existence except to serve man.[15]

Scientists continue to debate the precise extent of the environmental crisis we face. But no one can deny that there is a crisis, whatever its proportions. After all, if the hole in the ozone over the Antarctic is as big as Europe, then the world has to be in poorer health than if there was no hole at all. And most people believe that, if there is a solution somewhere, it will definitely have no connection with Christianity. One of the major claims regularly made in support of the emerging 'New Age' spirituality is that, unlike Christianity, it is environmentally friendly, because it regards the whole cosmic system – people included – as joined together in a deep spiritual unity. Many Christians dismiss environmental concern as irrelevant to the task of evangelization, and regard people like Lynn White as ill-informed and irresponsible. There is certainly a lot of misinformation being put about concerning Christian attitudes to the environment, and it does no harm to point out that Christians have not spoiled things single-handedly. The Baltic Sea is at least as polluted as the Mediterranean – and that was the work of an atheistic communist ideology, while Buddhists in Thailand started cutting down rain forests there at least 50 years before anyone in the Christian West thought of doing the same thing. But that is the easy part, for it is absolutely undeniable that the leaders of the Industrial Revolution who started all the pollution were Christians, motivated not only by the Calvinist work ethic but also by the conviction that God had put the world and its resources at their disposal. They were of course also deeply influenced by the secular materialist values of the Enlightenment, with its pretentious optimism about human potential – but this self-centred individualism in turn nourished its roots in the insistence of Reformed faith that every individual is solely responsible *for themselves* to God, and while the Reformers themselves may not have said so, it was not long before their successors took it for granted that this involved a corresponding reduction in responsibility both towards other people and for the wider environment.

This is one of those points where Christians need to be prepared to live with their past, and accept responsibility for it. Repentance might be a more appropriate attitude than self-justification. But we also need to do some hard thinking about our own theology, especially notions of the fall, sin, and blessing.[16] Three assumptions about the environment seem to permeate the thinking of many Christians. First, that creation exists solely for the benefit of people, and therefore can be exploited no matter what the cost. Secondly, that God is entirely transcendent and 'out there', totally separated from creation and no longer involved in it. And third, that everything physical is sinful in comparison to the spirit or the powers of reason. Put otherwise, many Christians have a Newtonian view of the universe in which everything is a big machine operating according to fixed 'laws of nature'. Therefore, while Christians might believe God created the universe, many also believe that God lost interest in it because of sin – and that is why people have to manipulate it as best they can for their own benefit.[17] This understanding has prevailed for the greater part of the last 200 years, if not with the explicit approval of Christianity, then certainly with no effective opposition from it. I remember hearing an American tele-evangelist

taking part in a debate on Christian attitudes to the environment, and he put it bluntly: 'animals belong to the jungle,' he
said, 'and men [sic] belong to God.' He might have been a
chauvinist, but he was certainly not out of tune with the Christian tradition. Back in the fifteenth century, Thomas à Kempis
said much the same thing, albeit in a less strident way: 'Every
time I go into creation, I withdraw from God.'[18]

Historically, many Christians have been uncomfortable not
only with the physical universe, but with their own physical
existence, which is one reason the Church finds it so incredibly
difficult to make any useful contribution to current debates
about the nature of sexuality. Christians who think of the Fall as
a hierarchical tumble from spiritual perfection to material sin-
fulness are bound to regard the physical as second-rate and
spiritually unsatisfactory. This view itself owes a lot to our self-
centred Western individualism, and beyond that has its philosophical roots in the ancient Greek dualism between matter and
spirit. The Bible however takes a broader view of both fallenness and redemption, in which sin and salvation are not about
metaphysics but about relationships. A spirituality that regards
the created world and our own physical existence solely as a
backdrop for personal salvation has an inadequate understanding of sin, and consequently a deviant view of salvation.

Matthew Fox has not exactly endeared himself to the mainline Church, and his questions are generally better than his
answers, but he is right when he claims that too many Western
Christians are covert Docetists, more comfortable in the esoteric world of spirit than in the physical world God created –
and his concept of 'original blessing' as the starting-point for
the gospel has blown through much theological debate like a
breath of fresh air, even if it does need a more careful expression than he has given it.[19] Instead of a 'fall-redemption' model
of Christian theology, he proposes a 'creation-centred spirituality'. He argues that Christians should understand nature

itself as a blessing from God, to be accepted and received – and by accepting ourselves and our own creativity, we will not only renew our own lives, but we can also enhance God's ongoing creativity by participating in that work. Fox traces an alternative Christian history exemplifying this paradigm shift, finding expression in the works of mystics such as Meister Eckhart, St Francis, St John of the Cross, Mother Julian of Norwich and others. Much of his analysis is simplistic and inaccurate. In particular, he tries to rewrite history in a way that simply goes against the known facts. All those past church leaders and theologians whom he praises as having a 'creation-centred spirituality' also had an awareness of sin as an objective moral reality. Fox is unrealistically optimistic about human nature, and as a result he is unrealistic about sin, especially the experience of the marginalized and oppressed who find themselves systematically sinned against.[20]

Having said that, however, he has drawn attention to this issue in a way that no one else has, and in form that invites critical engagement with it. We surely need to be reminded that fallenness is not something that exists or happens without people. The essence of sin is a breakdown of relationships – between people, between people and the natural world, and between people and God. This understanding is basic to any talk of effective evangelization, for our view of the nature of sin and blessing (and the relationship between them) affects our understanding not just of the environmental crisis, but issues of gender, race, economics, and other aspects of our broken world to which Christ offers wholeness.

PEOPLE AND THEIR NEEDS

Who are the people who need to hear and respond to the gospel? What is the human condition? The traditional answer to that question has generally been something along the following lines: people are sinners, they need to be saved from their sin, and they can achieve that by trusting in Christ. Different Christian traditions might wish to use their own terminology, and other elements would need to be added for a more comprehensive statement. And it is all broadly faithful to the New Testament. But it is only half the picture. How about those people who say, 'I'm quite happy as I am. My life is perfectly satisfactory without God. I'm not a sinner, and even if you label me that way, I don't feel guilty about it anyway'? Some of those who say that are never going to hear the call of Christ, because they have closed it off as an option for their life. But there is another human reality with which we need to reckon. For it is a simple fact that many people today experience the power of sin in their lives not directly as a result of their own personal sin, but primarily because they are sinned against. One of the characteristics of modern culture is that our world is full of victims. People are the victims of economic and political exploitation, of abuse and violence, of personal alienation. To tell such people that they are responsible, and they should choose to follow Jesus instead, is not the gospel – or at least, not if 'gospel' is 'good news'. There are many people for whom personal responsibility and the freedom to choose are meaningless concepts, for they have so internalized their experience of being sinned against that their basic human capacities have been all but destroyed. This no doubt helps to explain why so many who so obviously need the kind of personal transformation and direction that Christ offers simply have no expectation of finding that in the Church, because their experience of Christians is of people who put them down and, in effect, victimize them even further.

A few years ago, I was involved in helping a woman at a time of crisis in her home life. She was on the fringes of Christian faith, and attended church from time to time though she probably would not have described herself as a believer. One day she came to see me. 'I've been reading the Bible,' she said, 'especially the bits about Jesus.' She explained that, like many, she was attracted by what she read, and could easily follow Jesus. 'But,' she went on, 'I really have enough problems of my own without joining the church.' That phrase has stuck with me ever since. In a world that is fragmented at so many levels, people are searching for acceptance with no strings attached. That, in another way, is what the gospel is about. So how can we affirm broken people and lift them up – and then challenge them to discipleship? Jesus had a unique capacity for doing both those things, while we find it so difficult to do either.

The reality is that for a person in that situation, the gospel will not offer unjust condemnation by claiming that 'You are responsible'. It will hold out hope, by saying: 'You can become responsible; with Christ's help you can be made whole'. For those who are wounded, that is really good news. Though he did not express it this way, John Finney's findings underline how important it is that we recognize this, for a massive 49% of those he interviewed came to faith in Christ without any sense of guilt at all – and only 18% felt some specific sense of guilt related to their own personal shortcomings.[21]

This discussion further highlights one of the most tragic divisions to have afflicted the Church in modern times. I refer to those who, on the one hand, have identified themselves with a so-called 'social gospel', and have attempted primarily to share the love of Christ with those who are sinned against, and on the other, those who have placed a high and exclusive priority on calling people to personal faith in Christ. Yet the stories of Jesus show both these concerns to be of equal importance. They are two sides of the same coin: empowering people to address their circumstances is part of evangelism, and inviting people to follow Jesus is part of giving that empowering. Jesus saw people as lost for two reasons: people sin, and they are sinned against. We seem to have somehow lost sight of this theological reality, and I suggest the reason for this is that much Western Christianity has a shallow – and unbiblical – understanding of sin as something that people do, rather than as a cosmic universal reality that affects everything. This is perhaps one of those points at which (under the influence of Enlightenment values) we have become so aggressively individualistic that some of the most fundamental aspects not only of the gospel but also of human life itself have been ignored.

In mentioning the environmental issue, I have already argued that sin is ultimately about the breakdown of relationships. Jesus consistently spoke about the renewal of relationships as the heart of the gospel, while Paul included in his understanding of salvation the renewal of the physical environment and human culture, as well as of individual lives, since all are transformed through the cross and resurrection of Jesus, and the gift of the Holy Spirit (Romans 8:18–24). We will return to some of these issues in the next chapter, as we explore how Jesus addressed them.

In terms of sharing faith with others, one of the practical consequences of this insight is that a consciousness of personal sin, and the possibility of forgiveness and healing, will for many people not be part of the content of the message to which they respond, but will itself be a part of their response. That lesson came out quite clearly in our examination of the stories of Peter, for whom repentance and faith in the conventionally-understood sense were not his entry point to discipleship, but were part of his subsequent interaction with Jesus.

SHARING FAITH

This understanding of the human predicament and the nature of discipleship is naturally going to affect the ways in which we invite others to follow Jesus. If I was correct in my earlier characterization of the 'McDonaldization' of spirituality, then we will need to develop a less predictable and more relational style (for which, again, I believe we can identify the model in Jesus himself). Picking up an earlier discussion, instead of supposing that we are bringing God to other people, we will begin from an acknowledgement that God is already present in the world beyond the church. Because we share a common humanity, we will not be issuing an invitation to discipleship from a position of power and control (still less superiority), but as partners. We will be more ready to identify with the struggles of others as they try and make sense out of the journey that is life – or, to use a different metaphor, we will invite others to join us as we ourselves discover how the frayed pieces of our own lives can be transformed into a beautiful patchwork with the aid of the most creative designer of all, who is Christ. In the process of working this way, we will release evangelization from the hands of experts who work only in the formal settings of big events, or even regular church services, and place it back where the New Testament locates it, in the everyday lifestyle of ordinary Christians. Instead of placing all the emphasis on professional preachers, we will discover afresh the power of conversation between friends. We will listen, as well as speak – and we will often do both not in safe environments where we are in control, but on other people's territory, where we may feel a little unsafe. At the same time, almost unconsciously, we will find ourselves recreating and redesigning the church in such a way that it will be concerned with the needs of people rather than with programmes, personalities, buildings and bureaucracies.

I have already commented several times on the irony of the fact that at a time of very obvious spiritual search in Western culture, so few people seem to expect to find spirituality in the churches. One of the reasons for this is that some churches are simply so hard to join that not many will make the effort. This particularly affects churches which would describe themselves as 'gathered congregations', where there are often so many hurdles to be jumped and hoops to be gone through that it is a wonder anyone at all ever makes it through to full acceptance and membership. Those inside tell themselves these things are necessary in order to preserve the purity of the church. To those outside, they look suspiciously like barriers specifically designed to exclude everyone else. 'Most people are not attracted to active, closed groups, which can often function like pressure groups. If Christianity is to increase it will be by people joining us not because they have to, but because they want to. We must show love not just for one another but for those outside too. Bridges must be built into the non-Christian world.'[22] Trying to take this seriously could be a more painful process than many people imagine.

I have a Christian friend who works with drug addicts in Edinburgh, and I remember her telling a story about one particular addict who was in the final stages of breaking free from his addiction. In order to help him through this time, my friend had committed herself to being with him as near to 24 hours a day as she could possibly manage. It was demanding, but if he made it she knew it would have been worth the effort. One day, he said, 'There's a big horse race on today, and I need to place a bet.' Now my friend was one of those abstemious Christians who had never in her entire life contemplated the possibility even of going into a betting shop, let alone placing a bet on a horse. As a matter of fact, she was unsure whether or not she approved of such activities. You can imagine her moral dilemma when this person made such an announcement. Did she let him go by himself – and maybe risk him dodging off somewhere else to purchase drugs? Or did she put her scruples to one side, and go with him? She decided on the latter course of action. There was just one outstanding problem: she had never been inside a betting shop before. She began to wonder what people do in such establishments. Do they stand up, or sit down? Do they talk to one another? And so on. She began to appreciate that it would be extremely threatening to go through the door without having at least some idea what might meet her on the other side. Then she came up with a brilliant plan. The betting shop was on the opposite side of a rather busy main road, with a pedestrian crossing almost directly outside the door of the shop. They would walk to that crossing, and while waiting for the traffic to stop she would take a good look through the window and see what everyone else was doing. That way she would be prepared for the experience. Her plan worked like clockwork – until she lifted her eyes to look across the road into the window. Anyone who has ever tried to look into a British betting shop will know why. The windows are all blanked out by law, precisely to prevent people outside from seeing what goes on inside! 'I was terrified,' she subsequently reported, 'as we walked through the door my heart was beating so fast I thought I would pass out. It was one of the most horrific experiences of my entire life.' And that was from someone working regularly with drug addicts!

As I heard that story, I made some immediate connections with the church's evangelistic task. Have you ever tried to look through the windows of a church? Crossing the threshold of a church building is likely to be a highly threatening experience for most people in today's world. 'What is it like inside?' 'What do people do?' 'How can I be sure I'll not do the wrong thing and embarrass both myself and the rest of them in there?' These are just a few of the thoughts that will no doubt cross the minds of those few who even entertain the possibility of a visit to church – while the rest (the majority) will just find the whole idea so threatening (not to say irrelevant) that there is no way they would ever venture onto such alien territory.

Most modern evangelism is on our territory, in places and circumstances where Christians feel safe because they know the ropes – and where others feel threatened because they don't. We will not reach many people that way. On the other hand, there are many signs that in places where we might feel threatened, God is at work in people's lives. If we take seriously the example of Jesus and the practical implications of our incarnational theology, then we are the ones who will need to allow ourselves to be threatened by sharing the good news on territory that to us seems foreign. In the process, the churches we now have will need to change quite radically – perhaps more radically than most of us are prepared for. In recent years, it has become trendy for Christians to speak the language of mission. But so many still only engage with unchurched people on their own terms, which always seems to mean eventually getting people to come to churches which we ourselves enjoy and feel comfortable with. That kind of church, and those Christians, have an ever decreasing chance of surviving, let alone growing, in the twenty-first century.

THE NATURE OF GOD

At the bottom of much of this is a defective view of God. This quite often manifests itself in the pessimism that many Western Christians have as they contemplate the evangelistic task before us. On the one hand is a defeatist kind of pessimism, as Christians take a realistic view of contemporary culture, and see the increasing marginalization of the Church. All the statistics in the West show decline in membership and church attendance, and as a result many Christians, including church leaders, are just giving up. They acknowledge that talk about renewed mission can lift their spirits for a while, but ultimately they are concluding that the task will overwhelm them, and hope for the future is rapidly diminishing. That is probably where a majority of people in mainline churches find themselves today. On the other hand, in some circles a kind of triumphalist pessimism is much in vogue. This view assumes that the decline of the Church is all down to the work of the devil. The whole world is in the control of evil forces, the Church is on the defensive in some kind of spiritual battle, and there is not much that ordinary Christians can do about it, because maybe in the end of the day it is God who seems to be losing the battle.

I find myself deeply uneasy with both those kinds of pessimism. I do not believe – nor do the figures support – the notion that the Church is in terminal decline. What is happening in world Christianity shows that quite the reverse is the case, in mainline denominations as well as in new, indigenous expressions of Christian community. We Western people need to be more open than we have been to learn from growing churches in other parts of the world. I also find enormous theological problems in accepting the other viewpoint, that the world is in the control of the devil. The Bible unequivocally affirms that this is God's world, and if we believe that then God must be at work in the world. Could it be that Western Christians have developed a defective view of God, that is in turn leading to a dysfunctional Church? And does that defective theology begin from the way so many of us seem to have no concept of the fact that this is God's world and God is at work in it? Frankly, if this is not God's world, and if God is not at work in it, then we are wasting our time talking about being Christians, or evangelization, or indeed anything else in relationship to biblical faith. The relationship of this to practical evangelistic strategies has already been discussed in chapter 3. Here I want to draw further attention to a key theological concern.

When Christians talk of sharing their faith, who is the God whom they are trying to communicate? For many people today, this question focuses on the kind of imagery used to describe God. Traditionally, God has been described in exclusively male terms, even by those who would argue that God is without gender, and who recognize that the Bible itself has any number of passages where female imagery is applied to God (for example, Deuteronomy 32:18; Isaiah 42:14, 46:3–4, 66:12–13; Matthew 23:37). Some Christians – especially in Britain – are inclined to dismiss debates on such matters as trendy nonsense. But it is a serious issue and we neglect it at our peril. The truth is that it is about far more than just language; in Marshall McLuhan's well-known phrase, 'the medium is the message'. The language we use both influences and articulates our whole understanding of who God is and the ways in which God works.[23] To give a very simple example, in a world of abused families the imagery of mothering is likely to be far more user-friendly than the language of fathering. But it goes deeper than that. Is God angry or nice? What does God require of people? What kind of response are we looking for when we share the gospel with those who as yet are not Christians? Part of the over-emphasis on rational categories as a way of expressing faith has been the unthinking acceptance of other aspects of that Western imperialism which both created and ultimately has destroyed the Enlightenment vision. By returning to the more holistic model of discipleship presented by Jesus, we are challenging that on a personal level. But there are other aspects of the Western heritage that also need to be addressed. In reflecting on who God is, most of us have felt happy to concentrate almost exclusively on understanding God as transcendent and all-powerful. Like many other aspects of our history, we cannot change this, though we should not be surprised by it. At a time when our culture was driven by imperialist expansion into distant lands, it was convenient for our forebears to have an imperialistic God. In Europe, most church buildings reflect power and authority, not only in their actual construction but also in the way people congregate in them. To sit in rows is to model a transcendent view of who God is.[24]

Two things in particular make me uneasy with all this, one of them theological and the other more practical. Where does our image of God come from? The image of God taken for granted by many people – including some Christians – has its origins in the world of Greek philosophy, in which 'God' was in supreme splendour, controlling things all the time through the exercise of an all-encompassing and terrifying power. Why else would anyone imagine that God ought to step in and stop all the disasters and tragedies that happen in the world? In the Christian faith, however, that is not the image of God. God's purposes and God's person are at the heart of the gospel, and that is found not in the categories of Greek (or any other) philosophy, but in the incarnation of Jesus Christ. That is where we should be looking for images of God. And that is where we find the most serious challenge to our inherited images. For the incarnation is not about transcendence and power, but about weakness, vulnerability and powerlessness. At the centre of the gospel is the extraordinary fact that God became a child. No doubt if almighty God had wished it, God could have entered our world as a full-grown, macho adult male. Much traditional imagery comes close to implying that anyway, especially the lyrics of some traditional hymns. But we can only go down that route by disregarding the central core of the New Testament. To the extent that Christians fail to take seriously this incarnational model both in lifestyle and evangelistic communication, they are in danger of betraying the very gospel that they claim to represent.

This theological observation relates also to a practical issue. For in a generation which has rejected the trappings of transcendence and imperialistic power (and that means the majority of today's spiritual searchers), we will not make much progress with a purely transcendent gospel. I would go so far as to say that our perpetuation of overt images of transcendence is actually impeding the evangelistic task. If we truly believed in a God who is 'in the midst', many things would have to change, among them our buildings, styles of worship and the ways we teach and expect people to learn.

In concluding the argument of this chapter, readers need to recall our starting point, in particular the emphasis that this redefinition of faith is not about ditching what has gone before, but rather on reaffirming some things that, for various reasons, have been lost or hidden. If I have not referred much to what we already have – whether in terms of belief or practice – that is primarily because I assume we can take it for granted, not because I don't believe it or don't like it. But I am pleading that, in order to be faithful to a holistic, biblical gospel, we should give urgent attention to the issues highlighted here; and I am further asserting that to do so will help us to begin to address the questions of people in today's world in a more relevant and challenging way than has hitherto been possible. The diagram below summarizes the key issues that will be involved in this redefinition.

REDEFINING THE FAITH

	INHERITED MODEL	HOLISTIC BIBLICAL MODEL
The Bible	Propositions	Stories
	Theology	Experience of God
	Words	Actions
	Ideas	People
	Answers	Questions
The World	Human resource	Gift of God
	Physical	Spiritual
	Dead	Alive
	Sin	Blessing
People	Sinners	Sinned-Against
	Fallen	Made in God's image
	Male-in-Charge	Male and Female in Partnership
Personal Sin	'You are Responsible'	'You can be Responsible'
	Part of the Gospel Content	Response to the Gospel
	Repent–Believe–Belong	Discipleship. 'Follow Jesus'
Sharing Faith	Formal	Relational
	Bringing God to People	God is already Present
	From Above	Being Alongside
	Speaking	Listening
	'Missions'	Worship
	Church Territory	Other People's Territory
	Stressing Difference	Expressing Solidarity
Conversion	Event	Process
	Destination	Journey
	Crisis	Growth
	Impersonal	Personal
The Church	Organization	Organism
	Programmes	People
	Control	Service
	Authority	Spirituality
	Structures	Purposes
	Maintenance	Mission
God	Transcendent	Immanent
	Leading	Nurturing
	Power	Power of Powerlessness

If all this seems a large and risky project, let us remind ourselves why it is worth doing. There is a group of Native Americans who used a simple signal on the doors of their homes to indicate whether or not they were ready to entertain visitors. The door was secured by a catch on the inside, which when lifted opened the door. In the middle of the door was a small hole, through which a rope could be passed to connect with the catch on the other side. Any visitors seeing the rope knew they were welcome. Without further ceremony, they simply pulled on the rope, the catch was raised, and they went in. If there was no rope showing, the message was simple: the inhabitants were not able to receive visitors. All over the world today, the ropes are hanging out of the doors of people's lives in a very obvious fashion. They are ready to receive visitors who will facilitate their spiritual search. Even 20 years ago, they were not so likely to have an open door. No one knows for how long the present spiritual search will continue, though it is a safe guess that it will last at least for some time into the new millennium. But how can Christians grasp the rope and enter as welcome guests, so that their message will be recognized for the good news they believe it to be? For our final glimpse at a possible answer to that question, we must now turn to Jesus as the model evangelist.

CHAPTER 8

THE PERSONAL TOUCH

Dumbfounded! That was how I felt as I drove back home through the cold air of a December night. Skirting the edge of the Scottish Highlands, it was not the sort of road on which you can drive very fast at any time. In mid-winter, there was a good chance of ice – and perhaps even a hungry stag looking for supper on the grassy verge. So I had plenty of time for thinking, even though the journey was little more than 20 miles – and there was no doubt my mind was working overtime. I had been to a party! The sort of party that, until it's over, you never really know whether you want to go. In some ways, it was a pretty quiet affair. Nine or ten couples, some married, some living together unmarried, along with a few single people. When we arrived, most of us had never met before, so we had some introductions to make. In typical Western fashion we all described ourselves by reference to our work. We were a very mixed bunch, with wide-ranging expertise. An electrician, a surgeon, a forester, a bureaucrat, an engineer, social worker, teacher, personnel adviser, car mechanic – and more besides. Then there was me.

I remember agonizing over the most appropriate way to introduce myself in this situation. 'Remember, this is a party,' I kept telling myself, 'these people have come here to enjoy themselves. You'd better not come over too strong on religion.' And so when it came to my turn I restricted my self-introduction to saying that I worked in a university. I don't mind admitting I was deliberately trying to be as vague as possible – and even at that one or two looked as if they might already have been turned off by the prospect of spending an evening with some ivory-tower academic whose knowledge was probably limited to all the things that nobody else had ever wanted to know about. But others were curious. Was I perhaps a wizard with computers? Or some kind of scientist or technologist pushing forward the frontiers of human knowledge? So the inevitable supplementary soon followed: 'And which department do you work in?' Now I knew from experience that this could be tricky, so I opted for a fairly general reply ('religion'), and muttered it as fast as possible, hoping that not too many would hear. That alone can usually be guaranteed to create a slight hiatus in the conversation – and so it did. But having got this far, why turn back? Especially if you're curious to know whatever could possibly attract an apparently normal person to spend their life thinking about such a subject. In any case, it needn't be all boring: perhaps I was an expert in Islam, or Zen, or some other esoteric subject that would be good for at least a couple of minutes' worth of polite conversation at a Christmas party. And, who knows, it might even be interesting. So someone piped up, 'I suppose that will be comparative religion, then?'

I had a good idea what would happen next. For the true answer to that question can go down like a lead balloon in some circles: 'Well no. Actually I'm interested in Christianity, and the Bible.' Sure enough, there was an audible gasp from someone, followed by a general horrified silence. For what felt to me like an eternity – but cannot have been longer than about two seconds – no one spoke. The floor and the ceiling suddenly became subjects of compelling fascination! But not for long. What I had said was like letting a genie out of a bottle. Soon, everyone was talking – to each other, but especially to me. 'Do you believe in God?' the hostess asked me (a particularly apposite question for a theology professor, I thought). Then, 'How can a book as ancient as the Bible still make sense today?' 'What do you think happens when people pray?' 'What happens when people die?' 'Do you think Jesus was an extraterrestrial?' 'How about the prophets – were they spirit mediums, channeling in messages from some other world?' And so it went on. I can't remember whether anyone else got the chance to introduce themselves! Even when the group subsequently split up into smaller circles, those who attached themselves to me still wanted to talk about religion – and they did, until the early hours of the next morning, covering everything from the origins of evil to the power of spiritual healing, and touching all points in between. I know for certain that I and my partner were the only ones who would have qualified as 'Christians' by any definition of that word. Yet everyone else clearly believed in God. They were all educated and intelligent people (a very broad cross-section of our culture, I would say) and they were fascinated by the spiritual and supernatural. And despite the fact that none of them could see much relevance in the Church as they knew and experienced it, they all had an obvious fascination for the Bible, and its central figure, Jesus Christ.

There are millions of people like that today all over the Western world. The fact is that allegedly 'secular' people are far more religious than for many generations. Twenty years ago, being religious was often regarded as a sign of weakness, or even psychological deficiency. Now, it's almost *avant-garde* to be engaged in the spiritual search. That search might easily encompass all manner of seemingly bizarre and incredible beliefs and practices, but it is unlikely to have a place for whatever the Church has to offer. On hearing my opinion about the things they were interested in, some of the partygoers actually asked me, 'If you believe all this, what are you doing in the Church?' These people were not spiritually uncommitted – far from it. Nor, for that matter, were they against Christianity. They saw Christians as, on the whole, good, kind and caring people who in their own way were making a worthwhile contribution to the life of their community. But they did not see Christians as being in any sense concerned with a spiritual search, and the way Christians expressed their faith in church Sunday by Sunday just made no connections with them.

Moreover, on those few occasions when they had been vaguely interested in the Church, they had a hard time even making contact with it. A few weeks after the party had alerted me to that, I had a salutary experience myself of the non-welcoming attitude the Church can adopt. The occasion was a student mission in a university in the north of England. I was to speak at the opening meeting on a Saturday evening, and then in a local church the following morning. My student hosts did their best to entertain me in style, but by 6 am the next morning I was awake, alone and freezing (I later discovered that this particular student residence had been a medieval castle, and in the meantime not much had changed). With little to detain me over breakfast, I had some time to kill before I needed to be at the church, which was a ten-minute walk from where I was staying. An even shorter walk, however, took me to the cathedral which was a major focal point of this particular city: a grand and ancient building, which I decided to explore. Being all alone in a medieval cathedral early on Sunday morning was an interesting experience. With freedom to wander, I explored all the nooks and crannies that, had there been more visitors, I would probably not have entered. Then I became aware that I was not entirely alone. I was being followed. I could hear footsteps behind me, but since their owner was not yet in sight I played games with him by running as fast as I could round different corners in the cloisters. He knew the short-cuts better than I, and eventually we met face to face. 'I'm sorry,' he said, 'but I'll have to ask you to leave.' Thinking that my little game of hide and seek had upset him, I prepared to apologize. But that was not the problem. 'They're going to have a service,' he explained, 'and it won't interest the likes of you.' With that, I was unceremoniously bundled out of a side door so that 'they' could come through the main entrance. As I made my way to the other church where I was to be the preacher, I wondered what could possibly have given this man the impression that I would not be interested in Christian faith. I concluded it could have been the way I was dressed (jeans and a leather jacket). That itself would say something. But when I related this experience to my family, they agreed that it was probably just an unfortunate one-off experience. More recently, I found myself with all my family in the same city, with time to spare (on this occasion it was early evening), and guess where they suggested we go? And guess what took place at the cathedral door? You've probably got it in one: all six of us were shown the way to the car park, with these words ringing in our ears, 'I'm sorry, but they're about to have a service.' Few churches would bundle people out in this officious way (though there may be more of them than I think). But our body language can easily communicate the same message. If people think they will get the brush-off from us, they are unlikely to make the effort, no matter how serious their spiritual search might be.

LEARNING FROM JESUS

What is the appropriate way to respond to the spiritual seekers of our generation? I believe the answer to that question will be found in a fresh appreciation of how Jesus ministered. We usually read the gospels looking for answers to questions of a historical, literary or theological nature. But they are not the only possible questions, nor are they necessarily the most useful ones in terms of evangelization. How about asking what was actually going on in the gospels? What was Jesus looking for? How did he relate to the people he met? And what did he intend to happen? Asking questions like that might easily unearth some useful guidelines for faith sharing today. There are any number of stories we could home in on, but there are two passages which are particularly illuminating. These are the story of the woman at the well (John 4:1–42) and the story of the couple on the road to Emmaus (Luke 24:13–35). It will be worthwhile to spend some time on them. In some ways, they are contrasting stories. Most obviously, they come from different gospel traditions. But for that very reason, what they have in common is more interesting than their differences.

In Luke 24, Jesus met a married couple who were similar to many people today. They were certainly not card-carrying, committed disciples: if they had been they would have been in Jerusalem with the others, not on the road back home. They were, in a sense, on the fringes of the Church. Yet they had not given up on belief. Quite the reverse, for their conversation revealed that they were searching for meaning in life, and they would even like to believe in Jesus. But somehow it had not come together for them, which is why they were heading away from the uncertainty and insecurity of Jerusalem (where the real action was) back to the safety of their own home. Do you recognize them? Are they 'nominal' Christians, I wonder, people who would never be found in church, but still like what they know of Jesus? The woman in John 4 was in a different category. She shared some of the same questions, but her situation was further complicated by what we might call an esoteric spirituality, not to mention the fragmentation of her relationships for reasons that might well have alienated her from people like the couple in Emmaus.

Jesus bumped into both these people only once, and neither meeting took place in particularly promising circumstances. Yet in the course of these short encounters, they recognized their need of God, they began to understand who Jesus was – and then went off to share the good news with their friends. No one ever meets Jesus and stays the same. What can we learn from this? What was Jesus' secret?

GETTING ALONGSIDE PEOPLE

Putting it simply, Jesus was there, where these people actually were. It seems almost too obvious to say, but Jesus would never have met these people had he not been by the well and on the roadside. He was a partner in their world, and was sufficiently at home in his own culture to be able to meet people on their own territory. Clergy in particular are not supposed to hang about at wells or on roadsides. At least, that's what we would tell ourselves today. They should be in church to serve God. Of course, in a church where all the members are mobilized for faith-sharing, even that would hardly be a problem. But we often give the impression that to share faith effectively, all Christians really need to be in church buildings. So far as evangelism is concerned, modern churches generally prefer to play all their games at home, by inviting others to join us on territory where we feel safe, rather than making ourselves vulnerable by getting alongside them where they are. No matter how 'seeker friendly' we try to make services in church, it will never be the same thing as sharing the good news on other people's territory. Even if we hire a cinema or a sports stadium that is not necessarily going to be the same thing as being alongside other people. It is all too easy to turn the cinema or stadium into a church for that occasion, and the Christians will still be in control. Just being where other people are can be painful: it might take us into places where we would not normally venture. It will always be challenging. But if we believe that God is at work out there, then we can be confident that evangelistically productive things will take place. Knowing that God is at work in the world should empower us for witness. Jesus calls us to evangelize in the world, sharing the good news on other people's terms, in territory where we are vulnerable, and willingly so. Jesus is our model: to follow him, we are going to have to take all this more seriously than we typically do.

AFFIRMING PEOPLE'S VALUE

Notice Jesus' opening remarks in both these episodes. At the well, he says to the woman, 'I see you have some water. I'm desperately thirsty: would you be willing to share your water with me?' Right from the start, the woman knew this was going to be something different. For a start, here was a rabbi who had needs. More than that, they were needs that he thought she could meet – and unlike other men she had encountered, he was not looking for sex. He accepted there was something good and positive about this woman, while also expressing his own weakness and making himself vulnerable. She could easily have told him to get lost, but already she was feeling good about herself. Here was a man who was able to listen as well as to speak.

That is exactly what Jesus did with the couple on the Emmaus road too. He walked alongside them listening to their questions. There are plenty of talkers around today. Our ears are bombarded on all sides by people with a product to market. If the only thing Christians can do is to join this cacophony, not many people will hear their message. We need to learn that sharing our faith can often begin with saying nothing at all. Dietrich Bonhoeffer expressed it well:

Christians, especially ministers, so often think they must always contribute something when they are in the company of others, that this is the one service they have to render. They forget that listening can be a greater service than speaking. Many people are looking for an ear that will listen. They do not find it among Christians, because those Christians are talking where they should be listening. But he who can no longer listen to his brother will soon be no longer listening to God either...One who cannot listen long and patiently will presently be talking beside the point and be never really speaking to others, albeit he is not conscious of it. Anyone who thinks that his time is too valuable to spend keeping quiet will eventually have no time for God or his brother but only for himself and for his own follies.[1]

Now think of all this in relation to so much of what passes for evangelism. I remember once asking a group of students to draw an impression of what came into their minds when they heard the word 'evangelist'. They were of different religious persuasions themselves, and their cartoons reflected that diversity. Paid up members of the student Christian group typically drew ministers standing in pulpits preaching sermons. Other slightly more adventurous souls drew ministers at street corners, but still standing up and preaching sermons. There was only one truly creative sketch among them, and that was a full-colour depiction of Rambo, the fictitious 1980s Hollywood movie character who single-handedly saw off enemy soldiers without ever being hit himself. The person who drew this image explained that this had been his experience of evangelists: people with rapid-fire religious guns, loaded with slick questions and answers with which to shoot down the opposition. Certainly, people who only knew how to communicate in one direction, and whose body language, let alone their words, conveyed just one message: 'You listen to what I have to say, and then decide what to do about it.'

Society is littered with the broken lives of those who have been the victims of this kind of processing. Wounded people lie all around us, crushed by those who are self-assured, assertive and directive. If Christians can only offer more of the same, why should we expect anyone to listen to us – still less to take us seriously? A lot of modern evangelism starts by putting people down. I have already suggested this happens because we have a shallow view of sin. As a result, there is little compassion in our evangelism, and hurting people head off elsewhere to find value and acceptance.

The gospel, however, always lifts people up.[2] Faced with the woman at the well, Jesus affirmed her and recognized her value as a person. Can you imagine the field-day some of today's moralistic busy-bodies might have had with a woman with her lifestyle? Jesus could see well enough that she was a sinner, but he had no need to tell her because she knew that only too well herself. He did, however, see her as someone who had been seriously sinned against, and had compassion on her – and that certainly marked him out as different. Many of those to whom we are called to witness are in the same predicament, and saying – as Jesus did – 'You are a person of value', can easily lead to a great evangelistic harvest.

A Christian worker was walking round a housing estate one Sunday afternoon. The rain was lashing down, and a gale was blowing. There seemed little possibility for faith-sharing here. The only sign of life was someone up a ladder trying to repair a leaking gutter. As he walked nearer, the Christian could see that the person up the ladder was a girl about seven years old. The rain was cascading like a waterfall over the door, inside which a drunk man was sheltering, shouting instructions to the child on the ladder. It turned out that he wanted to go to the bar for another drink, but needed the gutter fixed so he could leave home without getting soaked through. The church worker summed up the situation, and decided to help the girl. He went up the ladder, and fixed the gutter. The girl was delighted: she was saved from her precarious perch. So was her father: he got his drink. But the Christian had mixed feelings, for he was actually employed by his church to be an evangelist to this community – and what could such an action possibly have to do with sharing the gospel? About two weeks later, he got the answer to his question. The man and the girl – and other members of the same family – turned up out of the blue at the church. For somebody to care that much for a little girl whose father was in a drunken stupor had spoken powerfully to them. The father knew he had done wrong: he needed no one to tell him. If the evangelist had told him so on that wet afternoon, he would probably have cursed and sent him packing. As it was, the family came to faith. That incident happened in Scotland, but similar things are happening around the world when Christians see others as sinned against and, like Jesus, have compassion on them.[3] We have too many evangelists like Rambo, and too few like Jesus.

ADDRESSING PEOPLE'S NEEDS

We have already considered the importance of addressing people at their point of need. It makes no sense to repeat it here. But it is worth reading these stories carefully to see how Jesus worked in this respect. The Emmaus couple had a problem with the Old Testament because they could not reconcile what they understood of its teaching with what had happened on the cross. Jesus joined them in their discussion, and using the methodology we highlighted in chapter 7, he helped them to address their questions to the text, moving them on in their reflections, and giving them an opportunity to learn from their experiences. We are unlikely to meet too many people with questions about the Old Testament – or, for that matter, the New Testament. Of course, we feel happiest talking about such topics, which is why we are tempted to do it all the time. But if we insist on setting our own agenda, we ought not to be surprised if no one else is interested. Jesus followed an adaptive strategy. He was not primarily message-centred, but people-centred. The message was not expressed in the same terms for everyone. Jesus knew he would only connect with others if the message was relevant for each person and situation.

Martin Luther observed that people are 'captivated more readily by comparisons and examples than by difficult and subtle disputations. They would rather see a well-drawn picture than a well-written book.'[4] People today still discover faith this way. I must have preached thousands of sermons in the last 20 years, many of them very good sermons. But sermons rarely have the same power as pictures to challenge and change people's lives. My wife has a specialist Christian ministry in the creative arts, particularly clowning, and particularly in worship (which, you will recall, is an essential part of authentic evangelization). I remember an occasion when she joined a dance group who were working with the song 'Shine, Jesus, Shine'. Attracted by the colour and the music, Valentine the clown came in, hesitantly at first, and was gradually drawn into the movement, ultimately transformed as she knelt at the foot of the cross. A social worker said afterwards, 'That was me at the foot of that cross.' Or another occasion in Perth, Western Australia, where the crosses over Valentine's eyes were used to spell out the message that for true transformation we need to look at the world the way God sees it – through the cross – and a teenage boy who was there found his concerns about the environment, peace, justice and violence, picked up in such a way that he too was drawn closer to Christ. I can think of a workshop on spirituality in southern California, where people were moving in a circle dance to the song by Scots musician Ian White, 'Praise the Lord, all you servants of the Lord' (Psalm 134). In the circle, we put our hands palm to palm with the people next to us, and raised them to form a giant crown in praise of God the sovereign – and that action alone brought healing and freedom into the life of more than one person who had previously been sexually abused. I could go on. People's needs are all different. Jesus calls us to recognize them, and then to address them in appropriate ways – and that will not always mean in words. Remember that other text about loving the Lord with the heart, soul, and strength, as well as the mind.

WAITING FOR PEOPLE TO JOIN US

Jesus always gave people space to work out how to respond to him. Take the couple at Emmaus. He had moved them on in their understanding, and when he got to the door of their home he gave them the chance to go on – in a direction of their choosing. They had the freedom either to leave the encounter, or to invite him to join them. Jesus did not pressurize them, or force them into a corner. He recognized their freedom as persons, and the couple chose to invite him in.

At Emmaus Jesus had no need to create a space. It was already there, as the trio arrived at the front door: the natural dynamic of the situation meant a choice had to be made. Jesus respected that, and did not invite himself. The opposite, in fact, for Luke says 'he walked ahead as if he were going on' (Luke 24:28). With the woman at the well, Jesus needed to create a space. In this instance, he did it by suggesting she went to get her husband. As soon as he said that, she knew she had the opportunity to make choices. No doubt Jesus could have criticized her relationships, but to do so would have been incompatible with the way he had already affirmed her as a person. It is worth noting that Jesus' approach, valuing her and addressing her need, did not lead (as some might imagine) to a woolly gospel. It actually put Jesus in a uniquely credible position from which to challenge her. True evangelism always starts where people are, but then opens up opportunities for them to move closer to God.

In Luke 15, Jesus told three parables about lost things. It is instructive to observe how those lost things were found.[5] In two cases (the sheep, verses 4–7, and the coin, verses 8–10), their owners took an active role and went out to find them. But in the third case (verses 11–31), the father did not follow his lost son into the far country, nor go looking for him among the pigs. He stayed at home, and waited for his return. Expectantly waiting, of course, prayerfully waiting no doubt – but waiting all the same. There is nothing contradictory between these two dynamics of evangelization. Sometimes activism is appropriate. It is certainly an easier posture than waiting, for it enables us to think we are doing something, and we all like to feel busy. But waiting will always have a key role in effective evangelism. No one was ever intimidated into God's kingdom. 'True witness follows Jesus Christ in respecting and affirming the uniqueness and freedom of others…The Spirit of God is constantly at work in ways that pass human understanding and in places that to us are least expected…'[6]

QUESTIONS AND STORIES

The style of communication modelled by Jesus generally included three things. First of all, he always listened to people. Then, having heard their concerns and struggles, he asked questions and told stories in order to create spaces within which new possibilities might be identified. And in addition, he lifted people up. These are things that on the whole we seem to have lost the capacity for doing. We do not know how to affirm and stand alongside others without somehow feeling that we are compromising ourselves, or the Church. And we do not know how to challenge people. Jesus had the marvellous facility for just being available to people, and then almost casually digging them in the ribs and saying, 'Oh, by the way, do you fancy being my disciple?' We have something to learn from him on all this. Because this is not a programme we have to buy into, sharing faith this way will not require costly investment from limited church budgets. Nor will we need to import experts to evangelize for us. Every Christian, no matter who they are, can work this way. The weaker we are, the more successful we are likely to be. Once we grasp that we have something to share with others not because we are different from them, but precisely because we are no different maybe that will be really good news – for us as well as for those who are not as yet following Jesus.

APPENDIX

CONVERSION AND FAITH DEVELOPMENT

In discussing the nature of conversion in chapter 4, reference was briefly made to the work of various Christian educators, and the possibility of relating the faith journey to the life cycle, particularly by utilizing insights from developmental psychology that might help to explain how and why faith seems to take on different forms at different stages of life.

The idea that the life of faith passes through various stages is nothing new. In their book *The Critical Journey*, Janet Hagberg and Robert Guelich trace it back into the early Christian centuries, and identify an impressive array of people whose experience of faith seems to have been like this: Augustine, Julian of Norwich, Teresa of Avila, Francis of Assisi, Ignatius – and then, into modern times, with Søren Kierkegaard, Evelyn Underhill, Scott Peck, and others. 'It soon becomes apparent that, if not agreement, at least some parallels exist in the description of the direction by many writers/faith seekers on the journey of faith.'[1]

In biblical terms, the idea that faith is a journey rather than a single ecstatic episode in a person's life goes right back into the Old Testament, where the journey motif is all-pervasive, and being nurtured as part of the community of faith is central to personal faith-commitment. The same emphasis comes through in many parts of the New Testament, where it is stressed that following Jesus is more than just making a single choice: it also involves learning, being built up in faith, and, indeed, ultimately becoming like Christ.[2] That all makes sense in the light of the passages we have studied previously, for if conversion is more than just an instantaneous episode, then it must potentially be a lifelong process: 'Christianity must touch all areas of a person's life: thinking, feeling, and doing'.[3]

But how does the faith journey work? James Fowler has been a pioneer in this field. In the ideas of developmental psychologists Erikson, Piaget, and Kohlberg, he found a useful framework within which to express a concept of 'stages of faith'.[4] The six stages of faith that Fowler identified are listed on the diagram, along with Erikson's eight ages of man for comparison. In recent years, these notions have given rise to widespread debate, and Fowler has continually revised his model, though always within the six-stage framework.[5]

'Faith' itself is one concept that has generated much discussion. Fowler (adopting the ideas of one of his own teachers, Wilfred Cantwell Smith) assumed that 'faith' is something everyone has, and it is not the same thing as believing in religious systems and structures, but is the basic way in which we all make sense out of things.[6] On this understanding, 'faith' becomes something like 'worldview', as long as we think of that not in propositional but in personal terms as 'the stories I use to make sense out of it all'. This opinion has much to commend it inasmuch as it reminds us that faith can be a verb as well as a noun,[7] and in the context of evangelism it helps us understand why, for instance, Paul could use the (mistaken) views of the Athenians as pegs on which to hang the gospel, or why Jesus, instead of getting involved in complex debates about theology, contented himself with pointing to a different (and better) way of seeing things than his questioners had.[8]

Inevitably, there are many detailed questions that could be addressed to this kind of scheme. If we think of it as a rigid structure into which everyone's experience of God must be made to fit, then it will be less than useful. In reality, these stages of faith are rather like stills taken from a particular movie. They are not therefore normative for what should be in every other movie. They describe what faith is, and how it develops, but they do not prescribe what faith must be for every person. Much of the criticism of Fowler has centred around this point, in particular the view that his stages are based on a male (even macho) way of understanding human development.[9] They certainly need to be broadened out to include more of the emotional side of human experience.[10]

But there can be no doubt that Fowler has demonstrated that life, and faith, develop hand-in-hand, and to try to address the one without taking account of the other is likely to be a futile undertaking. Even Neill Q. Hamilton, who is critical of any attempt to link psychological development with Christian faith, still insists that life is about change, and evangelism must therefore relate to that.[11]

One of the most promising expositions of all this is in the work of Janet Hagberg and Robert Guelich, not least because they have been prepared to use their own personal faith stories to illustrate their work. They have been able to pick up many of the criticisms of Fowler's early work, and eliminate some of his weaknesses while building on his strengths. They place themselves firmly in the mainstream of the Protestant theological tradition, and take both theology and the Bible seriously. Their description of stages corresponds very closely to Fowler's, as the diagram shows. But they adopt a more flexible approach, describing their work as 'a loose guide, a globe rather than a road map'.[12] For them, movement within the life of faith revolves around two pivotal points: God's actions in a person's life, and the personal response itself. This corresponds quite closely to what we identified in the life of Peter, where faith seems to be about making active choices, and letting God into different areas of life, something which can be described as 'a continual process of growth rather than a point of arrival'.[13] A two-dimensional diagram does not, however, fully reflect the dynamic nature of this model of faith development. For on this model, faith does not proceed in a linear progression from one stage to another. It is, for example, possible to get stuck in different stages, even to move back to earlier stages. The image of a coiled spring referred to in chapter 4 is a better visual aid here.

In thinking about all this in relation to evangelism, it seems to me that understanding where people are at in their faith journey will help us to communicate the gospel in relevant ways. To help people find Christ, we need to know their starting points, otherwise how can we set up effective signposts to move them in the right direction? There will be for everyone an appropriate response to God at each stage of life and faith, and there are probably different kinds of challenge and change that will be relevant at different stages. Some try to distinguish between two different types of 'conversion' experience, and that may be a helpful way to think about it. R. Moseley, for instance, differentiates 'structural' conversion (the reorientation of basic assumptions), from 'lateral' conversion (changes in the contents of one's faith).[14] In terms of Peter's story, 'structural conversion' may be an appropriate way to describe his first encounter with Jesus, while 'lateral conversion' could approximate more closely to some of the other episodes (though what took place at the house of Cornelius looks much more like a 'structural' change). However we label things, there is wide agreement that change from one stage to another does not happen automatically, but is brought about by 'crises, novelties, and experiences of disclosure and challenge which threatens the limits of the person's present patterns of constitutive-knowing'.[15] That is what was happening on the Emmaus road and at the Samaritan well, where Jesus either created or utilized spaces in which challenges could be faced and new choices made. Indeed, one author actually traces five significant stages of faith development within the Emmaus story, which he believes can be taken as a paradigm for the total conversion experience.[16]

Placing the story of Peter alongside the other models helps to anchor all this in a particular Biblical example. The various points of challenge and change which can be identified in his coming to faith actually parallel fairly clearly the stages identified by Hagberg and Guelich in particular, and their delineation of the various stages can be correlated quite easily with the episodes in the life of Peter. Their notion that it is possible to go back a stage, as well as forward, appears over and over again in Peter's experience (most notably, perhaps, after Caesarea Philippi and again after the episode in the house of Cornelius). Hagberg and Guelich do not themselves adopt Peter as a model, preferring others from Old Testament as well as New. But in biblical terms, Peter's seems to be the most comprehensive example of the faith journey, probably because it is so well documented, though with more intensive scrutiny I believe Paul could also be used to demonstrate the same thing.

In terms of practical faith-sharing, we would of course place our own experience of faith within this matrix, as we set 'the hope that is within us' alongside the faith journeys of others to whom we witness, confident in the knowledge that since God is at work out there, something creative will happen. This then becomes another tool helping to clarify the interactive relationship between the three dynamic elements of mission outlined in chapter 3: God's story, the Bible stories, and personal stories (our own and other people's).

Stages of Life and Faith Development

Eric Erickson Eight Ages of Man	James Fowler Stages of Faith	Janet Hagberg and Robert Guelich The Critical Journey	Peter New Testament
1 BASIC TRUST Infancy: "Somebody is there and somebody loves me"	1 INTUITIVE/PROJECTIVE "God is like my mum and dad" Discovery through relationships	Influenced by External Sources and Stimuli 1 THE RECOGNITION OF GOD "Who is God? Who am I?"	1 "I BELIEVE IN GOD" Personal and spiritual growth within Judaism
2 ACHIEVING AUTONOMY Age 2–3: "Let me do it"	2 MYTHICAL-LITERAL "What's fair is fair" Getting things into order	2 THE LIFE OF DISCIPLESHIP Sense of belonging/group identification	2 "JESUS SEEMS A GOOD GUY" Adoption of a role model/a place to belong (Mark 1)
3 EXPANDING IMAGINATION Age 4–6: "I am what I can imagine I will be"	3 SYNTHETIC CONVENTIONAL "I believe what the church believes" Conforming to other people's expectations	3 THE PRODUCTIVE LIFE "Giving to and for others – within limits"	3 "I NEED TO THINK THIS OUT" Jesus is the Messiah! (Mark 8)
4 A SENSE OF INDUSTRY Age 6–12: "I can really do it" – learning and making	4 INDIVIDUATIVE/REFLECTIVE "As I see it God is ..." Thinking things through	Centred Around Self Discovery and Transformation 4 THE JOURNEY INWARD Re-evaluation of faith and life: "What am I worth, and to whom?"	4 "CAN I REALLY LOVE HIM THIS MUCH?" (John 18, 21)
5 IDENTITY Adolescence: "Who am I?"	5 CONJUNCTIVE "Distinguishing the map from the territory" Seeing a broader picture, especially in relation to emotions	'The Wall'	5 "WHO IS GOD, WHO AM I, WHAT AM I ABOUT?" Acts 10/Gal. 2:11–14)
6 INTIMACY Young adult: need to belong, participate	6 UNIVERSALIZING "I have a dream" The big vision	5 THE JOURNEY OUTWARD "Living with uncertainty"	6 "SHARING MYSELF AND MY FAITH" Galilee, Antioch, Rome, 1 Peter etc.
7 GENERATIVITY 30s–60s: making, producing – achievements, family, etc.		6 THE LIFE OF LOVE Loving God, self, others	
8 FACING DEATH "It has all been worthwhile"			

ENDNOTES

CHAPTER 1   FAITH, CULTURE AND THE 21ST CENTURY

1 J. L. Steffens, *Autobiography* (New York: Literary Guild 1931), p 799.

2 Joanna Lumley, *Stare Back and Smile*, quoted in *Woman's Weekly*, 9 October 1990, p 26.

3 *TS Beat* issue 9 (1990), p 6.

4 M. Ferguson, *The Aquarian Conspiracy* (London: Paladin 1982), p 77.

5 For extensive discussion of this question, see Lesslie Newbigin, *Foolishness to the Greeks* (Geneva: WCC 1986); *The Gospel in a Pluralist Society* (London: SPCK 1989).

6 Cf the personal testimony of Kenneth Wapnick, the New Age author of *Forgiveness and Jesus* (Roscoe, NY: Foundation for 'A Course in Miracles' 1983), who contrasts the way that 'Christianity has been a religion of sacrifice, guilt, persecution, murder and elitism' with 'Jesus its primary symbol – he whose gospel was only love, forgiveness, peace and unity', and goes on to observe somewhat ruefully that 'Christianity has not been very Christian' (p 9). For a more comprehensive analysis of how Christianity has failed to provide the West with a meaningful spirituality, cf also (among many others) F. Capra, *The Turning Point* (New York: Simon & Schuster 1982); J. Needleman, *Lost Christianity* (Garden City, NY: Doubleday 1980).

7 Petronius, *Satyricon* 17.
8 By contrast, there are only 30,000 Christian clergy of all types. In France 40,000 professional astrologers are registered for tax purposes, compared with 26,000 Roman Catholic priests. Cf *MARC Newsletter* 93/3 (September 1993), p 2.
9 On Hitler, cf Nicholas Goodrick-Clarke, *The Occult Roots of Nazism* (Wellingborough: Aquarian Press 1985); for the influence of neo-paganism on Hitler, through Wagner, see M. Brearley, 'Hitler & Wagner: the Leader, the Master and the Jews', in *Patterns of Prejudice* 22/2 (1988), pp 3–22.
10 R. L. Ackoff, *Creating the Corporate Future* (New York: John Wiley & Sons 1981), pp 4–5. For a readable and well-informed analysis of the nature and rate of change by a Christian writer, see Russell Chandler, *Racing Toward 2001* (San Francisco: HarperCollins 1992).
11 S. Weil, 'Some thoughts on the love of God', in R. Rees (ed), *Science, Necessity and the love of God* (London: OUP 1968), p 148.
12 Quoted by Charles Krauthammer, 'The Greatest Cold War Myth of All', in *Time* 142/23 (29 November 1993), p 84.
13 On the Western press and Islam, see N. Daniel, *Islam and the West: the making of an image* (Edinburgh: Edinburgh University Press, 1960); E. W. Said, *Covering Islam: how the media and the experts determine how we see the rest of the world* (London: Routledge & Kegan Paul 1985).
14 In the 1980s, an average of one new mosque opened every two weeks in Britain, a rate of growth paralleled also in France and Germany. Much of the growth of the Islamic community is due to births and immigration. But increasing numbers of Western people are converting to Islam, mostly as Western women marry into Muslim families, but also among people who are attracted by the moral demands Islam places on believers, and Afro-Caribbeans alienated by prevailing cultural values.

15 These and other statistics relating to the growth and decline of the Church are mostly taken from *The World Christian Encyclopedia*, edited by David B. Barrett (New York: OUP 1982), and updates published by him in a variety of journals, most regularly the *International Bulletin of Missionary Research*. In many Western countries, Church decline is accelerating fast. In Scotland, for example (the country I know best), something like 230 people leave the Church every week – the equivalent of a good-sized congregation – and projecting the figures forward in a straight line seems to lead to the extinction of the Church in the first three decades of the twenty-first century. Introducing an age-profile factor into this shows the Church in serious crisis long before that, as its members are predominantly older people. Cf Peter Brierley and Fergus Macdonald, *Prospects for Scotland 2000* (London: Christian Research Association 1995). Churches in North America have managed to resist this decline up until now, but the same trends are now obvious there as well, with serious decline in the mainline churches which, in spite of growth elsewhere, is still leading to an overall reduction of the proportion of the population who would describe themselves as Christian.

16 According to recent projections, by the year 2000 55% of all Protestant missionaries will be non-Western, and the figures are similar for the Roman Catholic Church. Cf J. H. Kraakevik and D. Welliver, *Partners in the Gospel* (Wheaton: Billy Graham Center 1992), pp 161–175.

17 For a stimulating account of all this, see Charles Handy, *The Age of Unreason* (London: Business Books 1989).

18 See *Social Trends 1993* (London: Central Statistical Office); and *Family Lifestyles* (London: Mintel 1993). Tom Griffin, editor of *Social Trends 1990*, observed then that 'If this trend continues, by the end of the century no baby will be born in wedlock.'

19 For an analysis of this central issue, and some indication of possible Christian responses, see John Drane and Olive M. Fleming Drane, *Happy Families?* (London: Marshall Pickering 1995).

20 Peter and Sue Kaldor, *Where the River Flows* (Homebush West, NSW: Lancer 1988), p xxiii.

21 Tom Forrest, 'An opportunity not to be lost', in *New Evangelization 2000* 13 (1990), p 8.

CHAPTER 2   WHERE DO WE GO FROM HERE?

1 The title of the first chapter of M. McLuhan, *Understanding Media* (London: Routledge & Kegan Paul 1964)

2 Anyone who doubts that latter claim need only select at random any commentary on any book of the Bible written in the last couple of centuries, to discover that they all start from the assumption that we can best understand things by taking them to pieces. Theories on source documents and ultimate origins of the biblical materials all feature prominently in the basic tool-kit of today's Bible interpreter. We have convinced ourselves that, once you can discover what a piece of literature is made of, you also know what it means. You don't, of course: if you are very lucky, you might just manage to come up with some approximate idea of what it is made of. But such is our love affair with the reductionist model that very few stop to make that observation.

3 See, for example, R. L. Ackoff, *Creating the Corporate Future*, esp. pp 3–24; M. Ferguson, *The Aquarian Conspiracy*, esp. pp 397–426.

4 Philo of Alexandria, quoted by Matthew Fox, *Whee! We, Wee All the Way Home* (Santa Fe: Bear & Co 1981), p 4.

5 The pioneer in this field was Roger Sperry, who won the 1981 Nobel Prize in Physiology and Medicine for his research. Cf his early paper, 'Brain Bisection and Consciousness', in *Brain*

& *Conscious Experience*, ed. J. Eccles (New York: Springer-Verlag 1966). For an accessible survey of subsequent research, see Sally P. Springer and Gertz Deitsch, *Left Brain, Right Brain* (New York: Freeman 1993, 4th ed.). A practical application of these insights would be Tony Buzan's *The Mind Map Book* (London: BBC 1993) or, for a distinctively Christian application, see Walter Wink, *Transforming Bible Study* (London: Mowbray 1990, 2nd edn).

6 Cf Dave Tomlinson, *The Post-Evangelicals* (London: Triangle 1995), pp 84–103. The diagram here is an adaptation of his classification of culture into 'scientific' and 'poetic' worldviews.

7 Charles Handy, *The Empty Raincoat* (London: Hutchinson 1994), p 17.

8 Barry McWaters, *Conscious Evolution* (Los Angeles: New Age Press 1981), pp 111–112.

9 Lawrence M. Krauss, *The Physics of Star Trek* (London: HarperCollins 1996), pp xi-xiii.

10 Influential examples of this kind of analysis would be Marilyn Ferguson, *The Aquarian Conspiracy* (Los Angeles: Tarcher 1980), or Fritjof Capra, *The Turning Point* (New York: Simon & Schuster 1982). For a history of Western thinking which arrives at broadly similar conclusions, cf Richard Tarnas, *The Passion of the Western Mind* (New York: Ballantine 1991).

11 Of course, the further back in time one goes to look for antecedents, the more difficult it is to achieve precision. The alleged existence of a pre-patriarchal goddess-centred matriarchal culture is an example, where most scholars believe ancient history has been rewritten and distorted by the imposition of modern western values. Cf Mary Jo Weaver, 'Who is the Goddess and Where does She get Us?' in *Journal of Feminist Studies in Religion* 5/1 (1989), pp 49–64; Sally Binford, 'Are Goddesses and Matriarchies

Merely figments of Feminist Imagination?' in *The Politics of Women's Spirituality*, ed. Charlene Spretnak (Garden City NY: Doubleday 1982), pp 541–549. For a survey of all this from a Christian perspective, see Aida Besancon Spencer, Donna F. G. Hailson, Catherine Clark Kroeger and William David Spencer, *The Goddess Revival* (Grand Rapids: Baker 1995).

12 For a readable account of the rise of transpersonal psychology, see R. S. Valle, 'The Emergence of Transpersonal Psychology', in R. S. Valle and S. Halling (eds), *Existential-Phenomenological Perspectives in Psychology* (New York: Plenum Press 1989), pp 257–268.

13 Starhawk, *The Spiral Dance* (San Francisco: Harper & Row 1989), p 214. A good example of what Starhawk complains about would be the way Westerners have taken over and reinterpreted Eastern concepts of reincarnation. In the East, reincarnation always has a moral basis: how a person will come back next time depends on the way they behave now. Westerners, however, have too strong a sense of their own individual importance to accept that, and so typically talk of choosing their own karma, and deciding who they will be in each life – thereby destroying and distorting the very basis of the belief they claim to be espousing. For an example of this, cf J. L. Simmons, *The Emerging New Age* (Santa Fe: Bear & Co 1990); and critical comment in my *What is the New Age saying to the Church?* (London: Marshall Pickering 1991), pp 95–134. As part of the same process, the history of Christianity is regularly rewritten and misunderstood, while Christian belief is misrepresented. For example, it is widely taken for granted that, if there is such a person as the 'real Jesus', he is not to be found in the pages of the New Testament but in esoteric Gnostic gospels that circulated on the fringes of Christianity in the third and fourth centuries and were allegedly repressed by early Church leaders for essentially political reasons. Nor is there any shortage of

people who will claim (against all the historical evidence) that the canon of the Bible itself was concocted in the fourth century by nasty male chauvinists whose main concern was to put women down and to disinfect its contents so as to remove notions like reincarnation which allegedly were there in the beginning, but became an embarrassing inconvenience to the Church's political philosophy. For an example, see Shirley Maclaine, *Out on a Limb* (London: Bantam 1983), pp 234–235.

14 David Spangler and William Irwin Thompson, *Reimagination of the World* (Santa Fe: Bear & Co 1991), p xvi.

15 Ernest Gellner, *Postmodernism, Reason and Religion* (London: Routledge 1992), pp 22–23.

16 The literature on modernity and postmodernism is enormous. For general orientation, see Hans Bertens, *The Idea of the Postmodern* (London: Routledge 1995); David Harvey, *The Condition of Postmodernity* (Oxford: Blackwell 1989); Keith Tester, *The Life and Times of Post-Modernity* (London: Routledge 1993). For Christian perspectives, see Philip Sampson et al, *Faith and Modernity* (Oxford: Regnum 1994); Stanley J. Grenz, *A Primer on Postmodernism* (Grand Rapids: Eerdmans 1996); David S. Dockery (ed.), *The Challenge of Postmodernism* (Wheaton IL: Bridgepoint 1995).

17 D. W. Bebbington, 'The Enlightenment & Evangelicalism', in *The Gospel in the Modern World*, ed. M. Eden and D. F. Wells (Leicester: IVP 1991), p 76. For more discussion of the same theme, see Alister E. McGrath, *A Passion for Truth* (Leicester: Apollos 1996), pp 163–200, who concludes that 'Certain central Enlightenment ideas appear to have been uncritically taken on board by some evangelicals, with the result that...the movement runs the risk of becoming a secret prisoner of a secular outlook which is now dying before our eyes' (173).

18 Shirley Maclaine, *Out on a Limb*, p 215.

19 Bhagwan Shree Rajneesh, *I am the Gate* (New York: Harper & Row, 1977), p 18.

20 Jacob Needleman, *Lost Christianity* (Garden City NY: Doubleday 1980), pp 4, 35.

21 George Barna, *Baby Busters: The Disillusioned Generation* (Chicago: Northfield 1994), p 93.

22 Barna, *Baby Busters*, p 69.

23 The answer will not be too different from one tradition to another. For whereas some Protestant churches were established precisely to exclude what could be felt, tasted, seen, or touched, it is also the case that since Vatican II the Roman Catholic Church has been heading very fast in the same direction, to such an extent that some RC circles are almost more 'protestant' in this sense than the Protestants! Though it would be difficult to prove, the thought has crossed my mind more than once, whether there is not some intrinsic connection between the rise of 'new age' spirituality with its heavy emphasis on the tactile and experiential/sacramental/mystical and the generally more cognitive direction now taken by much RC spirituality.

24 Barna, *Baby Busters*, pp 150–151.

25 *Finding Faith in 1994* (London: CRA 1995).

26 Matthew Fox, *Creation Spirituality* (San Francisco: HarperCollins 1991), pp 75–76; emphasis added.

27 Douglas Coupland, *Life after God* (New York: Simon & Schuster 1994), p 359. For a classic exploration of the spiritual search of young adults in the West, see Coupland's earlier book, *Generation X* (New York: St Martins Press 1991).

CHAPTER 3   BACK TO THE BEGINNING

1 On Galilee, see S. de Freyne, *Galilee from Alexander the Great to Hadrian* (Wilmington: Glazier 1980). For the view that Galilee was more sophisticated and religious than is usually

supposed, see Shmuel Safrai, 'The Jewish cultural nature of Galilee in the first century', in M. Lowe (ed.), *The New Testament and Christian-Jewish Dialogue: studies in honor of David Flusser* (Jerusalem: Ecumenical Fraternity 1993).

2 On the hermeneutical challenges presented by the letter form of the New Testament, see M. D. Hooker, *Pauline Pieces* (London: Epworth 1979), pp 7–20; C. J. Roetzel, *The Letters of Paul* (London: SCM 1983), pp 1–80.

3 E. W. Blyden, *Christianity, Islam and the Negro Race* (London: W. B. Whittingham & Co 1889, 2nd edn), p 65.

4 William J. Bausch, *Storytelling, Imagination & Faith* (Mystic CT: Twenty-Third Publications 1984), p 28.

5 For a judicious survey of these and other issues, see B. Stanley, *The Bible and the Flag* (Leicester: Apollos 1990).

6 On Paul's lifestyle in relation to his strategies for evangelization, cf R. F. Hock, *The Social Context of Paul's Ministry* (Philadelphia: Fortress 1980).

7 *Mission and Evangelism – an ecumenical affirmation* (Geneva: WCC 1982), section 28; emphasis added.

8 Reported in *LandMARC* (New Year 1990), p 3.

9 Haddon Robinson, 'Listening to the Listeners', in J. D. Berkley (ed.), *Preaching to Convince* (Waco, TX: Word 1986), p 46.

10 On communication issues in general, see C. H. Kraft, *Communication Theory for Christian Witness* (Nashville: Abingdon Press 1983); J. F. Engel, *Contemporary Christian Communications* (Nashville: Thomas Nelson 1979).

CHAPTER 4   THE CALL TO FOLLOW CHRIST

1 Augustine, *Confessions* viii. 12.

2 *Views from the Pews* (London: BCC & CTS 1986), p 37.

3 John Finney, *Finding Faith Today* (Swindon: Bible Society 1992), pp 23–24.

4 *Finding Faith Today*, p 25. It is worth observing, however, that this research also discovered that, even in those churches with no tradition of dramatic or crisis conversion, some 20% of converts actually had such an experience.

5 The classic exposition of the distortions this has caused is K. Stendahl, 'Paul and the Introspective Conscience of the West', in *Paul among Jews and Gentiles* (Philadelphia: Fortress Press 1976), pp 78–96. For a more recent (and more wide-ranging) discussion of similar questions, see Neil Elliott, *Liberating Paul* (Maryknoll NY: Orbis 1994).

6 On the significance of Paul's Damascus road experience as the source of his distinctive theological understanding, see the classic work of Seyoon Kim, *The Origin of Paul's Gospel* (Grand Rapids: Eerdmans 1982). For a brief summary, see my *Interpreting the New Testament* (Oxford: Lion 1986), pp 361–367.

7 For one of the most striking expositions of the total and radical nature of conversion, see Jim Wallis, *The Call to Conversion* (Lion: Oxford 1982). Wallis's work is specially instructive, as he came from a background where the single instantaneous moment of crisis was the normative view of conversion.

8 Cf T. A. Droege, *Faith Passages and Patterns* (Philadelphia: Fortress Press 1983), pp 7–26.

9 'The one preaches the Gospel of bodies without souls, while the other preaches the Gospel of souls without bodies. The first is a corpse and the second a ghost.' (quoted by B. Hathaway, and attributed to E. Stanley Jones, in *Quadrant*, November 1993, p 5).

10 On Peter, cf Oscar Cullmann, *Peter* (London: SCM 1962); R. E. Brown, K. P. Donfried, J. Reumann, *Peter in the New Testament* (Minneapolis: Augsburg 1973); R. E. Brown and J. P. Meier, *Antioch and Rome* (London: Geoffrey Chapman 1983). There are of course many historical and critical questions

raised by the presentation of Peter in the various New Testament books, though I believe that enough can be known about him for the purposes of charting the course of his life of discipleship. In any case, given that Peter was one of their great heroes, we may assume that the model he embodies must have represented the early Church's widely held concept of the nature of discipleship.

11 Cf Hans Ruedi Weber, *Jesus and the Children* (Geneva: WCC 1979).

12 On this, see R. A. Batey, *Jesus and the Forgotten City: new light on Sepphoris and the urban world of Jesus* (Grand Rapids: Baker 1991).

13 *Mission & Evangelism – an ecumenical affirmation*, section 7.

14 The story in John 1:35–42, though obviously from a different set of traditions, displays very similar characteristics to the story in Mark 1:16–20. In the fourth gospel, Peter shows the same motivational attachment to whatever he thinks Jesus stands for, and is following at a distance. When Jesus unexpectedly addresses him, he covers his embarrassment by asking what seems an irrelevant question ('Where are you staying?') – but he still ends up going after Jesus.

15 *Mission and Evangelism – an ecumenical affirmation*, section 13.

16 W. Temple: see S. Neill, *The Unfinished Task* (London: Lutterworth 1957), p 45.

17 J. Hagberg and R. A. Guelich, *The Critical Journey* (Salem WI: Sheffield Publishing Co 1995), p 15.

18 Cf J. Finney, *Finding Faith Today*, pp 49–50.

19 There is a vast and growing literature on this subject. Significant texts include the following: J. W. Fowler, *Stages of Faith* (San Francisco: Harper & Row 1981); J. W. Fowler, *Becoming Adult, Being Christian* (San Francisco: Harper & Row 1984); J. W. Fowler, K. E. Nipkow, F. Schweitzer (eds), *Stages of Faith and Religious Development* (London: SCM

Press 1992); J. Westerhoff III, *Will Our Children Have Faith?* (San Francisco: Harper & Row 1976); V. B. Gillespie, *The Experience of Faith* (Birmingham, Alabama: Religious Education Press 1988); W. E. Conn, *Conversion* (New York: Alba House 1978); J. Astley and L. Francis (eds), *Christian Perspectives on Faith Development* (Leominster: Gracewing/ Grand Rapids: Eerdmans 1992).

CHAPTER 5   THE CALL TO WORSHIP

1   *International Review of Mission* LIV (1965), p 455.

2   'To make evangelism the primary concern of the church is to give it a misplaced and exaggerated position in our lives. The first task of the church is to worship…' (William Abraham, *The Logic of Evangelism* (London: Hodder & Stoughton 1989), p 182.

3   George Ritzer, *The McDonaldization of Society* (Thousand Oaks CA: Pine Forge Press 1993).

4   Ritzer, *The McDonaldization of Society*, p 130.

5   Ritzer, *The McDonaldization of Society*, p 26.

6   Shirley Maclaine, *Out on a Limb* (London: Bantam 1987), p 198.

7   Cf Michael J. Fanstone, *The Sheep that Got Away* (Tunbridge Wells: Monarch 1993); William D. Hendricks, *Exit Interviews* (Chicago: Moody 1993).

8   They also raise theological questions for some people. Describing a visit to Willow Creek Community Church in Chicago, Anthony B. Robinson asks, '…is what it offers recognizable as the church? Or has the worshipping congregation been transformed into an audience? Are the weekly services more entertainment than worship?' ('Learning from Willow Creek Church', in *Christian Century* 23 January 1991, p 69). The same question could of course be addressed to more traditional churches as well.

9 In 1949, China had 800,000 Protestant Christians. Forty years later that had grown to 4 million, even according to the figures of an unsympathetic Chinese government. Other sources put the number closer to as many as 40 million. For a well-informed account, see Raymond Fung, *Households of God on China's Soil* (Geneva: WCC 1982).

10 For a classic treatment, see C. G. Jung, *Modern Man in Search of a Soul* (London: Routledge & Kegan Paul 1933); and cf the role of Transpersonal Psychology, as mentioned in chapter 2 above.

11 Raymond Fung, *The Isaiah Vision* (Geneva: WCC 1992), p 13.

12 Raymond Fung, *The Isaiah Vision*, p 14.

13 On this, see Robert Banks, *Going to Church in the First Century* (Beaumont: Christian Books 1990); and for a modern application of it, Robert and Julia Banks, *The Church Comes Home* (Sutherland NSW: Albatross 1986).

14 Ernst Käsemann, 'Ministry and Community in the New Testament', in *Essays on New Testament Themes* (London: SCM 1963), pp 63–94 (quotation is from p 81).

15 For detailed accounts of this consult Peter Honey and Alan Mumford, *The Manual of Learning Styles* (Maidenhead: Peter Honey 1992, 3rd edition).

16 *Finding Faith Today*, p 25.

17 William Abraham, *The Logic of Evangelism*, p 171.

18 Walter Wink, *Transforming Bible Study*, p 74.

19 There was no shortage of people even in the early centuries who found all this highly threatening, of course. Docetists and Gnostics soon began to deny that Jesus could possibly have been fully divine from his birth, and instead saw him as receiving a divine spirit at baptism, or on some other occasion. In practice, if not in theory, quite a few Christians today are crypto-gnostics on such matters, which probably explains the almost total absence of any satisfactory theology of childhood in all our traditions.

20 Ian Wray, 'Buddhism & Psychotherapy', in G. Claxton *Beyond Therapy* (London: Wisdom Publications 1986), pp 160–161.

21 Raymond Fung, *The Isaiah Vision*, pp 14–15.

22 For a discussion of some of the key challenges this presents to the church, see John Drane and Olive M. Fleming Drane, *Happy Families?*, pp 89–143.

23 John Naisbitt and Patricia Aburdene, *Megatrends 2000* (London: Pan 1991), pp 53–76.

24 Epistle to Diognetus 5.

25 Michael Marshall, *Renewal in Worship* (London: Marshall, Morgan & Scott 1982), p 65.

CHAPTER 6   THE CALL TO BE CHURCH

1 By 1989, though, there was a more circumspect understanding of what this might mean, and even in the opening address of the Lausanne II Congress, chairperson Leighton Ford admitted that 'It is even possible that Jesus Christ may do this greatest work through some people who aren't at this Congress and might never be invited.' See J. D. Douglas (ed.), *Proclaim Christ Until He Comes* (Minneapolis: World Wide Publications 1990), p 54.

2 On the way in which these incidents might be fitted into the overall context of Paul's life, see my *Introducing the New Testament*, pp 277–280; D. A. Carson, D. J. Moo and L. Morris, *An Introduction to the New Testament* (Leicester: Apollos 1992), pp 223–231, 289–296.

3 On the wider issues relating to how we may date Paul's life, see G. Lödemann, *Paul Apostle to the Gentiles: studies in Chronology* (London: SCM Press 1984); R. Jewett, *Dating Paul's Life* (London: SCM Press 1979).

4 For the evangelistic relevance of church planning, see Jeffrey Harris, 'Structural Considerations', in M. Hill (ed.), *Entering the Kingdom* (London: MARC Europe 1986), pp 69–83.

5 The Emperor Claudius formally excluded the Jews from Rome in AD 49, and it was several years later before his successor Nero allowed them back again (Suetonius, *Life of Claudius* 25.4). In an edict to the inhabitants of Alexandria in Egypt, the same Claudius described the Jews as 'a general plague throughout the world'. Many Greek writers of the time depicted the Jews in a bad light. For a particularly extensive catalogue of anti-semitic misinformation, see the Latin author Tacitus, *History* V.1–13.

6 Gilbert Murray once described it as a 'failure of nerve': 'It is hard to describe. It is a rise of asceticism, of mysticism, in a sense, of pessimism; a loss of self-confidence, of hope in this life and of faith in normal human effort; a despair of patient enquiry, a cry for infallible revelation; an indifference to the welfare of the state, a conversion of the soul to God.' (*Five Stages of Greek Religion*, Oxford: OUP 1925, p 155). This diagnosis of the spiritual condition of the Hellenistic age has more than a few similarities with the spiritual climate of Western culture today – something which ought to give us confidence (if we needed it) to root our solutions firmly in the New Testament.

7 On Paul's creative use of the letter form, see W. G. Doty, *Letters in Primitive Christianity* (Philadelphia: Fortress Press 1973).

8 Quoted in James D. Berkley (ed.), *Preaching to Convince* (Waco: Word 1986), p 41.

9 For recent efforts to set the record straight, see Brian J. Dodd, *The Problem with Paul* (Downers Grove IL: InterVarsity 1996); Neil Elliott, *Liberating Paul* (Maryknoll NY: Orbis 1994).

10 For more on this, and a comparison of the evangelizing styles of Paul and Jesus, see my 'Patterns of Evangelization in Paul and Jesus: a way forward in the Jesus-Paul debate?' in J. B. Green and M. M. B. Turner (eds.), *Jesus of Nazareth, Lord and Christ* (Grand Rapids: Eerdmans 1994) pp 281–296.

11 R. Fung, 'Mission in Christ's Way', in *International Review of Mission* LXXIX (1990), p 8.

12 The expression of John P. Meier, *Antioch & Rome* (New York: Paulist 1983), p 12. For a succinct account of Christianity in Antioch, see also W. Meeks and R. Wilken, *Jews and Christians in Antioch* (Missoula: Scholars Press 1978).

13 On Antioch as a model New Testament church see M. Green, *Evangelism Now and Then* (Leicester: IVP 1979), pp 33–52; M. Green, *Evangelism through the Local Church* (London: Hodder & Stoughton 1990), pp 82–103.

14 *Essays on New Testament Themes*, pp 80–81. For further evidence, Käsemann draws attention not only to 1 Corinthians 12, but also 1 Peter 2:5–10. This is not an eccentric view: mainstream New Testament scholarship would agree with it. James Dunn's comments are typical: 'There is no such thing as passive membership...to belong to the body is to have a function within the body, a contribution which the member must make...the idea of mono-ministry, of all the most important gifts concentrated on one man (even an apostle) is foolish nonsense to Paul...Paul has no concept of a hierarchy of offices.' See his *Jesus and the Spirit* (London: SCM Press 1975), quotations from pp 264, 268.

15 On such organizations in general, see Charles Handy, *Understanding Voluntary Organizations* (London: Penguin 1990).

16 Bryant Myers, 'Christian leadership in the nineties', in *MARC Newsletter* 91/1 (March 1991), 3. On emerging leadership styles in the Church, see Kennon L. Callahan, *Effective Church Leadership* (San Francisco: HarperCollins 1990); C. Jeff Woods, *Congregational Megatrends* (Bethesda MD: Alban Institute 1996).

17 R. Ackoff, *Creating the Corporate Future* (New York: John Wiley 1981), p 30.

18 R. Ackoff, *Creating the Corporate Future*, p 33.

19 For some of this, see Charles Handy, *The Age of Unreason*, pp 137–402; also his *The Empty Raincoat* (London: Hutchinson 1994).

20 R. Fung, 'Mission in Christ's Way', pp 8–13, 16–17; *The Isaiah Vision*, especially pp 43–47.

21 For more on this concept from a management point of view, cf Charles Handy, *Understanding Organizations* (London: Penguin 1993, 4th edn) – though he observes that even the 'stakeholder' model will soon be forced towards a more genuine sense of community ownership and accountability: 'In order to give proper expression to the ideas of stakeholders and community the power of ownership will not... reside in the centre but in the parts... making the centre truly the servant of the whole, not the master of it' (p 366). For Christians to grasp that would require a major change in our present attitudes to non-church culture, as well as (encouragingly) a return to some fundamental values espoused by Jesus.

22 Jim Dethmer (a leader in Willow Creek Community Church, Chicago), quoted by Russell Chandler, *Racing Toward 2001*, (San Francisco: HarperCollins 1992), p 210.

23 *Mission and Evangelism – an ecumenical affirmation*, Preface.

24 Roland Allen, *Missionary Methods: St Paul's or Ours?* (Grand Rapids: Eerdmans 1962; originally published in 1912). See also David Paton and Charles H. Long (eds), *The Compulsion of the Spirit: a Roland Allen Reader* (Grand Rapids: Eerdmans 1983).

25 Foreword to the 1962 edition of *Missionary Methods: St Paul's or Ours?*, pp i-iii. John Stott also comments that Allen's 'principles have been remarkably vindicated in recent years', see his *Message of Acts* (Leicester: IVP 1990), p 235.

26 Cf J. D. G. Dunn, *Unity and Diversity in the New Testament* (London: SCM Press 1977). According to some, the diversity was more than merely cultural: cf W. Bauer, *Orthodoxy and*

Heresy in Earliest Christianity (London: SCM Press 1972); and, for a critical assessment, Thomas A. Robinson, *The Bauer Thesis Examined* (Lewiston: Edwin Mellen Press 1988).

27 A. Maslow, *Toward a Psychology of Being* (New York: Van Nostrand Reinhold 1968, 2nd edn).

28 For biblical perspectives on the Church as community, see Robert Banks, *Paul's Idea of Community* (Peabody MA: Hendrickson 1994); David L. Bartlett, *Ministry in the New Testament* (Minneapolis: Fortress 1993).

CHAPTER 7   REDEFINING THE FAITH

1 For further reflection on gospel and culture issues, see my article 'Salvation and Culture', in Donald English (ed.), *Windows on Salvation* (London: Darton Longman & Todd 1994), pp 166–180.

2 See Richard Clark Kroeger and Catherine Clark Kroeger, *I Suffer Not a Woman* (Grand Rapids: Baker 1992).

3 For more on this, cf John Drane and Olive M. Fleming Drane, *Happy Families?* (London: Marshall Pickering 1995).

4 John Finney, *Finding Faith Today* (Swindon: Bible Society 1992), p 20.

5 The rise of Liberation Theology is perhaps the most striking example of this trend, though it is not the only one. Cf P. Berryman, *Liberation Theology* (London: Tauris, 1987); T. Witvliet, *A Place in the Sun* (Maryknoll, NY: Orbis, 1985); Robert McAfee Brown, *Liberation Theology, an introductory guide* (Louisville: Westminster/John Knox, 1993).

6 I have deliberately not said anything here about theories of the Bible's authority and/or inspiration. In his otherwise stimulating – if over-cautious – book, Dave Tomlinson (*The Post Evangelical*, London: Triangle 1995) misses the most fundamental aspect of Bible use to which we need to address ourselves today, which is not about theories of

inspiration but about hermeneutics, or how we use the Bible. Theories of inspiration – if we need them – can never be the starting point, telling us how we ought to interpret the Bible, but should emerge naturally out of the way we actually handle and interpret it. In the past, so-called 'liberal' and 'evangelical' views of this subject have both been based on a set of rationalist-inspired assumptions about the nature of authority, which means that engagement with that debate is not only a secular Enlightenment agenda, but is also for that very reason increasingly irrelevant to the questions of today's spiritual searchers.

7 For critical analysis of this model and its development, cf W. Hankey, 'The Bible in a Post-Critical Age', in W. Oddie (ed.), *After the Deluge* (London: SPCK 1987), pp 41–92; Alasdair I. C. Heron, 'What is Wrong with Biblical Exegesis?', in Andrew Walker (ed.), *Different Gospels* (London: SPCK 1993), pp 86–104.

8 Of course, despite its eager adoption by scholars of all theological persuasions, the historical-critical method never has been a value-free objective science. Cf Helmut Koester's opinion that it was 'designed as a hermeneutical tool for the liberation from conservative prejudice and from the power of ecclesiastical and political institutions', in B. A. Pearson (ed.), *The Future of Early Christianity* (Minneapolis: Fortress 1991), p 474.

9 That is not to say that such study has nothing to offer. By placing the story of the near-sacrifice of Isaac, for example, into its historical context it is possible to appreciate that, in the context of a patriarchal society, 'a man's children are seen as extensions of his own value and significance and are not considered as uniquely important human beings in their own right', so 'Isaac is that which Abraham values and prizes the most, effectively his most precious possession' (R. W. L. Moberly, 'Christ as the key to Scripture: Genesis 22

Reconsidered', in R. S. Hess, P. E. Satterthwaite, G. J. Wenham, *He Swore an Oath*, Cambridge: Tyndale House 1993, p 156). But while such observations may tone down some of the text's implications for modern readers, they do not begin to address the contemporary situation, nor indeed to show how stories like this relate to the wider Christian theological tradition, not least the teaching of Jesus where children seem to be given a rather special significance (Mark 9:33–37, 42; 10:13–16).

10 For the use of masks in exegesis, worship, and spirituality, see Prof. Doug Adams, 'Facing the Cain in Ourselves', in *Church Teachers* 20/2 (1992), pp 58–59.

11 Even in the original context of the Genesis story there is significance in the fact that it is God who steps in to rescue Sarah (12:17–20), Hagar/Ishmael (21:14–20), and Isaac (22:11–14).

12 For discussion of the differences between the two, cf E. V. McKnight, *Post-Modern Use of the Bible* (Nashville: Abingdon Press 1988). For presentation and critical examination of more interactive ways of textual interpretation, see C. Rowland and M. Corner, *Liberating Exegesis* (London: SPCK 1990); F. Watson, *The Open Text* (London: SCM Press 1993); R. S. Sugirtharajah (ed.), *Voices from the Margin* (London: SPCK 1991).

13 R. McAfee Brown, *Liberation Theology*, pp 81–82.

14 See R. McAfee Brown, *Unexpected News* (Philadelphia: Westminster Press 1984), pp 21–32.

15 L. White Jr, 'The historical roots of our ecological crisis', *Science* vol. 155 (March 10, 1967), pp 1203–1207.

16 For a more detailed discussion of some of these issues, cf my article 'Defining a Biblical Theology of Creation', in *Transformation* 10/2 (April/June 1993), pp 7–11; also my *The Bible, Fact or Fantasy?* (Oxford: Lion 1989), pp 125–150.

17 Anyone who doubts the influence of this view need look no further than some of the political theorists who most

inspired the development of Thatcherism in the 1980s, and emphasized exactly this point as a way of providing a religious (Christian) foundation for their socio-economic ideas. Cf M. Novak, *The Spirit of Democratic Capitalism* (New York: Simon & Schuster 1982); J. Davies (ed.), *God and the Marketplace* (London: Institute of Economic Affairs 1993); D. Anderson (ed.), *The Kindness that Kills* (London: SPCK 1984).

18 Cited in M. Fox, *Original Blessing* (Santa Fe: Bear & Co 1983), p 11.

19 Cf M. Fox, *Original Blessing; Whee! We, Wee All the Way Home* (Santa Fe: Bear & Co 1981). For a discussion of Fox's position in relation to biblical exegesis, see Andrew Deeter Dreitcer, 'A New Creation', in *The Way* 29/1 (1989), 4–12. In the same issue of *The Way*, Thomas E. Clarke gives a useful introduction to the subject ('Creational Spirituality', pp 68–80). I am myself far from uncritical of Fox's arguments, but I believe what he says about sin and blessing is drawing our attention to some issues that are fundamental to the task of evangelization at this point in history. His other book, *The Coming of the Cosmic Christ* (San Francisco: Harper & Row 1988) raises different kinds of questions, and promulgates what I would regard as a deviant Christology, but that should not be allowed to detract from the validity and usefulness of his other works. For a personal perspective, cf his autobiography (*Confessions: The Making of a Post-Denominational Priest*, San Francisco: HarperCollins 1996).

20 For critiques of Fox, cf Ted Peters, *The Cosmic Self* (San Francisco: HarperCollins 1991), pp 120–131; Jane E. Strohl, 'The Matthew Fox Phenomenon', in *Word & World* 8 (Winter 1988), pp 42–47; M Brearley, 'Matthew Fox: Creation Spirituality for the Aquarian Age', in *Christian Jewish Relations* 22/2 (1989), pp 37–49; M. Perry, *Gods Within* (London: SPCK 1992), pp 76–84; C. Noble, 'Matthew Fox's Cosmic Christ – a

critical response', in *Crux* (XXVII) 1991, pp 21–29; Rosemary Radford Ruther, 'Matthew Fox and Creation Spirituality: Strengths and Weaknesses', in *Catholic World* July/August 1990, pp 168–172; Margaret Goodall and John Reader, 'Why Matthew Fox Fails to Change the World', in Ian Ball et al, *The Earth Beneath* (London: SPCK 1992), pp 104–119.

21 John Finney, *Finding Faith Today*, pp 33–34.

22 Peter Brierley, *Christian England* (London: MARC 1991), p 206.

23 For an outstanding and balanced treatment of this whole subject area, see Aida Besancon Spencer, Donna F. G. Hailson, Catherine Clark Kroeger and William David Spencer, *The Goddess Revival* (Grand Rapids: Baker 1995), especially chapter 6, 'God is Not Male'.

24 Charles Darwin was the first to note the significance of non-verbal aspects of communication: see his *The Experience of the Emotions in Man and Animals* (London: John Murray 1904, first published 1872). Albert Mehrabian discovered that words account for only about 7% of the total impact of a message, while 38% of it comes from vocal messages (tone of voice and so on), and a massive 55% is non-verbal, or body-language. See A. Mehrabian, *Silent Messages* (Belmont CA: Wadsworth 1971). Others have rated the influence of the non-verbal even more highly, for example R. L. Birdwhistell, *Kinesics and Context* (London: Allan Lane 1971). All this is of enormous importance for evangelism, as well as church design.

CHAPTER 8   THE PERSONAL TOUCH

1 D. Bonhoeffer, *Life Together* (London: SCM Press 1954), p 75.

2 Not quite always. It will do us no harm to reflect on the fact that out of all the people Jesus met, the only ones he consistently put down were the Pharisees – and they were

religious types, like us.

3 See R. Fung for other examples from around the world ('Mission in Christ's Way', pp 20–23; *The Isaiah Vision*, pp 17–18, 29–31, 36–37, 40).

4 Luther, quoted in J. D. Berkley, *Preaching to Convince*, p 113.

5 On this understanding of Luke 15 and the two dynamics of going and waiting, see R. Fung, 'Mission in Christ's Way', pp 6–9.

6 *Mission and Evangelism – an ecumenical affirmation*, sections 41, 43.

APPENDIX: CONVERSION AND FAITH DEVELOPMENT

1 Janet Hagberg and Robert Guelich, *The Critical Journey*, p 7.

2 Cf E. L. Hayes, 'The Biblical Foundations of Christian Education', in W. Graendorf, *Introduction to Biblical Christian Education* (Chicago: Moody 1981). William Barclay, *Educational Ideals of the Ancient World* (Grand Rapids: Baker 1974).

3 J. Wilhoit, *Christian Education and the Search for Meaning* (Grand Rapids: Baker 1986), p 22. See also V. B. Gillespie, *Religious Conversion and Personal Identity* (Birmingham, Alabama: Religious Education Press 1979), a study which integrates 'conversion' as part of the life cycle itself.

4 Erikson's concept of the 'eight ages of man' was a useful starting point, though it was Kohlberg's notion of six stages of moral development that provided the structure for Fowler's own theory of 'stages of faith'. Cf Fowler, *Stages of Faith*, pp 98–105. In *The Psychology of Moral Development* (San Francisco: Harper & Row 1981), L. Kohlberg himself tentatively proposes the addition of a seventh stage, which in his terms would be a 'religious' stage.

5 For other selected contributions to the discussion, see note 19 in chapter 4.

6 W. Cantwell Smith, *Faith and Belief* (Princeton: Princeton University Press 1979).

7 In biblical Hebrew, faith is never a noun, always a verb: cf James Barr, *The Semantics of Biblical Language* (Oxford: OUP 1961), pp 161–205.

8 C. E. Nelson questions Fowler's definition of faith, claiming 'It is noteworthy that the Hebrew word for faith is never used for faith in false gods' (*How Faith Matures*, p 238). This is a significant question for exegesis, though it is not strictly relevant to understanding faith in the context of evangelization, especially in the light of the biblical models provided by Jesus and Paul.

9 Cf Carol Gilligan, in J. W. Fowler, *Becoming Adult, Being Christian*, p 38.

10 Cf C. E. Nelson, 'Does Faith Develop? An evaluation of Fowler's position', in *The Living Light* 19 (1982), pp 162–173.

11 N. Q. Hamilton, *Maturing in the Christian Life: A Pastor's Guide* (Philadelphia: Geneva Press 1984).

12 J. Hagberg and R. Guelich, *The Critical Journey*, p xix.

13 *The Critical Journey*, p 4.

14 R. Moseley, in a 1978 Harvard dissertation referred to by Fowler, *Stages of Faith*, pp 285–286. See also Fowler, *Becoming Adult, Being Christian*, pp 138–141.

15 Fowler, 'Faith and the structuring of meaning', in Fowler, Vergote, Brusselmans (eds), *Toward Moral and Religious Maturity* (Morristown NJ: Silver Burdett Co. 1980), p 67.

16 See James E. Loder, *The Transforming Moment: Understanding Convictional Experiences* (San Francisco: Harper & Row 1989), pp 97–115. See also J. E. Loder and J. W. Fowler, 'Conversations on Fowler's Stages of Faith and Loder's 'The Transforming Moment', in *Religious Education* 77/2 (1982), pp 133–148.